To Jane

With best wishes —

[signature]

How to Capture the Advertising High Ground

Other books by Winston Fletcher

The Admakers
Teach Yourself Advertising
Meetings, Meetings
Super Efficiency
Commercial Breaks
The Manipulators
Creative People
A Glittering Haze

How to Capture the Advertising High Ground

by

Winston Fletcher

First published 1994
© Winston Fletcher 1994

All rights reserved

Winston Fletcher has asserted his rights under the Copyright, Designs and Patents Act, 1988 to be identified as the author of this work.

First published in the United Kingdom in 1994
by Century Limited
Random House, 20 Vauxhall Bridge Road, London SW1V 2SA

Random House Australia (Pty) Ltd
20 Alfred Street, Milsons Point
Sydney, NSW 2061, Australia

Random House New Zealand Ltd
18 Poland Road, Glenfield
Auckland 10, New Zealand

Random House South Africa (Pty) Ltd
PO Box 337, Bergvlei, South Africa

Random House UK Limited Reg. No. 954009

ISBN 0 7126 6007 0

Set in Bembo by SX Composing Ltd, Rayleigh, Essex
Printed and bound in Great Britain by
Clays Ltd, St Ives plc

For Miss Brownston

Contents

Foreword

1	The Future of Advertising	1
2	The Future of the World	18
3	The Future of Agencies	35
4	How to be a High Ground Client	61
5	High Ground Creativity	78
6	Smart Targeting	98
7	Testing, Shmesting	116
8	Launching a High Ground Agency	132
9	How to Make Clients Happy	154
10	How Advertising Works	171
11	Your Brilliant Career	191
12	Playing Politics	212
13	Joys and Woes	220

Index 225

Foreword

About thirty years ago a small torrent of successful advertising books flooded the book stores. Pierre Martineau's *Motivation in Advertising* (1957), Martin Mayer's *Madison Avenue USA* (1958), John Gunther's *Taken At The Flood* (1960), Rosser Reeves' *Reality In Advertising* (1961), David Ogilvy's *Confessions of an Advertising Man* (1963), and Jerry Della Femina's *From Those Wonderful Folks Who Gave You Pearl Harbor* (1969) all portrayed and revealed advertising as it then was, each from its own vantage point.

Taken together – and with the addition of Vance Packard's *The Hidden Persuaders* (1957), which was just a potboiler – those books painted a picture of the advertising business which is still widely accepted today. Yet advertising has changed radically during the last three decades – and that picture is in many ways now out of date.

How to Capture the Advertising High Ground is about advertising in the 1990s. It simultaneously charts the major recent and future trends while identifying those deep-rooted, immutable forces in advertising which so easily get forgotten in the daily sound and fury.

I have pillaged those ideas from my previous scribblings which have stood the test of time (surreptitiously jettisoning those which have not) and drawn up a detailed map of advertising as it approaches the millennium – pinpointing the peaks and the swamps. I look forward to scaling the former while gingerly sidestepping the latter.

Finally I must emphasize that the views expressed are my very own, and are not necessarily shared by Bozell corporately, by my colleagues, by my clients or by the Advertising Association.

1
The Future of Advertising

To listen to the sourpuss soothsayers you would think that the end of advertising – like the end of the world – is nigh. They have been prophesying it for years, from their podiums and in print. So people who should know better are beginning to believe them.

The impending obsolescence of advertising is based on three premises:

    i   The growth of retailers' own brands.
    ii   The burgeoning of other means of marketing.
    iii The ever-increasing clutter of commercial communications.

All three, of course, are real enough, but none of them presages advertising's demise.

Let's investigate each in turn.

'The Brand Is Dead' (or at the very least terminally sick) has been a recurrent headline for more than two decades. Recent variants have included 'Brands: who needs them?' (*The Times*); 'Private Label Nightmare' (*Advertising Age*); 'Shoot-out at the check-out' (*The Economist*); and 'Brand Graveyard Beckons' (*Marketing*). Sometimes I harbour nasty suspicions that the identical article keeps popping up, again and again over the years, with only the headline changed to conceal the flimsiness of the evidence. In 1977 a piece I published in the *Financial Times* began: 'Contrary to prevailing market wisdom, manufacturers' brands are by no means losing out in the battle against own-label' – so 'The Brand Is Dead' must have been a commonplace headline even then. At that time retailers' own labels accounted for some 26% of grocery sales. They now account for about 29%. Their growth has not been unremitting: their market share declined steadily between 1982 and 1989. They may possibly grow further in future. Equally, there are good reasons for thinking they may not. One can't say fairer than that.

In any event the future growth of retailers' own brands (if any) in no way implies the end of advertising. Indeed to a cheerful soothsayer – but cheerful soothsayers are nowadays as rare as cures for baldness – the figures could indicate that the glass is not half empty, but half full. Because they mean that manufacturers will need to spend more money on advertising to promote and protect their brands, not less.

If manufacturers slash their brand advertising they'll go out of business quick as a flash and the retailers will have them for breakfast with their corn flakes. (Not that retailers' own-label corn flakes amount to much. Kelloggs, Shredded Wheat, Weetabix and the other manufacturer brands still account for some 85% of breakfast cereal sales.)

There is now no doubt at all that media advertising will protect a brand's sales. Dr Stephen Buck, of Taylor Nelson AGB, has demonstrated beyond peradventure that those consumers who see most brand advertising are least likely to buy retailers' own labels. And vice versa. Dr Buck has shown that people who watch lots of television advertising buy about 30% fewer retailer private labels than people who watch little television advertising. And this holds good for all social classes and for all regions of the country. To quote his conclusion: 'It is extremely difficult to move from statistical relationships to causal connections . . . but the figures go a long way towards demonstrating that advertising works to maintain brand franchises and limit the growth of own label.'

And after carrying out a survey correlating retail price with brand image, the Henley Centre recently concluded: 'The evidence suggests no reversal of the long-run demands for quality and, critically for branding, the importance to people of the images and meaning of the things they buy.'

So manufacturers who want to keep selling their brands will need to spend, spend, spend.

This would all be obvious to even the dimmest of soothsayers if they ever bothered to study the annual reports of the world's great brand owners – of Nestlé and Unilever, of Grand Metropolitan and Guinness, of Procter and Gamble, Pepsico and Phillip Morris. As unit trust advertisements never tire of telling us, what goes up may well come down, but the world's major branded goods companies have grown their sales, are growing their sales, and will continue to grow their sales with advertising.

Not that things are *quite* as simple as that.

In some product sectors retailers do indeed now rule the roost. Retailers' own labels have grabbed more than half the sales of cooking oils, jams and honeys, aluminium foils and dry pasta, to mention but a few. Whereas manufacturers' brands still dominate the markets for pet foods, instant coffee, cooking sauces, canned soups, beers, household cleaners and detergents, toothpastes, toilet soaps and tampons, to mention a few more.

Why have retailers made such successful inroads in some product fields but more or less failed in others? Sadly I cannot claim this is just due to advertising. During the past decade there has, I believe, been a small revolution in marketing which has passed largely unnoticed by the soothsayers.

Ever since the 1950s it has been accepted wisdom that the world is full of very similar products which are differentiated from each other only by their advertising and packaging. This is naturally music to an adman's ears; and admen have not been slow to promulgate the message. They will prattle on about it incessantly given half a chance. But retailer power is changing things. In those markets where there were many brands with indistinguishable formulations, the retailers have produced their own equally indistinguishable substitutes.

Naturally they have given their own offerings lots of shelf space, sold them at lower prices, and elbowed the manufacturers' brands. But in the markets where the manufacturers' brands are truly superior, the best that retailers have been able to do is produce something not quite so good. This will be instantly confirmed by anyone who has ever bought a jar of retailers' instant coffee and then watched it linger lovelorn in the larder while new consignments of

Nescafé continuously come and go. Or by anyone who has dallied – but will not have dallied for long – with a sickly supermarket own-brand cola. Not being a cat it is harder to be sure about the quality of cat food, but my own moggies' meal-time fussing suggests that much the same applies to pet foods. (It seems unlikely that my cats are persuaded by the commercials.)

As Unilever chairman Sir Michael Perry puts it: 'When retailers' private labels thrash manufacturers' brands it is because the manufacturers haven't been doing their job properly.'

Advertising can, and does, successfully emphasise, glamorise and indeed exaggerate the differences between similar brands – provided there are differences to emphasise, glamorise and exaggerate. To rely upon advertising alone to differentiate your brand is, in the 1990s, a recipe for disaster. To quote the Henley Centre again: 'There are many manufacturers who neglected functionality in the 1980s as their advertising agencies emphasised the importance of the image attributes of brands. They forget that to add value, you have to have something to add it to.'

There certainly was a time, in days of yore, when many of my clients would brief me thus: 'My product is no different from any of its competitors. So it's up to the advertising to differentiate it. Just do me a great campaign. And get cracking. I'm relying on you.'

Happily that brief is rarer than an empty commercial break nowadays. People who haven't been watching what is going on still talk about competitive brands being exactly the same as each other but for their advertising. Well, it is true that a few long-established brands have built such powerful loyalty over the years that they can continue to fend off the depredations of retailers' products which are equally good. But nobody who was not especially keen, and in a hurry, to declare themselves bankrupt would today launch with massive advertising a brand based on a parity formulation – unless it enjoyed some other clear and demonstrable advantage such as price or availability, or packaging, or parentage.

It cannot be done. Them days are gone and will not be coming back.

All the best and most successful clients I have ever worked with have been fanatical about product quality and dotty about product superiority. To mention just a dozen that spring instantly to mind, from all kinds of markets and in no particular order: Unilever, Pedigree Petfoods, International Distillers and Vintners, the Halifax, Panasonic, Chrysler, P & O, Seiko, Kimberly-Clark, SmithKline Beecham, Wellcome and L'Oréal. And there are many many more – many too many to list.

The world thinks of them all as formidable marketing companies. And they are too. But it is their products which are closest to their hearts. Most of them spend far more on research and development and on quality control than they do on advertising.

The new law of the marketplace is unequivocal: if you cannot build a better mousetrap don't bother to market it. (But NB the meaning of the word *better* is a good deal more complicated than it used to be, and we'll need to return to that later.)

In markets where the quality of the retailers' products is truly on a par with that of the manufacturers' brands, the retailers are bound to win out. Even the heaviest brand advertising cannot sell a duff product. And the truth – much as we admen hate to face it – is that nowadays advertising will not succeed in selling a parity product for long.

Though that isn't bad news for advertising either. And it certainly isn't bad news for consumers. It may mean that as some manufacturers do a little less advertising, retailers will do a little more. (Retailers currently spend £540,000,000 in the media each year – that's 9% of all consumer advertising.)

Valuing brands is far from an exact science. For major brands it is easy to be wrong by a few million bucks either way. But here is the American magazine *Financial Week*'s valuation of the world's ten top-notch brands in 1993:

Brand	**Value ($ million)**
Marlboro	31,200
Coca-Cola	24,400
Budweiser	10,200
Pepsi-Cola	9,600
Nescafé	8,500

Kellogg	8,400
Winston	6,100
Pampers	6,100
Camel	4,400
Campbell	3,900

The combined value of these ten brands alone is a whopping $112,800,000,000. Imagine then – if you can carry enough noughts in your head without getting dizzy – the potential value of all the brands in the world. And then remember that all of them were built, in no small measure, by media advertising. (Lander Associates recently identified 6,000 *multinational* brands, to which would need to be added the zillions of national brands.)

All of which makes the proliferation of articles proclaiming that 'The Brand Is Dead' bewildering.

The retailers don't want to kill off manufacturers' brands: it's not in their interests at all. Manufacturers' brands make handsome profits for them. Without manufacturers' brands, how could they demonstrate that their prices are cheaper than those of their competitors? Without manufacturers' brands their turnover would fall. Without manufacturers' brands they would be forced to initiate all their own product development. Without manufacturers' brands they would be forced to spend a great deal more on their own advertising. Without manufacturers' brands, how could they establish the cheapness and value of their own-label offerings? To demonstrate the depths of their discounts, the warehouse discounters, especially, need and adore manufacturers' brands.

As do consumers. A recent study by Dr Simon Broadbent of Leo Burnett Brand Consultancy showed that consumers are willing to pay – *do* pay – an average price premium of 37% for manufacturers' brands. Item for item, that means consumers believe manufacturers' brands to be worth more than one-third more than the retailers' products.

Without manufacturers' brands consumer choice would be minimised. And the evidence shows that consumers are far less loyal to store brands. They chop and change. And they frequently change back to manufacturers' brands. That is why manufacturers' brands achieve such longevity. Old brand names almost never die. In sixteen major American markets the 1923 brand leader was still brand leader seventy years later. Even in the trendy booze business, of the world's top hundred alcohol spirit brands ninety-three are more than twenty-five years old.

Far from growing less important, brands are growing more important. In the early 1990s, despite deep economic recession, almost every significant brand, in almost every significant market, increased its sales significantly. And most did even better. And those brands that spent more on advertising did best of all. In a study of 127 fast moving consumer goods brands The Billett Consultancy showed that during 1991/92 those brands which increased their spend (average +7%) increased their market shares, while those which cut their spend (average −8%) lost market share. Whatever else suffered during the recent recession, it was not the major brands. Indeed retailers' own labels made surprisingly little headway, though they might have been expected to. In many sectors – baked beans is a fair example – retailers' labels actually lost market share during the early 1990s.

Why? Because consumers know brand names mean quality and reliability. Brands are woven deep into our social fabric. People use brands to integrate themselves with some social groups and to differentiate themselves from others. If you still drive a Citroën 2CV you are flaunting your independence of spirit, your non-conformity; whereas if you run a Ford Escort you are happier lost in a crowd. If you drink Heineken you are one of the boys; if you sip Stella Artois you're someone slightly special.

That is why novelists, with subconscious sensitivity, use brands to reveal their characters' characters. They know readers will recognise people by their predilections for Armani suits or Aramis, for Raybans or Reeboks or J & B Rare. Cigarette packs and beer brands litter most modern novels, especially the sex-and-shopping sagas. You won't find many brand names in the Brontës or Balzac.

Brands have become so intricate and integrated a part of our lives that we would feel lost without them – as we are in foreign parts, when faced with an array of indecipherable shampoos or toothpastes. (And how relieved we are when we recognise a pack with a friendly face!)

Moreover, in examining the future of advertising and the growth of retailers' labels, we have so far mostly considered only groceries. Admittedly the way they are extending their tentacles to embrace an ever wider and wider range of goodies, it sometimes seems as though supermarkets are taking over the world. Nonetheless there are hugh swathes of advertising where the retailer versus manufacturer battle is irrelevant, or hardly relevant.

Automobile advertising. Financial advertising. Utilities advertising. Entertainment advertising. Government, charity and travel advertising. In 1993 expenditure on those sectors alone notched up a hefty £1,150,000,000 and they are all thriving. Of the top fifty UK advertisers nine are car manufacturers, six are financial institutions, four are utilities, and thirteen are themselves retailers. (And none of the retailers is likely to become a car manufacturer or a building society or an electricity company in a hurry.)

So much then for retailers' private label brands. Don't get me wrong: I am not saying they are unimportant. But they are not going to dismember advertising.

Nor, to shift the spotlight, are other means of marketing communication.

Nobody knows when the very first advertisements appeared, nor who invented advertising. This prestigious accolade is usually awarded to the call girls of Pompeii, whose below-the-belt promotional material can still be deciphered on some of the once-buried walls of the once-naughty city.

At about the same time Aesclyptoe, an early Athenian Max Factor, promoted his lotions and potions with a commercial which might have sprung yesterday from a highly paid copywriter's word-processor:

> For eyes that are shining, for cheeks like the dawn,
> For beauty that lasts after girlhood has gone,
> For prices in reason, the women who know
> Will buy their cosmetics from Aesclyptoe.

This catchy little jingle would have been one of many crooned by the ancient Greek town criers, as they wandered about the Parthenon proclaiming new laws, and earning themselves a few extra drachma on the side by interspersing their official announcements with commercials. (Just as Hellmann's Mayonnaise and the Halifax interrupt the ten o'clock news.)

And doubtless, on hearing it, any Athenian damsels in the market for reasonably priced shining eyes and dawn-like cheeks dashed off smartly to the Acropolis Boots.

Media advertising, in other words, is no Johnny-come-lately fly-by-night way to win sales and influence people. Anthony Trollope published a novel about advertising, *The Struggles of Smith, Brown and Robinson*, in 1861. It is not one of the world's greatest works of fiction, but for anyone in advertising it confirms the depressing truth that there is little new under the sun. (Trollope, incidentally, defined advertising as 'The poetry of euphemism'. Nice.)

All of which is history. And old orders change. The Athenians fought their wars with swords and spears but we don't. Maybe the new marketing weaponry of databases, and sponsorship, and telemarketing and inter-active media will soon make advertising as obsolete as the cutlass and the lance.

Well, maybe. But the facts do not support that thesis.

Let's first consider the size of the main marketing communications sectors:

	£
Media advertising	7,825,000,000
Sales promotion (est.)*	1,000,000,000
Direct mail	945,000,000
Sponsorship	304,000,000
Telemarketing	46,000,000
TOTAL	**10,120,000,000**

*The best available estimate of non-price-related sales promotions, produced by the Advertising Association in 1987. The figure will have increased since then but – taking account of the recession – not greatly. The other figures relate to 1992.

In other words, media advertising still accounts for a clear 77% of all marketing communication. Little evidence there of an incipient corpse.

But then size, as they say, isn't everything. How about growth? Everybody knows, don't they, that media advertising is on the skids while its competitors are bustin' out all over. Well, reading the business and marketing press you might, once again, easily come to that conclusion. And indubitably it is what the direct marketing wallahs and the sponsors of sponsorship would like you to believe. But it ain't necessarily so.

As always there are lies, damn lies and statistics. In 1982 expenditure on direct mail – or database marketing as its protagonists modishly call it – accounted for 9.8% of all advertising. Ten years later that figure had climbed to 10.5%. Healthy growth, but hardly rumbustious. In the intervening decade the figure wandered between 7% and 11%. By choosing the right years for your argument you can prove that as a proportion of all advertising, direct mail was booming, dwindling, or unchanging. To put direct marketing in perspective, in Britain the average household receives eighty mailshots a year, about 1.6 per week – and sees some ten thousand commercials a year, about two hundred per week.

Far from being a dynamic new medium, direct mail, as it happens, is one of the oldest. I will bet my Victorian penny black to your Mailsort discount that direct marketing was much more important at the end of the nineteenth century than it will be at the end of the twentieth. (At the end of the nineteenth century there were no broadcast media, no cinemas, and no popular press.) In 1907 the Reliable Advertising Service (how we all miss them!) had a register of 30,000 car owners and a proto-Acorn geodemographic list of 170,000 London suburbanites graded according to the value of their rent. Reliable Advertising Services could handle 250,000 catalogues a day and over 9,000,000 mailings a year – without even the aid of a computer to mis-address a few envelopes.

That isn't to say that direct mail hasn't grown. But then – except in the recession – so have all other forms of commercial communication. And the figures do not suggest that direct mail, or anything else, has grown at the expense of media advertising. Happily, marketing communications is a big pool, and there is lots of room for everyone to splash cheerfully about in it.

Including sponsorship. Sponsorship has maybe doubled in size since the early 1980s, but it still accounts for only 3% of all marketing communications expenditure. Given the relaxation of the regulations that have controlled media sponsorship in Britain in the past, it will blossom a bit in the immediate future. But the total value of UK television sponsorship in 1994 will not exceed £50 million – the size of one small-ish advertising agency. Sponsorship will never seriously challenge advertising. It hasn't in the USA, where it has always been deregulated.

And compared to sponsorship telemarketing is but a tiny tot, a babe in arms, less than 1% the size of big Uncle Advertising. In any event telemarketing is truly a means of personal selling – not a communications *medium* at all. Its true competitors are Avon ladies and Tupperware parties, not advertising and direct mail.

So if none of the existing modes of marketing communication poses a serious threat to media advertising, how about interactive marketing – often dubbed the communications medium of the future?

Keen to explore this potentially powerful new marketing weapon, my own agency, Bozell Worldwide, has taken a long hard look at the development of interactive media in the United States, and has produced an authoritative tome titled *The Reality and Blue Sky Realms of Interactive Marketing, Media & Communications*.

Its conclusions? Don't hold your breath.

> Interactive media will not replace the traditional media vehicles, but in time may become another option for marketeers.

Patently the ability to respond immediately to a commercial message – the essence of interactive media – is occasionally useful to consumers. But the great majority of consumer goods are not worth being interactive about. They aren't worth making a phone call, or even pressing a few buttons, to have delivered. (Delivery is a costly business.) If you want some baked beans, or bacon, or burgers, the easiest and cheapest way to get them (and the thousands of other foods like them) is to nip down to the shop. But interactive media have lately received so much hype, particularly in the USA, that we'll examine them more closely in Chapter 6.

Throughout history ingenious pioneers have invented – or do I mean discovered? – new ways of advertising which they believed, and doubtless hoped, would quickly become the rage.

In 1911 an exceptionally creative adman developed a pair of boots into the soles of which were cut advertisement stencils, supplied with ink from a tube running down his trousers. Original, undoubtedly; but as an advertising medium it had no legs.

Fifty years earlier the impresario William Smith promoted one of his plays by affixing suitably printed sticky labels to everything in sight, including 'omnibuses, cabs, Windsor Castle, The Old Bailey court, Steamboats and measures in public houses both in London and the country.' Smith claimed his campaign to have been a great success – though there is no evidence of a full econometric analysis having been carried out – and for a while sticky labels became a groovy medium. (Which is more than could be said for stencilled boots.) But you don't see that many sticky labels on Windsor Castle and the Old Bailey these days.

Telegrams, too, when first invented, promised well. In 1875 a large furnishing firm despatched five thousand telegrams all timed to arrive 'at the fashionable dinner hour, when most of the best families would be assembled.' It was modestly described, as new media so frequently are by their sponsors, as 'one of the boldest advertisements carried out in modern times.' The telegrams medium boomed until at least 1906 when a 'nervous old lady' wrote to *The Times* complaining bitterly that she had been awoken in the middle of the night to receive a telegram which, on tremulous opening, was discovered to carry the urgent message 'Peter Robinson's Sale Now Proceeding.' Some advertisers always go too far.

Town criers, as we have already seen, have been around since Aristotle's days, but at one time London was also crowded with sandwich-board men. Now sandwich-board men's only clients seem to be The Wages Of Sin, Eating Too Much Fish and The End Of The World, which (unlike that of advertising) is Nigh.

In 1861 it was estimated that some 1,150,000,000 advertising handbills were stuffed into the unwilling fingers of passing pedestrians. But handbill distribution too has gone to the great advertising media cemetery in the sky.

More recently we have seen advertising on car-bumper stickers, and rear-windscreen stickers; audio-commercials in supermarkets; painted taxis and sponsored airport trolleys; strategically placed advertisements aimed at skiers while they are immovably strapped into ski lifts (gotcha! you can hear the advertisers cry). Best of all, advertising on the inside doors of loo cubicles – promoting which Mr Richard L. Weisman, president of Stallwords Inc., claimed immodestly, 'The only way not to read our ads is to close your eyes.'

(But so far the results have not been flushed with success. Ms Marion Dipoala, who spent $450 on Stallwords ads in local bars and restaurants, to promote her Florida tanning salon, declared the medium a bit of a bummer. 'I think the people who go into the bars drink heavily and are not really paying attention when they're in the stalls,' quoth Ms Dipoala. 'It's not a bad idea. It's just not as effective as I thought.')

More seriously, advertisers are currently experimenting with commercials on rental videotapes; commercials in kids' computer games; commercial TV monitors in classrooms and in doctors' waiting rooms; printing messages on eggs; monitors at supermarket checkout aisles and in airports. (Users of Charles de Gaulle airport in Paris will know the strange spherical objects which float above the travolators and on to which are projected advertisement slides which change every few seconds. *Très sophistique*.)

There are, in other words, a vast number of new ways to advertise on trial at any one time – some serious, some dotty – of which a few may survive. This, it seems to me, is vigorous and healthy. Except that it brings us to the third threat to advertising: clutter.

As each new manifestation of commercial communication appears, advertisers grow increasingly apprehensive that one day the pudding will be over-egged and the goose will finally and irreversibly be cooked. It is an understandable fear. Every day most people are exposed to hundreds, maybe thousands of advertisements.

Register MEAL – the UK's leading advertising expenditure analyst – picks up about 850,000 display advertisements in newspapers and magazines each year. That's some 2,350 per day. And Register MEAL only scrutinises 500 of the 9,000 or so publications currently available. Additionally, the average viewer sees about 1.5 hours of commercials, almost 200 different spots, each week. Plus, let us not forget the 1.6 mailshots a week (which seem to generate a disproportionate and to me mystifying volume of hostility).

And to the press, magazine and television advertisements, and direct mailshots must be added posters and point-of-sale material, radio commercials and perimeter placards, movie trailers and matchbox covers, seaside skywriters and blimps . . . not to mention handbills, ski-chair publicity and possibly even loo-cubicle advertisements.

Nobody knows how many of these the average person actually sees each day. Specious surveys have sought to establish an exact figure but you only need to think about it for a moment to realise that the question is all but meaningless. How many *people* do you see in a day? Should you count all the people on the buses, in the shops, on the streets? Should you count all the people at the extreme edge of your vision, or only those you really look at?

It is the same with advertisements. Should you count all the small advertisements as you turn over the pages of your morning newspaper, should you include the radio commercials that go in one ear and out of the other while you're thinking of something else, should you add all the billboards on the distant horizon?

No? But maybe you should, because if they contain something that truly interests you they will probably catch your attention.

How many advertisements does the average person see in a day? The most accurate answer that can be given is: an awful lot. So it can hardly be a surprise that the advertising industry is growing increasingly anxious about this clamorous clutter.

And Research in Germany has shown conclusively that the more commercials there are in a break, the fewer that people remember. But that simply proves that more short breaks are preferable to fewer long breaks: hardly an astonishing revelation. (In Germany they used to bunch all commercials together in mammoth – and unwatchable – advertising ghettos.)

Against the plethora of persuasive communications, how can your messages get through?

That is what the rest of this book is about.

However, it is worth noting that advertising folk are much more worried about the issue than anyone else. This is because the advertising industry confuses variety with clutter. The broadcast media are proliferating and fragmenting, which will indubitably – as we shall see – make media targeting a damn sight more difficult. But viewers can still only watch one channel at a time. So they don't know about – or anyway are not impacted by – the countless commercials being churned out by the stations they are not watching. That is doubtless why the public does not care a fig about clutter. In November 1993 ITV briefed The Research Business, one of Britain's top ten market research companies, to investigate viewers' perceptions of clutter. Their conclusions:

> It was notable across the research groups we conducted, on the subject of 'clutter', that it was not an issue for consumers. It is evident that 'clutter' has *not* emerged on the consumer agenda as a topic worthy of comment. Indeed we had to push and probe very hard to elicit any responses or comments on the topic. We became aware that the viewers saw us as somewhat silly to spend an hour and a half talking to them about this non-issue!

A careful analysis of channel switching, which was part of the same study, showed that viewers are far more likely to switch during programme credits than during commercials – unless the commercial break exceeds five minutes. (This confirms the German finding above.) Indeed people switch just as much during programmes as during commercials. So the infamous 'zapping' problem isn't a problem at all.

More evidence: in the UK, studies regularly carried out by the Advertising Association established that throughout the 1980s, when advertising boomed and the number of advertisements burgeoned like tropical flowers in a hothouse, the public's liking for advertising grew steadily. And by the end of the 1980s nearly 90% of Britons expressed generally favourable views about advertising.

Even in the United States, where surveys consistently prove that advertising is more unpopular than it is in Britain, a study carried out in 1993 showed that advertising and marketing people were much more hostile than the public at large to advertisements in 'new' media – rental videotapes, grocery carts, TV monitors in doctors' waiting rooms and the others.

None of this, of itself, proves that the swelling welter of advertisements is not becoming counterproductive – that because each new advertisement has to fight so much harder to be heard, it is marginally less cost-effective. Like so many other aspects of advertising it is a hypothesis that cannot be proved or disproved. But there is plenty of circumstantial evidence to suggest that it is wrong.

Every week sees the launch of new campaigns which rapidly reach very high levels of awareness. *Marketing* magazine tracks these campaigns and they frequently hit awareness levels of 80% plus within a few weeks. There is no evidence whatever that it is becoming any more expensive (in real terms) to achieve these high awareness levels. Survey evidence in West Germany, which attempted to correlate advertising expenditures with awareness, for 150 campaigns, during the years 1985–1989, showed no such trend.

Similarly, direct response advertisements continue to pull as well as ever (excluding the effects of the recession). More relevantly, if you want a financial advertisement to pull coupon response, put it on the financial pages where it will jostle against its competitors. The pages are seemingly overcrowded with competitive coupon ads: they nearly all pull.

Advertising clutter is not a major issue. (Brand clutter, as we shall see later, is another matter.) The aforementioned William Smith, ingenious inventor of sticky-label advertising, was also a pioneer market researcher. One Thursday morning in 1851 he counted over

250 handbills foisted upon him as he strolled through London. Now that *is* clutter. And litter, too. Handbill foisting is also much mentioned in Anthony Trollope's novel of the same period. But advertising has survived.

Brands are not dying. Media advertising is not losing out to other types of marketing communication. Consumers haven't even noticed any clutter. Far from becoming *less* effective, advertising can become, should become, and probably will become more and more effective. Or anyway, more cost-effective when properly deployed.

How will this come about? Not by accident, not without effort, that's for sure.

Agencies will need to adapt themselves, their systems and their disciplines to the dramatically changing marketplace.

Advertisers will need to think a good deal harder about how to make sure their agencies provide them with the best (not just the cheapest) advertising for their bucks.

Everyone – including the creatives themselves – will need to learn how to motivate creative people to produce sharper, more remarkable, more accurately targeted commercials and campaigns.

Researchers will need to be less slapdash, media buyers less catchpenny.

And all of us will need to learn to live with the vagaries and curious local eccentricities of this shrinking globe.

That is the agenda for the future of advertising, the agenda for more cost-effective advertising, the agenda for capturing the high ground.

Advertising is much more like farming than like physics. Even the most successful farmer cannot forecast next year's crop – but he will consistently outperform his competitors. Higher yields with lower costs, that's what successful farming is all about. So is advertising.

2

The Future of the World

Human beings the world over are all the same – driven by the same potent urges: greed, hunger, ambition, sex . . . .

Sigmund Freud gave these universal urges respectable classical names, like *ego* and *libido*. But hidden deep in our subconscious is another universal urge, every bit as powerful as the others, which the great founding father of psychoanalysis failed to discover. The urge to be exactly the same as everyone else, but different. It is this potent urge which is at the heart of all global marketing problems – and opportunities. (Indeed it is this urge which is at the heart of most global economic and political wrangles too.) And because it is so important I have, like Freud, dubbed the urge to be the same as everyone else but different with a dignified classical name: *globus confusingus*.

While *globus confusingus* is ubiquitous – as common among Australian aborigines as among Beverly Hills billionaires – it is at its most pervasive in Europe, whose nations constantly strive for homogenous diversity. And so it is in Europe that the challenges of multinational marketing are currently most acute.

We all know the world is shrinking daily, as McDonald's, Coke and Benetton (to mention but a few) sweep across the map with a nonchalant disregard for national borders and national differences. Despite appearances to the contrary, such brands proclaim, people everywhere are exactly the same.

And yet everyone knows different nations speak different languages, in different dialects, with different accents; and that they eat, drink and dress differently (how can anyone say the Italians dress like the English?). We all carry in our minds distinct national stereotypes. We refer to them daily. Spaniards are as unlike Swedes as Israelis are unlike Iranians; we even believe we can differentiate Austrians from Germans, Aussies from New Zealanders and the English from the Scots. (Anybody who thinks the Scots and the English are as alike as peas in a pod had best not express this view north of the border.) Peoples, *en peu de mots*, are as different as chalk and *chèvre*. That's *globus confusingus* at work.

Nowadays the first of the two above views is much the more fashionable. Professor Theodore Levitt first postulated it in his classic work *The Marketing Imagination*. He put forward a series of arguments which have since become marketing dogma. Levitt argued, as did John Naismith in *Megatrends* (and many others since), that city-dwellers have more in common with other city-dwellers than they have with country bumpkins, even if the bumpkins come from their own country – that Londoners have more in common with Hamburgers than they have with the denizens of Great Snoring.

To which hypothesis *globus confusingus* replies, without a moment's hesitation, yes and no.

There are of course many things that all the world's townies have in common: traffic jams and car-parking problems, high-rise flats and high-rising rents, sedentary jobs and keep-fit clubs, fashionable shops and first-run cinemas, one-way streets and pedestrian precincts, concert halls and three-star restaurants, lots of crime and little punishment. And most of the world's inhabitants share, in addition to McDonald's, Coke and Benetton, a cornucopia of sophisticated and unsophisticated brands. Gucci and Kellogg, Marlboro and Mars, Sony and Seiko and Smirnoff – the all-about brands which reassure us and guide our choices on our travels.

Nor is this conformity confined to famous brands. Look at the teenagers in every town in the world. Their uniform is, well, uniform: denims, T-shirts and trainers – plus occasionally, though nowadays less often, multicoloured spiky hair and chain leather jackets. On an (even) more humdrum note, there probably isn't a town of any size in the world which doesn't boast a Chinese takeaway. (Which came first, the sweet and sour chicken or the egg burger?)

This uniformity is not nearly so new as Professor Levitt and his disciples believe. The cosmetics and perfume companies – Coty and Chanel for example – have been operating multinational marketing and advertising policies for well over half a century; so have movies, airlines and automobiles, albeit less rigorously. If the world is shrinking, the contraction began many decades ago.

And it still has a long way to go. For while much divides London from Great Snoring, their inhabitants still share innumerable tastes which they don't share with their cousins in Germany, let alone in Greece or Guatemala. *Coronation Street*, warm bitter, cricket, Yorkshire pudding and mushy peas, the Halifax Building Society – and the English language – to mention but a few.

Similar lists could easily be drawn up uniting Parisians with the charming village of Condom, Frankfurters with the people of Worms, New Yorkers with the folk from Poughkeepsie. Similar but utterly different of course.

Warm bitter is hardly the only idiosyncratic drink in the world. Few outside of Greece imbibe retsina with unbridled relish, any more than non-Italians down grappa in great gulps. Have you ever tried Chinese rice wine? The Chinese like it a lot. Such eccentricities are legion. The Belgians drink three times as much beer as the French, the Italians drink three times as much wine as the Germans, the Spanish drink twice as much spirits as the Austrians, sake still hasn't caught on anywhere except Japan, tequila is small beer outside Mexico, and nobody sups nearly as much cider as the British.

Despite all of which, in any bar you visit in Great Snoring or in Worms, in London or Poughkeepsie the chances are you'll find Courvoisier, Cointreau, Carlsberg and a multitude of other major international brands on offer – though they may not always taste the same. (Nescafé comes in twenty different international flavours.) It's that old *globus confusingus* again.

Nor is it only the potions. Every country in the world has its own favourite foods, from haggis to bouillabaisse. Did you know that per capita the Spanish devour twice as many potatoes as the Danes, the

French consume three times as much butter as the Italians and nibble twice as many biscuits as the Germans?

And why do the Germans own three times as many dishwashers per household as the Dutch? Happily the Dutch get their own back by owning twice as many video cameras as the Belgians. The Belgians score by owning no fewer than nine times as many freezers as the Spanish. The Spanish have an awful lot of gas cookers though.

Would you have guessed that the Swiss have twice as many telephones, per ear as it were, as the British, French or Germans, and more than three times as many as the Dutch? In fact the Swiss own more telephones than anyone else in the world: even the Americans lag a long way behind. Maybe it has something to do with their mountainous terrain. There must be a Ph.D. thesis lurking in the correlation between mountains and telephone ownership. Or maybe it's something to do with the holes in their cheese. And while we're on the subject, which other country puts great big holes in its cheese?

Even when the product is the same everywhere, it may be perceived and used differently. Take the humble Kit Kat bar. An award-winning paper presented at the 1992 ESOMAR market research conference showed that Kit Kat is viewed as a snack in Britain, a crispy chocolate in France, a relaxing product in Germany and as a quality chocolate in Italy. The same paper, incidentally, showed that a Kit Kat television campaign which had worked brilliantly in the UK achieved quite different results (some even better, some a lot worse) in Belgium, Holland, Italy, France and Germany.

Unsurprisingly perhaps, colours too have local meanings. Scantest, probably Europe's leading colour research specialists, state that the appeal of different colours, shades and textures varies widely. Modern brown crockery, beloved by the British and Germans, is anathema to the French. But the French are more than willing to pop purple pills, a colour considered far from healthy by the rest of us.

Note that I have not spotlighted the differences between rich countries and poor ones, between affluent Western economies and the impoverished Third World: that would be too easy. Nor have I so far focused on the most stultifying of all the many stultifying factors in the international marketing *mélange*: language.

If it weren't for the little local language problems, Noilly Prat, Pschitt, Crapsy and Sic would doubtless be as popular in Manchester as they are in Marseilles; BUM snacks would be chewed as cheerfully in Maidstone as in Madrid; and Super Piss would be as widely used to unlock frozen car doors in Hull as it is in Helsinki. Kellogg's Bran Buds means 'burnt farmers' in Swedish, Castlemaine XXXX has had problems in the USA where Fourex is a leading condom brand, and Esso apparently sounds like 'stalled car' in Japanese. (Small wonder that, to avoid such predicaments, of the 3,000 new brand names registered in Japan in the early 1980s, 1,000 were innocuous names of Italian towns, rivers or regions.)

All of which circuitously brings us back to *globus confusingus* and the problems it poses for multinational advertising and marketing. Some things are the same everywhere, others are completely different. And still more confusingly, others are loosely similar but not exactly the same. The problem for advertising is to identify which is which.

An incorrect assumption of homogeneity where it doesn't exist will lead to campaigns which fail. An incorrect assumption of diversity will lead to missed opportunities. The former will generally be more expensive than the latter. That is probably why the growth of multinational advertising has been much slower than many pundits predicted – particularly in the early 1980s when Ted Levitt, ably abetted by Saatchi and Saatchi, appeared to be promising that all advertising would be global by next Thursday.

The world will not be homogenous by next Thursday. Nor – it is to be hoped – by next Thursday a century hence. *Globus confusingus* will continue to reign for centuries to come. The diminishing diversity of our towns and villages is already deeply depressing: the same shops, the same designs, the same goods on every High Street. Imagine then a truly homogenous world.

Right now, nobody knows what percentage of all advertising is multinational. This is partly because it would be a truly massive task to collect the data – think of the complexities involved – and no one is even making the effort. But it is also because there are acute definitional problems which make precise measurement impossible.

Question: how much must an advertisement change, as it travels around the world, before it ceases to be the same advertisement?

If that sounds like an abstract how-many-angels can-you-get-on-a-pinhead type of question let me give some concrete examples.

Many advertisers issue style manuals, which define how all their advertisements and literature should look, throughout the world. Style manuals specify house colours, typefaces, spacing, design elements, logo sizes, when photographs may and may not be used, and how, and why, and many other things besides. Usually they are mind-numbingly detailed. (Not least because the design companies who produce them have to justify the mind-numbing fees they have charged.)

Rarely if ever do style manuals attempt to define what any advertising should say. Rarely if ever do they mention copy content at all (apart from controlling the use of the company slogan, if any).

Certainly such companies' campaigns look the same everywhere. But what if the words used in France, Italy, Germany and the UK are utterly different, as they frequently are? Is that multinational advertising? Yes and no, again. Once more *globus confusingus* has reared its head. The advertisements are the same but different.

For the *Financial Times* my agency has taken the style manual approach one stage further. Not only do our *FT* advertisements look the same throughout Europe, but we consciously aim for consistency of verbal style – for a consistently light, witty, approachable tone of voice in headlines and copy. Yet the messages have to vary, because the *FT*'s market situation, and its competition, vary from country to country. In the UK it is the only pink daily, while in Europe there are about thirty others. In the UK it dominates its market, in Europe it is the emerging contender.

So the campaigns throughout Europe enjoy a strong family resemblance. They look the same, feel the same, are stylistically the same. But they aren't the same. The words are different. (And words are not unimportant when you are advertising a newspaper.)

Another example. In order to minimise production costs – the total budget was far from massive – we recently used a fifteen-second American live-action sequence in a thirty-second Panasonic electric shaver commercial. In this instance the model of shaver on sale in the UK was different to that in the USA, so naturally the message was different, and the product sequence was different, and the pack-shot was different. But the central live-action sequence was the same, and with astute editing the end result (though certainly no cinematic masterpiece) was a clean-cut commercial. And it cleaned up, too.

But was it multinational? Well half of it was. More or less.

Historically, small advertising markets – Greece, Turkey, Scandinavia, countries in Africa and in the Middle and Far East for example – have long used local adaptations of American and British campaigns. Do those constitute multinational campaigns? Just about. If a German commercial is used in Austria or Switzerland, is that a multinational campaign? Hardly.

Currently a goodly number of Western commercials are being used in the ex-Communist bloc countries because they are a cheap and cheerful way for advertisers to dip their toes in the local water. The commercials were never written or intended for those countries. But by minimising entry costs they are enabling Western multinationals to get started quickly and cheaply. At the same time, and incidentally, the process is helping to build up the infant media and the advertising industries of Russia and Eastern Europe. Thus foreign advertisements are being used in many East European countries; but in most cases it would be glorifying them to describe them as multinational campaigns.

All of this shows that when people boldly quote precise figures for total multinational advertising – the chairman of one of London's top five agencies recently claimed publicly that 55% of all advertising is now multinational – they are talking through their global bums.

However, with those caveats firmly in mind it is possible to advance five (almost) irrefutable generalisations:

    i   Perhaps 15–20% of British consumer advertising now also runs in three or more other major markets with little or no significant change apart from translation. (After questioning

The Future of the World

a panel of 'experts' a couple of years ago *Campaign* magazine's best guestimate was 12%.) That means approximately £1,000 million is spent annually in the UK on multinational campaigns.

ii The percentage is slowly but steadily growing but is unlikely ever to exceed 50% because so many products (warm bitter and mushy peas . . .) will eternally be uniquely British.

iii The percentage varies greatly from product field to product field. For perfumes the figure may already be as high as 40%, for financial services it is probably under 3%. In addition to diverse national tastes, diverse national legislative controls have slowed the spread of multinational brands in many markets.

iv The percentage likewise varies, to some extent, with the size of the advertiser. Many large spenders are international corporations, with international brands; but as we saw in the last chapter, many large spenders (retailers, public utilities et al.) are still British through and through.

v The percentage also varies greatly from agency to agency. I guestimate that about one third of the top twenty UK agencies' income currently comes from multinational campaigns. (That is why the aforementioned agency chairman quoted so absurdly high a figure.) The percentage attributable to multinational clients is even higher – but multinational clients do not always run multinational campaigns. For most of the remaining 300 or so UK advertising agencies multinational business is still only a small proportion of their billings.

In summary, multinational advertising is big and growing bigger. It dominates the thinking of many multinational corporations and of the top London agencies. But it far from dominates the advertising landscape and it won't do so this side of the millennium, if ever.

In the light of all the confusion, maybe it is time to define just what a multinational campaign is. Or rather what multinational campaigns are, since there are three distinct varieties. The words 'multinational campaign' immediately conjure up in most people's minds Coca-Cola's historic 'I'd Like to Teach the World to Sing' commercials; but such universality is rare.

I have dubbed the three categories of multinational campaign:

    i   *Universal* – exactly the same everywhere.
    ii *Consistent* – the same campaign, local adaptations.
    iii *Diverse* – the same strategy and objectives, local interpretations.

(Before going one degree of longitude further on this transcontinental journey I must emphasise that these categories shade into one another on their global peregrinations; and that multinational campaigns are almost never truly global – it's as sure as death and taxes that in Kuwait or Kashmir or Kowloon or somewhere even the most carefully controlled multinational plan will run into a local glitch.)

Universal Campaigns

Coca Cola's 'I'd Like to Teach the World' campaign is the archetype. Others include Benetton, Smirnoff, Kodak and some of the British Airways commercials, expensive fragrances, designer fashions, and some toys. But there are not that many.

Essentially a Universal Campaign is planned, from its conception, to work in most countries, in most languages, unchanged in any respect. This precludes the use of lip-synch dialogue in television commercials, except for dialogue of the most basic kind ('Hello', 'Very Good' and 'I'd Like to Teach the World to Sing'). In most cases it pretty well precludes the use of people at all, being as how we all look and dress so differently.

Universal Campaigns minimise and amortise production costs wonderfully. They are marginally more common in print media than on the box. But they will never become common currency because they are so inflexible and so restricting.

Consistent Campaigns

This is the category of multinational campaigns which is burgeoning, and which is rapidly capturing the high ground in global marketing. However it is also the category which is most expensive and difficult to operate.

Consistent Campaigns conform to a formula which specifies the strategy, structure and message of every advertisement. The strategy, structure and message never vary, but commercials and print advertisements are often produced locally and take account of national styles and peculiarities. In advertising, that is the meaning of the hackneyed phrase 'Think Global, Act Local'. In my terms it is the taming of *globus confusingus*.

Often a particular section of the advertisement – perhaps an expensive photograph or product formulation sequence – will be used universally, without amendment, and the remainder of the advertisement will be built around it. But the complete advertisement will still be tailored to its local audience.

Most of the major international corporations increasingly employ Consistent Campaigns: Unilever, Mars Corporation, Kellogg, Procter and Gamble, Nestlé, Grand Metropolitan and their global comrades all run campaigns which are 'the same, but different', throughout the world.

To show how it works, here's a thoroughbred example. Pedigree Chum's 'Top Breeders Recommend It' campaign began in Britain in the 1960s. Almost instantly it proved successful and it has since travelled the world. However, for historic and trademark reasons the product is not called Chum in all countries; nor are the breeds of dog which people love and cherish the same in all countries. Most important of all, the top breeders change from country to country: no self-respecting British dog lover would dream of taking the advice of a French (let alone a Greek or Japanese) breeder!

So top breeders recommend the brand in a babel of languages, for a horde of breeds in a fair number of different packs. But the strategy, structure and message are fixed as the Northern Star – and always growl astonishingly well.

Diverse Campaigns

As rapidly as Consistent Campaigns are capturing the high ground, Diverse Campaigns are retreating into the valleys. While Universal Campaigns take as their starting point the established truth that people are all the same, Diverse Campaigns take as their starting point the contradictory established truth that people are all different.

Diverse Campaigns demand that the communications strategy should be universally consistent, but allow the structures and the messages in the advertisements to vary widely. This almost always involves the creation of new advertising in each country, which naturally whacks up production costs. But the Diverse approach is not without its protagonists, albeit a dwindling band. Nor is it without its merits.

It is built upon the precept – still widely accepted in most British advertising agencies – that the best, the most effective advertising is always embedded in a nation's culture. To be truly effective, the supporters of the Diverse philosophy argue, advertising must use language idiomatically, the way it is spoken; it must reflect shared knowledge (e.g., the use of local places and personalities) and shared values; it must be easy to identify with, be idiosyncratic and witty. None of these can easily be achieved in Consistent – let alone Universal – campaigns. Such multinational campaigns, their opponents insist, necessarily employ bland language and anodyne settings; idiosyncrasy and wit are *verboten* – they don't translate. So the price of increasing multinational standardisation is diminishing local effectiveness.

Moreover, the antagonists throw in for good measure, the traditions of advertising *itself* vary worldwide. *Vide* the Kit Kat campaign mentioned earlier. By and large we Brits don't like American ads, Italians don't like French ads, and nobody but the Germans has a single good word to say for German ads. This is not merely *confusingus*: it is outright *animus*.

Unarguably many of advertising's greatest campaigns support these arguments. It is difficult to imagine David Ogilvy's spiffing Rolls Royce headline 'At sixty miles an hour the loudest noise in this new Rolls Royce comes from the electric clock' in German: it would be longer than *War and Peace*. Nor would Heineken's brilliant 'Refreshes the Parts Other Beers Cannot Reach' travel well. Nor Bill Bernbach's classic New Yorker Volkswagen ad simply headlined 'Lemon'. These and a million others would have fallen at the first translation hurdle – as do most campaigns that depend upon wordplay. And that eliminates a lot of fine, effective campaigns.

As long as the brand's positioning and communications strategy remain steadfast, the Diverse Campaigners contend, it doesn't matter a toss if the advertisements vary from country to country. Few travellers watch local television or read local publications. Fewer still understand them. There is no need to worry about whether Mr and Mrs Mancunian will be exposed to different commercials for your brand when they nip off for a Bargain Break and end up in Munich, Madrid or Monaco. The last thing they are likely to do on arrival is couch-potato down in front of the telly. And if they do they won't understand a word. (Campaigns targeted at jet-setting businessmen, like those for airlines, and duty free – and the *Financial Times* – are atypical in this respect.)

It makes no sense, the Diverse Campaigners continue, to save a few thousand quid on TV commercial production costs – or even a few hundred thousand quid if the brand is a major one – if the campaign is ineffective on air.

In any event, as we have seen, only Universal Campaigns really save big bucks on TV production costs. Consistent Campaigns shave slivers off production costs, but the savings would be insufficient to justify risking a potentially ineffective – or even a less effective – campaign. In other words saving shekels, which most people believe to be the principle *raison d'être* for multinational advertising, is a secondary reason at best.

So why is everybody that's doing it, doing it?

The plain truth is that it is not possible to say whether multinational campaigns – in general – are more effective than local campaigns – in general. Or vice versa. Either proposition, when stated baldly like that, is laughable. The fact that fully grown advertising men (frequently including me, at one time) argue ferociously in favour of one side or t'other is pretty laughable too.

The equally plain but awkward truth is that many multinational campaigns are exceedingly successful and many local campaigns are exceedingly successful. Ditto unsuccessful. Ditto modestly successful.

So if you are marketing a multinational brand there is no way of knowing in advance – it just cannot be known in advance – whether a plethora of local campaigns will produce a greater increase in sales than a single Consistent Campaign. However, you don't need a Harvard Business School Ph.D. to see that running a raft of local campaigns is likely to have more disadvantages than advantages. There is more potential for downside risk than potential for upside gain.*

Moreover there seems to be little logic in advertising being so very different from all the other elements in a brand's marketing mix. If the brand name is consistent everywhere, the product specification more or less consistent, the packaging consistent, the price point fairly consistent, the consumer benefit presumably consistent – why on earth should the advertising be different?

Nonetheless it is clear that multinational advertising greatly ups the stakes. When you run a raft of local campaigns you hedge your bets: some you win, some you lose. Run a multinational campaign and you go for broke. It had better be good, or you'll find yourself with deeply unhappy shareholders (and maybe a largely unpayable mortgage).

In the eyes of many agency creative people the magnitude of such risks inevitably forces advertisers to seek unadventurous, unprovocative, unoriginal – 'risk free' – campaigns. Taken together with the translation and cultural differences involved in multinational advertising, they believe, the need to minimise risks when big bank notes are on the table results in insipid campaigns which aim to say everything to everyone and end up saying nothing to no one.

---

* In theory the dilemma could be resolved mathematically: estimate the average sales increase achieved by a multinational approach and compare it with guestimates of the total of sales increases achieved by a host of local approaches. In reality there are so many imponderables that such a calculation would not be worth the video screen it was displayed on.

These risks are real. But far from unavoidable. They can be pruned down, or they can be exacerbated.

They are exacerbated when campaigns are pre-tested, usually at concept stage, in a pot pourri of countries by a pot pourri of researchers all of whom deem it necessary to report back to base with a problem or two that is specific to their country. In France they report that consumers responded well but the beginning of the commercial is too obvious; in Italy consumers responded well but the product comparison is unclear; in Spain consumers responded well but the plot is a little confusing; in Germany they responded well but cannot remember the brand name afterwards; in Britain they responded well but wonder why the little girl is poking her tongue out at her grandma . . . but happily *everybody* responded well, so happily only a few small amendments are necessary. The outcome is not so much a camel, more a bouillabaisse-paella-spaghetti-carbonara-pig's-trotter-Yorkshire-pudding stew. Only blander.

Attempting to minimise risks by testing for negatives in a host of different countries at once will tear the heart out of any bold campaign.

The right way to develop strong multinational advertising is to create strong *national* advertising which you are sure will travel. To be that sure you do not need heaps of local market research. At the most you may need to consult your colleagues in other countries. It isn't difficult. Keep in mind from the outset that the advertising will be developed multinationally; but don't condemn it to death by a thousand improvements.

Far and away the best way to develop multinational campaigns is to extend advertising that has already proved itself in one country. For a multinational brand *every effective national campaign should be assumed to have multinational potential until proved otherwise.*

This is global marketing's equivalent of 'Every man is innocent until proved guilty.' And like its judicial equivalent it always needs to be examined and investigated rigorously. Local managers naturally tend to claim that all their advertising is marvellously effective: to admit otherwise would be unlikely to be career-enhancing. Working in an advertising agency you get used to hearing that such-and-such a campaign worked brilliantly in Uganda or Uzbekistan and is unquestionably worth a spin back home. Such fulsome claims need to be taken with generous pinches of salt. The rule applies only to those very few campaigns which can definitely be proved to have done the business.

To international marketeers countries are natural test markets. Rarely should it be necessary to 'go multinational' with a campaign which has not already shown its paces somewhere. The risks are too great, the international testing procedures too feeble. There are particular occasions, in particular markets, when the only way to win multinationally is to gamble multinationally. But more often than not, marketeers are seduced by the glamour which currently adheres to multinational campaigns and rush headlong into international action: more haste, less speed.

Good ideas must be whisked around the world with the greatest possible rapidity: the ability to do so is probably the multinational corporation's greatest single strength. This is not just true of advertising and marketing. Putting the know-how gained in one country to work in another, quickly, gives multinationals their muscle, their ultimate power. But that is quite different from a Gadarene rush to launch unproven ideas here, there and everywhere.

Advocates of the Universal Campaign approach patently cannot follow this national-to-multinational extension route. (And it is irrelevant to believers in the Diverse credo.) Those advertisers who espouse Universal Campaigns judge that the benefits outweigh the risks. As we have seen, Universal Campaigns are a small minority of the total – and I have no doubt that a case-by-case study would show that in every instance there are circumstances which make them atypical.

A tiny digression: until recently at least American corporations have adopted the Universal and Consistent approaches, while Japanese corporations have tended towards the Diverse approach. I suspect these two opposing points of view are derived from the two nations' histories. America, the great melting pot, knows that peoples of all nations were blended at Ellis Island into a single society, and this encourages a belief in the homogeneity of mankind.

Japan, one of the world's greatest isolationists, instinctively feels that peoples are culturally different from each other because they feel themselves to be utterly different from everyone else.

Back to the plot: having sung the praises of the Consistent way to develop multinational campaigns, I must conclude this package tour of global marketing by admitting that Consistent Campaigns have two major weaknesses. And they are weaknesses which will raise their troublesome heads again in the next chapter.

First, the Consistent approach inevitably provokes Not-Invented-Here responses. Second, and partly as a result, the Consistent approach is expensive to operate.

Universal Campaigns tend to be used by companies with lean but autocratic management structures: advertising isn't the only thing which comes from HQ and may not be changed. Executives who work in such companies accept the rules and play their own eccentric games. Diverse Campaigns, in contrast, allow national and local managers a good deal of freedom, with accompanying job satisfaction and personal commitment.

Consistent Campaigns, being hybrids, are harbingers of friction. Local advertising teams are required gleefully to accept, and to re-interpret, and develop, campaigns that have been foisted on them from another country. That is not something that talented advertising people much like. Talented advertising people like to create their own advertisements. And anyway they know that no copywriter or art director ever became rich and famous adapting other countries' ideas. It's no pathway to glory.

Nor, on the other hand, is it – or should it be – a mechanical hack job. If translation were all that were required (as with Universal Campaigns) it could be done by translators. That isn't the Consistent way: intelligent, imaginative flexibility within tight disciplines is called for. Few people have the right combination of personality and ability to be able to do the job well. Those who find the process antipathetic will grumble, and snigger behind their hands. It is a perfect breeding ground for divisive N-I-H fault-finding, and a consequential loss of local enthusiasm and commitment. All of which explains why it is expensive to operate – for advertising agencies even more than for clients.

To produce top-notch Consistent Campaigns it is vital for top-notch people to do a lot of travelling, a lot of explaining, a lot of persuading and convincing. This process cannot be carried out by juniors, nor by telephone, nor by fax. Top-notch people's time is expensive, and they like to travel comfortably: it cannot be done on the cheap. These costs may not easily be measurable, but they will greatly outweigh any savings made on production costs. As I wrote earlier, multinational advertising – contrary to popular belief – is not about cutting costs. It is about maximising advertising effectiveness.

Those who can conquer *globus confusingus* during the next few decades, by creating outstanding and effective and attractive multinational campaigns, will conquer the advertising world's highest peaks.

3

The Future of Agencies

In taking on my task at the IPA I've canvassed opinion quite widely and found pretty much unanimity on the threat we face. It is that business will come to believe that all there is to advertising is the dreaming up of the ad and the buying of the media, each of which can be bought for smallish fees from a specialist. Agencies might as well be studios. The challenge, then, is to the *thinking* in advertising – that this can be as well done at the client company, or by some third-party consultancy, or by a research agency, or not at all . . . . We have to re-establish the pre-eminence of agencies as *the* valuable source of advice and guidance in advertising, not merely as the doers of advertisements . . . we must make it clear that we are selling advertising solutions, not only creative ideas.
Chris Powell, Chief Executive BMP DDB Needham
(Inaugural speech as President of the Institute of Practitioners in Advertising, April 1993)

British advertising agencies are in the doldrums. Although the future of advertising is secure, and global advertising is growing apace, the agencies' role, the services they should provide, the way they should be paid and their relationships with their clients are all in jeopardy. There is much uncertainty, much debate, much nervousness, and not much sign of any resolution of the problems. How have agencies – supposedly populated by some of the cleverest brains in business – got themselves in such a pickle?

For at least half a century it has been a widely accepted truism that the agency business is about to polarise, any day now. At one end of the spectrum, opined the clairvoyants peering into their crystal balls, would be the large, lumbering department-store agencies, offering a trolley-basket full of strategic planning and marketing services, and producing workaday, uninspired advertising for big companies which want agencies to provide them with trolley-baskets full of strategic planning and marketing services, and workaday, uninspired advertising. (I have never met such a client but let's let that pass.)

At the other end of the spectrum, the clairvoyants continued, giving their psychic tea leaves a hearty shake, would be the small, lean, creative boutiques, offering nothing but dazzling campaigns of consummate genius to those enterprising, imaginative clients who want their agencies to provide them with dazzling campaigns of consummate genius and nothing much else.

In-between-sized agencies, which were neither large department stores nor small creative boutiques, and which attempted to bridge the gap, the clairvoyants confidently shuffled their playing cards and declared, were for the high jump. They had drawn the nine of spades and their days were numbered.

This polarisation thesis has always seemed to me to be fair old twaddle, not least because there are sackfuls of medium-sized clients for whom medium-sized agency partners are ideal. Such clients do not want to be small fish in large agency pools, but they demand more strategic planning and more marketing services than a creative boutique could provide. And to date the data has supported me. The market share of large, medium, and small agencies has varied little over the years. Polarisation has been a splendid theory, espoused by many agencies and reported upon at length by many journalists. Too bad it hasn't held water.

However, the worrying implications of the polarisation thesis lay not in the fallibility of its prescience, but in the nature of its analysis. The analysis implied that advertising creativity can be separated from strategic planning in the way that the yolk of an egg can be separated from the white. But when the yolk is separated from the white the egg dies. So it is with creativity and strategic planning.

Instead of the long-heralded polarisation – which will never

The Future of Agencies

happen – the advertising agency business is splintering into five groups:

 i   multinational agencies
 ii local agencies
 iii media specialists
 iv creative-only agencies
 v   multi-service agencies.

These groups are not mutually exclusive. Local agencies can be creative-only, or can be multi-service. Some media specialists operate within agencies, some are completely independent. It is all utterly bewildering – for agencies as well as clients.

The Multinationals

Let's first look at the multinational issue. Today an agency is either part of a worldwide network – a group with offices in thirty or more countries – or it isn't. There are just sixteen such worldwide networks:

Ted Bates	Grey
BBDO	Lintas
Bozell	Lowe
Leo Burnett	McCann Erickson
D'Arcy Masius Benton & Bowles	Ogilvy & Mather
DDB Needham	Saatchi & Saatchi
FCB Publicis	J. Walter Thompson
GGK	Young & Rubicam

These are, in practice, the only agencies that can efficiently handle worldwide campaigns. The British agencies that represent these networks claim total billings of about £2,000 million. Of that £2,000 million perhaps 40% – some £800 million – is spent on multinational campaigns. The remaining £1,200 million goes into local UK advertising.

Another £200 million or so is spent on multinational campaigns (giving a total of £1,000 million) and this is handled, willy-nilly, by the 300 or so British agencies who are not members of multinational networks, but who have loose trading agreements with agencies in other countries.

Within the multinational agencies the management, the client service executives, the planners, the finance folk and even the media specialists love their multinational clients to bits. Multinational clients provide big opportunities, big challenges, big budgets. For the chaps in suits, developing Consistent Campaigns and propelling them from country to country around the world can be both intellectually and socially stimulating.

The creative chaps, however, are by no means so enraptured.

The very best creative people, as I mentioned in the last chapter, do not relish adapting other agencies' campaigns for their local market. (Not even when the other agencies are part of their own network.) They know the work must be done: but they find it neither exhilarating nor invigorating. It is not at all the same as creating a new advertisement for an existing campaign, with which it is often, erroneously, compared. They do not even like *supervising* multinational adaptations, if they can avoid it. As far as creative people are concerned multinational campaigns are not a bundle of fun.

Historically, when there was far less multinational advertising around, this was no big deal. All good, professional creatives occasionally handle jobs they don't much like. Like everyone else, they grin and bear it.

The mushrooming of multinational advertising within the top agencies has shifted the goalposts. The creative supremos who find themselves spending more than one-third of their time handling multinational campaigns soon grow despondent. Some of the most talented have already quit and launched their own local creative boutiques. The money might or might not be as great; the job satisfaction is infinitely greater.

Patently the multinational agencies cannot afford to lose their most talented creative people. Above all, they need them to work with

The Future of Agencies

their local clients. The obvious solution is to split their operations – to run a local unit and a multinational unit. Some multinationals have already gone this route, but it won't wash, because the interface between local and multinational advertising is often blurred, as we have seen. And because most multinational clients appoint a multinational agency deliberately in order to handle Consistent Campaigns, which demand global/local creative integration. That is multinational agencies' *raison d'être*.

For high ground agencies, as for high ground marketing companies, the solution will be a complex matrix of interlocking responsibilities. The volume of multinational advertising allocated to any single creative bigwig will need to be carefully controlled, to be strictly rationed. This is in clients' interests, as well as agencies'. Living in a multinational world will not be simple.

Agencies in networks cannot afford to let themselves be dominated by their overseas business. Ideally the percentage of income derived from multinational business should never exceed 50%. If the overseas proportion greatly exceeds 50% then (a) the agency is not winning much local business, which suggests (b) that its local reputation is not much cop, which means (c) that it won't attract top-quality staff, which will eventually (d) result in its multinational clients being poorly served and then (e) the agency will be truly in the mire. That's the way the dominos fall.

All of which is a peculiarly British predicament, because for advertising, as for much else, Britain is the gateway into Europe for America and Japan. And naturally most multinational advertisers have a strong predisposition – it is not an inviolable rule, just a strong predisposition – to develop multinational campaigns in their own home markets. Unfortunately only a minority of major multinational advertisers are British (Unilever being the great exception). Most multinational advertisers are American or Japanese. So there will be a strong predisposition in coming decades for more and more campaigns to be born in America or Japan.

To overcome this handicap British agencies must convince multinational advertisers that the most talented advertising people in the world are to be found here in London. Few top British creative people mind *originating* multinational campaigns: they merely abhor adapting imported efforts.

We have a head start. British advertising is creatively admired and respected throughout the world. But it is also often thought – particularly by Americans – to be a trifle precious, too clever by half.

And British agencies have fuelled their critics' antipathy by being more than a wee bit arrogant, particularly in the late 1980s.

The British Agencies

Indeed it was in the late 1980s that British agencies' maladies began. So to understand fully the fragmented frazzle in which British agencies now find themselves we will need to take a stroll down memory lane.

Throughout the early 1980s British advertising men felt unstoppable. The principle reason for their cock-a-hoop jubilation was that British marketing communications companies were stock exchange heart-throbs, and love was blind. The financial journalists flattered and fawned upon them; the institutional investors lapped up their shares.

Advertising agencies tumbled on to the London stock market helter-skelter, like Smarties, at prices that eventually proved far too sweet to be digestible. Each new flotation spawned yet another crèche-full of teenybopper agency millionaires. And first Saatchi & Saatchi, then WPP became the biggest agency groups in the world.

In order to justify their toothsome share values, the agencies boasted of their profitability, and their profits seemed to grow exponentially, year by year. Clients, perhaps unreasonably but quite understandably, started to suffer from green-eye.

The view took hold that all advertising folk sped about the countryside in company-owned Porsches, breakfasted daily at the Savoy, lunched at Le Gavroche, downed a few cocktails in the Connaught, dined at Annabel's, weekended just outside Antibes, spent their winters commuting between the Caribbean and Megève, their summers in their Tuscan villas, bought their suits at Armani, their shoes at Lobb, their ties at Hermès, their shirts at Turnbull and

Asser, their wines at Berry Bros., their Schnabels at the Waddington, their riding boots at Gidden's and their guns down the road at Purdey's.

It was an image we British admen embraced and polished zealously. We puffed out our chests, sang 'Rule Britannia' and boasted, not without some justification, that British advertising led the world – both creatively and financially.

Advertising proclaims that success breeds success. And all admen believe that if you are perceived to be gigantically successful you will inevitably become gigantically successful. This is not entirely wrong. But in advertising, ostentatious displays of personal wealth raise lots of little local difficulties.

When agency people scatter money about like drunken deckhands, few clients manage to forget – or want to forget – the fact that it is *their* money being scattered about. Nor is it easy for modestly paid clients to cope with immodestly well-off agency blokes: it is a little like having assistants who are a great deal wealthier than you are. It strains relationships.

None of which causes too much *angst* in the normal course of events. Clients are big boys, and they know that making money out of one another is one of life's little luxuries. Profits are what it's all about.

As long as the profits are not excessive.

Unfortunately nobody knows exactly how to define 'excessive' when it comes to profits. It is a question which much exercises politicians, and economists, and investigative journalists (and nowadays the advertising industry). Investment analysts usually point to a figure which is 'the average for the industry', but the average for the industry is of no consequence if you happen to believe the entire industry is excessively overprofitable.

Despite these uncertainties, most people are convinced that they have an instinct, a nose, for grotesquely greedy levels of profit. And in the 1980s many clients came to feel that advertising agencies were making a great deal more than they should. Hence their Porsches. Hence their Schnabels. Hence their whopping share prices.

The feeling reached its zenith when Saatchi & Saatchi bought the

Ted Bates agency in America – almost sight unseen (the Saatchis never visited Bates' offices until after the deal) – for more than $450,000,000, and Ted Bates' diminutive president Bob Jacoby netted a sublime $110,000,000 personally. Jacoby made more out of the advertising business than anybody else, before or since; and he scooped an extra $5,000,000 by getting Saatchi's to cancel his contract within weeks of buying his agency.

It was a splendid deal for Jacoby, a lousy deal for Saatchi's – and an appalling deal for the advertising industry.

Saatchi & Saatchi's purchase of Bates and Jacoby's fat purse was publicised worldwide. From many clients' point of view this was the camel's-back-breaking straw. From then on clients began to look at agency finances with eyes that were not merely greenish, but deeply jaundiced. No longer were the perks and profits simply symbols of a lively lifestyle. As one of Jacoby's clients opined to me at the time: 'That's my money he's got.' At the same time, in France, the Gross brothers were coining lavish profits through their Carat media-buying operation. As one of *their* clients said to me: 'I don't mind anyone making a fair margin, but too much of my money is sticking to the Gross brothers' fingers.'

Suddenly, at the end of the 1980s, unheralded and out of the blue, came the recession. And with it the opportunity for clients to redress the balance, to put things right (as they have seen it); or to extort a little revenge (as most agency people have seen it).

But they probably could not have done so had not the terrain already been well prepared. It was.

In days of yore – we're talking the 1950s and 1960s here – British agencies were all paid 15% commission on the advertising they placed with the media, and would never have dreamed of competing with each other by price-cutting. Instead they competed by offering their clients more and more services. At that time the then president of the Institute of Practitioners in Advertising, the formidable Jack Wynne-Williams, stated: 'The commission system encourages competition among agencies by improved services, and discourages price cutting.' That was the textbook view.

As a result the larger agencies became mini-marketing

communications conglomerates: the department stores of the old polarisation theory. They offered their clients a myriad services, carried out a multitude of marketing functions. At J. Walter Thompson in Berkeley Square they even employed 'cardboard engineers'. These weren't engineers made of cardboard, but chaps who cunningly cut up cardboard in curious ways. J. Walter Thompson and the London Press Exchange (now Leo Burnett) both employed over a thousand people, twice as many as they do today.

In the late 1960s an Institute of Practitioners in Advertising brochure explaining how agencies worked included an organogram which showed that 'The Modern Agency' would include a public relations division, a merchandising and sales promotion division, a packaging and display division and a trade and consumer research division. All of which divisions, plus a good few more, were to be found in my first agency Mather & Crowther (now Ogilvy & Mather) when I joined it in 1959. I remember a splendid presentation from a chap in the sales promotion department – which was misleadingly called the marketing department – who had the nifty idea of selling advertising space on pub sausages: the sausages, for a price, would carry advertisers' brand names. Rather like today's tennis players, racing cars – and eggs. I don't remember how the sausages were to be emblazoned. Nor do I remember why the idea sizzled out. Too much like stencilled shoes perhaps.)

These marketing communications services were usually provided by the agency unprofitably, and often for free, to justify their 15% commission. In the peak year of 1966 British agencies employed over 20,000 people. That's almost double the number they employ now. In 1966 something like 6–7,000 of them were not directly employed in media advertising at all. They were engaged in commission-justifying ancillary activities: cardboard-cutting, sausage-branding and the like. Even in the booming, bubbling 1980s that 20,000 figure was never again reached. In the peak year of 1989 UK agencies employed 15,400 people – 25% fewer than two decades previously.

But then by the 1980s advertising agencies were no longer mini-marketing communications conglomerates – largely because the 15% commission system had already begun to crumble.

The Media Specialists

Traditionally the media had paid their 15% commission to recognised agencies, and to nobody else. The media didn't do this because they liked the colour of agencies' eyes. They paid the commission because they believed it to be in their own business interests – for three very good reasons.

i   The agencies were (as they still are) principals at law, responsible for their clients' debts. So the media only needed to collect money from 300 or so agencies, rather than 10,000-plus clients: that's simpler, quicker and safer.
ii The media knew the commission system would motivate the agencies to produce successful advertising. The more successful their advertising is, the more advertisers spend. The media like that.
iii The media wanted to ensure that the advertisements enhanced the appearance of their publications and programmes: they were (and are) anxious that they should be supplied with professionally prepared creative material on time and to the right specifications. That is well worth paying for.

Suddenly in 1978 the Newspaper Proprietors' Association changed its mind. Today it is widely believed that the 15% commission system was shattered by antagonistic clients. No so. It was the media themselves – and particularly newspapers – who cracked the dyke.

The NPA argued that the emergence of a then new breed of curious creatures called media specialists (in those days people called them media *brokers*, much to their fury) had forced their hand. Some clients, the NPA rightly said, had started to separate the media function from the creative work – and so the traditional 15% commission system no longer made sense. Far from being virgo intacta, the NPA claimed, the system had long ago been deflowered. The truth is that the NPA ditched the 15% system because the newspapers had decided that the agencies favoured television over print (probably right) and therefore concluded that they could sell more space if they bypassed the agencies altogether (definitely wrong).

Whatever the justice of the NPA's case, its decision profoundly changed the structure of the agency business. Today media specialists book some 55% of all display advertising: that's approximately £2,450,000,000 of billings. Slightly more than half of that £2.45 billion (£1.4 billion) is handled by the media subsidiaries of agency groups; the remainder (£1.05 billion) is handled by the independent media agencies. Another bit of splintering. And the independents' turnover has grown by about +230% in the last eight years – compared with traditional (creative) agencies' +33% – albeit from a smaller base.

Indubitably media specialists are very good at the specialist media job. They have improved media planning and buying colossally. They have developed sophisticated techniques and technology which are far in advance of anything that traditional agency media departments used to offer. But all these up sides have not been achieved without some down sides.

The Creative Agencies

Nowadays many creative agencies have few direct dealings with the media: they just send them ads to fill empty spaces that media specialists have booked, and will in due course pay for. It's a rum situation.

Like it or not – and I don't much – media buying, and often media planning, have been divorced from the creative function of most advertising agencies, probably forever. And this has thrown the advertising agency business into a series of seismic tremors. Advertising agencies, having previously dropped all their other ancillary activities, have now been divorced, unwillingly, from media selection and buying.

As a result the modern British creative agency is a highly specialised and refined species: a temperamental thoroughbred. It has pared down its functions, and now does very few things but aims to do them supremely well. It creates ideas for television, radio and cinema commercials, and for print and billboard advertisements. Or it adapts multinational ideas for advertisements. It then employs others to turn those ideas into advertising. Occasionally it also buys the space and time in which its advertisements appear. That's about it.

It is revealing, especially to outsiders, to realise the many things that this specificity of functions now excludes. Since the 1950s and 1960s most of the ancillary services which advertising agencies used to offer more or less for nothing have been spun off into separate, specialist units.

Major advertising agencies almost never nowadays include within themselves public relations operations, market research divisions, conference organisation facilities, telemarketing capabilities, sales promotion expertise, political lobbyists, point-of-sale designers, packaging and corporate image specialists, direct marketing units, exhibition stand contractors, promotional literature writers, recruitment advertising experts, artwork studios, photography studios, television and radio production facilities, printers, or even sponsorship dealmakers.

They don't have their own new product development specialists, marketing consultants, databases, poster inspectorates, they don't handle financial prospectus advertising, or medical advertising, or classifieds, either. And that's just a few of the things they don't do.

To confuse matters further many small agencies, and most out-of-London agencies, do perform lots of the functions listed above, within their own organisations. They continue to operate as multi-service agencies – small department stores rather than big ones. To some extent this is a result of smaller agencies' need to scrape a few quid wherever they can: lacking a bedrock of clients with big budgets, they need to be generalists and provide a wide range of services in order to earn their keep.

But to a far greater extent it results from the nature of their clients. In small client companies (or in large companies which do little advertising) a single person will usually be responsible for all the many different areas of marketing communications. For him it would be inefficient to deal with a raft of different suppliers, to each of whom he would be an unimportant customer. So he puts all his business through his advertising agency.

So smaller agencies are forced to be generalists while larger agencies, particularly in London, need to be specialists. That is what the majority of their clients now want. And the customer is always right. Even when he's called a client. Especially when he's called a client. (We'll return to the hot topic of integrated marketing communications in a second.)

The finely focused, honed-down role of large advertising agencies is far from universal throughout the world. In Japan major agencies undertake many of the functions that London (and New York) agencies spurn. Japanese agencies handle public relations, sales literature, exhibitions, sponsorship, company newspapers, market research, pack design – you name it, they'll do it.

And the same has been true, at least until now, of agencies in the East European countries. They too have been all things to all clients, following the Japanese rather than the Western model.

Different again, the East European agencies have not employed their own creative copywriters and art directors. Instead they use freelancers. In Prague alone there are 2,000 freelancers, none of whom work full time in an agency. The Prague agencies simply employ creative directors whose job it is to choose and supervise the right freelance creatives on a task-by-task basis. There are those who believe this way of operating will soon take hold in Britain. I'm not one of them.

In short, advertising agencies can and do come in a multiplicity of different shapes and structures; and those shapes and structures have changed radically over the years. And most of the different shapes and structures are now and will continue to be, simultaneously and confusingly, operative in the UK. There is no longer any such single, simple thing as an 'advertising agency'.

The splintered nature of today's marketing communications business gives many clients a headache, because they feel the need for an overall, co-ordinated, strategic approach to their multi-faceted marketing needs. And they feel this unified approach can and should be available from a single source. No dice. Marketing services have become as specialised as medicine: you don't consult a cardiologist if you've a detached retina.

There is proabably a gap in the market here for the equivalent of the general practitioner – somebody who can guide clients through the maze of marketing communications services and specialists. Such an adviser would need to assume the role of an independent marketing consultant. Without such a consultant it is a role clients must carry out themselves. It's part of their job.

The Multi-Service Agencies

In an attempt to plug the gap, most of the largest agency group holding companies – WPP, Saatchi, Omnicom, Interpublic and Bozell – now own specialist units which operate in several different marketing communications areas. They own PR companies, and sales promotion companies, and direct marketing companies, and package design companies, and the rest. These trade as completely independent operations, with their own managements, and their own profit targets, in their own offices, and they report direct to the group holding company which owns them. Many of them are dynamic, successful companies and they generate handsome profits for their holding company owners.

The holding company seeks to encourage cross-fertilisation between these various specialist subsidiaries, but generally fails. This is because (a) most clients do not like to put too many eggs in one basket; (b) within most large client organisations different individual managers are responsible for the different marketing functions, and each individual manager has his own favourite suppliers; (c) the various companies in a group are not all of the same quality – and never can be; but (d) most important of all, the managers of the individual subsidiaries see little benefit but plenty of risk in recommending their group partners: if their partners perform brilliantly they may gain some kudos for having made the recommendation, but if their partners screw up. . . .

Moreover the managers of the individual subsidiaries are competitive, and often don't like each other a lot. Turf wars do not disappear simply because the contestants are asked to stop fighting. (You can lead a manager to profits, but you can't make him deliver.)

One of the formidable strengths of the free enterprise economic system – compared to the now almost defunct centrally controlled systems – is that the marketplace determines how businesses should be structured. Which functions should be carried out within a business unit? Which should be delegated to outside suppliers – but controlled by the business? Which types of business unit make sense within a holding company? Those are always complex questions, not amenable to shoot-from-the-hip answers.

It has become a cliché to say that companies should stick to their core business, stick to their knitting. But this is rarely as easy as falling off a log. It can be uncommonly difficult to define a company's core business. Should retailers own their own suppliers? Should banks own their own insurance subsidiaries? Should publishers own their own printworks? Should brewers own their own food service businesses? With the wisdom of hindsight it is always easy – at least as easy as falling off logs – to spot when a company has miscalculated, and strayed into areas in which it has insufficient commercial expertise. Then lots of smart-arses smartly raise their heads above the parapet for just long enough to denounce the company's management as incompetent. 'They should have stuck to their knitting,' the smart-arses chant.

But in the present, splintered state of the market, it isn't at all clear what an advertising agency's knitting should be. As we have already seen, agencies have been and done different things at different times and in different places. The structure of advertising agencies is not God-given, nor is it cast in stone. The marketplace may in future determine that agencies should again extend their services to provide, in-house, all types of marketing services. Agencies may once more become mini-marketing communications conglomerates. This is the view held by many of the newer, younger, fashionable London agencies.

Without perhaps knowing that they are retracing agency history, they proclaim that they provide a wide and unified range of marketing communications services under a single roof. They call it 'integrated marketing' (which is a misnomer). They claim to offer 'seamless communication'. The fashionable phrase is 'through the line' – the line being that mythical, invisible boundary between media advertising and other types of marketing communication.

Despite the panache with which the proposition is being promulgated, and the apparent logic of the argument ('Why employ disparate suppliers when it is more cost-efficient to employ just one?'), I doubt whether this route will appeal to many clients. It offers convenience rather than quality. The best talents in all marketing services run their own, specialist shops. They do not want to be departments – and unglamorous departments at that – within an advertising agency. Indubitably clients should integrate their marketing communications. It is dumb to do otherwise. But that does not imply employing only one marketing communications agency. Nor, in reality, do any major clients do so – at most they integrate a *few* of their marketing communications needs. Sales conferences, exhibition stands, public relations, corporate identity, package design et al. are still handled by specialists, as they have always been. Any marketing manager who cannot get consistent and coherent communications from a diversity of suppliers isn't worth his mobile phone, and shouldn't be in the job.

The through-the-line approach will appeal in some degree, as it already has done, to consumer durable companies – who need plenty of back-up publicity material and direct marketing. It won't appeal to fast-moving consumer goods companies – who need very little. Moreover most major advertisers, as I have already said, employ different people – both internally and externally – to handle the different aspects of their marketing communications spectrum. In my view these clients are right. I am an unrepentant specialist.

As marketing communications grow increasingly sophisticated, and consumers grow increasingly advertising-literate, the creative skills needed to get through to them will grow increasingly specialised. So inevitably the high ground marketing communications agencies – whether in media, or sales promotion, or direct marketing, or advertising, or public relations, or whatever – will be the specialists.

Already, today, those people who are brilliant at creating television commercials are rarely as good at print advertisements. And vice versa. Those who are without equal at consumer goods campaigns are lousy at direct marketing. And vice versa. Those who design packs marvellously aren't much cop at brochures, those who write dreamy sales conference scripts can't even spell shelf-wobbler, and those with a perfect ear for radio commercials often have a myopic eye for posters. And vice versa. I could name names to prove each of these generalisations but that would be invidious. No names, no lawsuits.

Naturally, large agencies will aim to employ within their ranks all types of talent, a veritable cornucopia of creative abilities and skills. And they do. But the ethos of every agency will veer towards strengths in some directions rather than others. The ancient adage 'Jack-of-all-trades, master-of-none' is king.

If I were a client I would have no difficulty in selecting the best advertising agency for my business. But it would not be the same agency whatever my business. Even DFSD Bozell – hard as I find this to admit – would not be the ideal agency for *every* client.

Polymaths, like unicorns, are mythical beasts. Even the greatest artists are not infinitely versatile. Tolstoy was no playwright, Turner no portraitist, Brahms is not renowned for his operas.

So it now is with marketing communications. Specialisation is the order of the day; increasing specialisation will be the order of future days. It is not a clock that can be turned back.

Making Great Advertising

So if agencies simply create ideas for advertisements, aren't they merely creative boutiques, albeit of different sizes?

Why then do they need the profusion of account executives, and planners, and management boards, and controllers, the phalanx of organisation men who insulate the creatives from clients and botch the simplest of messages between advertiser and copywriter?

Without that top-heavy management, some major clients are now beginning to feel, the costs of creating and making advertisements could be decimated. And some clients – to date a small minority – are beginning to act upon their feelings. By applying sufficient pressure, and demanding nothing but ideas for advertisements, they believe they can slash their costs. This is the threat to which Chris Powell alluded in his inaugural speech as IPA President, at the beginning of this chapter.

Have advertising agencies, by becoming so specialised, really put themselves at risk of extinction?

That is not idle, academic waffle. It is a subject of profound concern to the advertising agency bosses. To celebrate its seventy-fifth birthday, the Institute of Practitioners in Advertising held its first major conference for over a decade. The title: 'Are Advertising Agencies History?' (A less than triumphant celebratory theme, you may think; but then the mood of the business has hardly been joyous.)

After much cogitation the speakers – almost all of whom came from agencies – explained that, having considered the matter objectively and at length, they had concluded that agencies are not history, not at all: agencies are absolutely wonderful.

As they whistled their happy tunes, however, there were many discordant notes:

> Our margins have been under constant attack; our workforce has been savagely hit; our relevance for today's marketplace has been questioned; and, above all, our future role is in some doubt in some people's minds.
> *Keynote address by Peter Mead, Joint Chairman and Chief Executive, Abbott Mead Vickers BBDO, President IPA (1991–93)*

> Some clients already think they should be able to buy advertising by the yard with a discount for bulk orders. If that approach took hold across the industry, agencies would become ad-factories . . . . If we take this route, life in the advertising agency of the future will be very, very different.
> *Graham Hinton, Joint Chairman and Chief Executive, DMB&B*

Some time ago I was invited to make a presentation at a major retailer's head office. I was dropped off at the address I'd been given. Over the door was a sign. It said 'Suppliers' Entrance'. I smiled, went in, had my briefcase searched . . . and took my seat in the waiting area with all the other suppliers. There's a phone you can use if you need it. But these days, of course, like me, most suppliers have mobile phones. Many of them were speaking frantically into them and scribbling, with sweaty palms, on to the pads they'd placed on the briefcases on their knees. Most of them were sweating. And I smelt it. I smelt fear . . . . And then I got really scared. Scared because I realised it could happen to us.

Andrew Robertson, Chief Executive, WCRS

To allay all those agency chieftains' apprehensive anxieties it is essential to establish that nowadays the underlying role of everyone in an advertising agency who doesn't create advertisements – the *only* important thing they do – is to ensure that the advertisements the agency creatives create are perfectly tailored to their task.

Ensuring that advertisements are perfectly tailored to their task is a whole lot more problematic than it may sound. It is a thorny process. It demands a complete fusion between strategic analysis and innovative creativity. The yolk and the white are interdependent. And this applies equally to both local and multinational campaigns.

Before the creatives ever lift a Pentel, the task must be sharply defined. What is going on in the marketplace? Who is the campaign to be aimed at? What do we know about them? Do we need to find out more? How do we want them to change their behaviour? Exactly what do we want them to think and feel? Are we seeking continuity or change? What are the strengths and weaknesses of the competition? What are the real benefits that our own brand offers the consumer? All hellishly difficult questions to answer.

But they must all be answered accurately – as accurately as knowledge permits – before the creatives start creating, because the answers will constitute the creative brief. And the creative brief – the document which defines what the advertising should communicate, and to whom – is the single most important piece of paper that agencies produce. Not a lot of agencies seem to know that.

Sloppy creative briefs make everyone unhappy. They lead to the creation of irrelevant ideas, which are rejected by clients. This wastes the creatives' time – the agency's most expensive resource. And it irritates the clients (not to mention the creatives themselves). Sloppy creative briefs are catastrophes waiting to happen.

Good creative briefs, in contrast, make everyone happy: clients, creatives and finance directors. Good creative briefs will ensure that the creative ideas are right for the marketplace, right for the brand, right for the budget available – in short, right for the advertising task, for the job to be done.

Creating creative briefs is itself a creative act. Drafting the creative brief is the joint responsibility of account planners working in collaboration with client service people. The account planners must know all there is to know about the marketplace, the client service folk must know all there is to know about the client and the product. Together they must investigate, analyse and finally generate an innovative, challenging brief.

Once this life-enhancing document has been finalised it must be presented – sold, if you like – to the agency's creative teams. And they must be motivated to pull out all the stops. Briefing creative people is rarely a once-and-for-all act: it is a continuous and often exhausting process of guidance, argument and supervision.

Then the agency must be certain – on the basis of judgement (always) plus market research (sometimes) – that the creative idea or ideas that have been produced do specifically meet the defined task, and not some other task with which the creative people have become infatuated along the way.

Next the creative idea(s) must be sold to the client, which may or may not prove difficult, and the client must be restrained from making improvements which would most definitely not be improvements (while being allowed the freedom to make improvements which really are improvements: not easy).

Finally the agency must make it all happen: the scripts and scamps and scribbles must be transmuted into brilliant commercials and artwork and typesetting. All within the budget and to time.

That's a skeletal précis of how ads are made. Naturally it involves

The Future of Agencies

a lot of leg work. And brain work. And computer work. And disputatious work – probably more disputatious work than anything else. And research work. And paperwork. And weekend work. And pub work.

And for maximum effectiveness all these good works must be interwoven with the planning and buying of media, whether this is being carried out by a separate media specialist or by a traditional media department, within the agency.

If it were all as easy as pie there would, indeed, be no need for advertising agencies. Clients would be able to brief copywriters and art directors themselves, and the copywriters and art directors would then deliver the goods. Heigh-ho, and off to lunch.

That it isn't all as easy as pie is down to two basic causes, both of which are inherent in the production of exceptional advertising:

i Exceptional advertising is by definition new, remarkable, original; and that means its creation will almost always involve harrowing birth-pangs.
ii Every advertising problem is different; you might have thought – I might have hoped – that after some thirty years in the business I would have concluded that all advertising problems are much of a muchness. Not so. On the contrary I grow increasingly aware, from day to day, that different products call for different approaches, and that each new campaign is a new challenge.

So that is what most advertising agencies now do. They offer a very great deal more than creative boutiques, but a very great deal less than the massive all-purpose, full-service juggernauts of yesteryear. They employ creative people and embed them in a framework designed to ensure that the advertising ideas they produce are spot-on. They guarantee that the yolk and the white interact and stay fertile until the campaign is born. And that is the way, the only way, to make great, effective advertising.

The Price

The final question currently generating lots of heat but little light is: how much should agencies be paid for doing it?

For agencies seeking the high ground, this will be one of the principle challenges of the late 1990s.

Unless they can devise a charging system which both provides them with healthy profits and is widely acceptable to clients then the future of advertising agencies is, indeed, bleak.

At present every agency charges every client in a different way (nervously insisting as it does so that this demonstrates its 'flexibility and open-mindedness'). In a splintered marketplace, this is less than surprising.

According to chartered accountants Willott Kingston Smith – who have made themselves specialists in agency finances – in 1993 agencies' income was sourced:

Media commissions	46%
Fees	39%
Production mark-ups	14%
Performance related payments	1%

When the data is analysed in more detail it becomes clear that agencies are grasping for remuneration every which way they can. This can hardly be astonishing after the long, painful income drought during the recession.

To quote Willott Kingston Smith:

> Two things seem clear. First, attempts at finding workable alternatives to traditional remuneration methods have not so far proved workable in practice. Second, whatever form remuneration methods may take in the future, they must breed profits among the agencies and confidence among their clients.

The inescapable fact is that there is no perfect system of remuneration in any high-salaried, talent-based personal-service industry.

The Future of Agencies

Study any similar professional industry and you will hear similar grumbles. Lawyers? Their charges are exorbitant. Accountants? They live off the fat of the land. Architects? Their scale rates are ludicrous. Dentists? Do you know how much dentists earn these days? Financial advisers? Their commission levels are a disgrace. So it goes on.

At the end of the day, as the cliché has it, and as Willott Kingston Smith pointed out, there are only three possible ways in which advertising agencies (and similar businesses) can charge for their services:

i   some type of commission system based on turnover
ii some type of time-cost fee package
iii some type of performance-related arrangement.

Each is flawed.

Commission systems, their detractors argue, make no sense at all. An agency's workload is only loosely related to the client's billings (turnover). Though it is more or less true that media-buying activity is directly related to billings, it is hardly true at all of creative activity. So how can commissions based on billings be relevant?

Yet time-cost fees are no better. The essence of any time-cost system is that it encourages people to work slowly, to invent jobs, and provides no incentive (indeed a disincentive) for efficiency: those who do things faster get paid less. Ask any plumber. Nor are time-costs a relevant way to pay for ideas. Sometimes ideas come instantaneously, sometimes they can only be dredged up laboriously, and painfully, and slowly.

But nor are performance-related payment arrangements the complete answer. In a marketplace where all kinds of communications are operative all the time, isolating the advertising effect is notoriously difficult. Moreover it is divisive: it makes client involvement in the advertising process almost impossible. If the client alters the advertisement, how can the agency then be held responsible? No agency wanting to stay in business could accept performance-related fees as more than a top-up.

Yet although each system is deeply flawed, each has great merits.

The commission system incentivises the agency to produce advertising which works, and rewards the agency when budgets increase. Budgets only increase when advertisers are successful, so it is an everybody-wins situation.

Time-cost fees ensure that the agency receives income even if the advertising budget is slashed after its creative work has been completed. And fees seem fair, and open, which is half the battle.

Performance-related payments patently motivate the agency to produce effective work and to avoid self-indulgence. The client can manage the agency on a loose rein, in the certainty that the agency will be totally committed to his success.

There are a myriad more pros, and a myriad-and-one more cons, that can be made for all three systems. The inescapable fact is that each of the systems – not to mention elaborate combinations of them – can and do work adequately, every day of the week, everywhere in the world. None is perfect, each is OK.

Having said this, I have no doubt that the commission system serves clients' needs best: and most experienced major clients agree. In the United States the majority of clients, having dabbled with time-cost fees, are now returning to commission. Not a fixed-level commission, but a gently sliding scale which takes some rough account of workload economies, while still motivating the agency to build billings.

Unhappily, right now the great majority of medium and small clients have lost faith in the commission system. And fascinatingly, all this has happened before. The commission system began at the start of the nineteenth century. At the end of that century, as a result of intense competition, it broke down. Media specialists sprang into existence, some charging as little as 1%. Creative agencies cut commissions; they worked for fees; they charged hourly rates.

Then in the 1920s the newspapers – led by *The Times* – decided the business was in a complete mess and reinstated the commission system. And it survived, more or less intact, until the NPA ditched it in 1978.

Maybe the media will once again mount their powerful stallions and come galloping to the agencies' rescue. Maybe. But I would bet a wagonload of Saatchi & Saatchi shares to a peak-time spot in *Coronation Street* against it happening.

The unavoidable, unappealing fact is that the flat 15% commission system is dead as a dodo, and no kiss of life will resuscitate it.

There will be no going back. There will never again be a price cartel among agencies. Ugly, unbecoming, ungentlemanly price competition is here to stay.

I do not see why this should scare us. Price competition permeates most industries yet they manage to make healthy profits. Good lawyers charge more than bad lawyers, and make fortunes. Ditto accountants, and architects, and butchers, and bakers and – for all I know – candlestick makers.

Clients should not be misled into thinking that their advertising services will come cheaper. But they will be able to choose how much they want to pay, and they will get what they pay for.

Many people believe that the increasing use of technology – video-telephones, faxes, conference calls, computer networks and all the electronic wizardry as yet undreamt of – will help agencies significantly to reduce costs in the next century. Not so. The cost impact of technology will be marginal, at best. All the expensive activities necessary in the development of high ground advertising demand personal contact. The benefits to be gained from hi-tech communications will be peripheral, and may not even compensate for the increased costs involved in handling both the increasingly complex media scene and multinational clients.

Quality, as always, will cost; those who pay peanuts will, as always, get monkeys. That is what happens in most walks of life. Soon it will happen in advertising. It will take a few more years to shake down. But after the turbulence it will be good news – for agencies as well as clients.

Advertising agencies have been around for almost two hundred years. Charles Barker, which is still trading, albeit somewhat transformed, opened its doors in 1812. N. W. Ayer, with which Barker's later merged, started trading in 1869. J. Walter Thompson is now a hundred and thirty years old, far older than Unilever, or Shell, or British American Tobacco – let alone young upstarts like IBM, Mars, General Motors and Hanson.

The popular notion that agencies are built on sand, that they have as little durability as candles in the wind, is manifestly mistaken. Like any other type of business they change, as they should, over the years. But they survive because producing effective advertising, continuously and consistently, is a difficult game: and over the long haul nobody else can do it.

4
How to be a High Ground Client

When I was but a babe-in-arms in this bewitching business I had a client who had been a lance-corporal until some ghastly quirk of career planning turned him into an advertising manager. His way of getting the best out of the agency was to telephone me every morning at 09.31 hours and issue my marching orders for the day. At the same time he would reprimand me for my misdemeanours of the day before.

'Fletcher,' his stentorian voice would bark through my early morning somnolence, 'Fletcher! You were briefed at eleven-oh-eight hours the day before yesterday. When are we going to see your proofs?' (He meant roughs.)

'Fletcher!' I held the phone several inches from my head, fearing permanent damage to the inner ear. 'There's another spelling mistake in this copy. You've spelt its it's. No. Perhaps you are right. It's it is. Correction dismissed.'

'Fletcher!' Balancing the phone in my right hand I reached for the Alka-Seltzer with my left. 'Where are those bloody media schedules? Asked your secretary for them p.m. on the seventeenth instant. Beginning to wonder if there isn't some funny business between you and her, yer know. Should have been fired months ago. Lazy bitch.'

I grew terrified of each morning's alarm call. Sometimes I deliberately arrived late, hoping that having missed me at 09.31 hours he might get caught up in drill parades or button-polishing and forget to phone again. No such luck. 'Late again, Fletcher! Breakfast meeting, was it? Ha ha! I'll be having a word with your commander-in-chief if you don't extract your digital! Not used to service like this. Unacceptable, yer know.'

Pleading incipient insanity, I was eventually transferred from the lance-corporal's parade ground to work on the late William Hill's account. This proved little better. 'Call that an advert?' the great bookmaker once bawled at me as I presented to him the layout for an aesthetically delightful little *lion d'or* winner. 'Call that an advert? I could do better with my knob and a pot of paint.' A difficult point to refute, really; for all I know he had an exceptionally versatile weapon.

On another occasion he turned upside down all the masterpieces I had presented to him. 'Lots of people read adverts in other people's papers,' he opined, 'in the tube and suchlike. You get double your money that way. Don't suppose you Mayfair arty-farties ever go in the tube, do you? If it's a good advert it can be read upside down. And this lot can't.' Not one of the tests which advertising textbooks often mention. Not without merit, though. Years later I sold a campaign to a client by inverting the advertisements and quoting the William Hill dictum. It happened to be a campaign which looked rather good upside down.

On yet another occasion the managing director of one of Britain's leading Japanese companies picked up an advertisement layout to which he had taken an exception and flung it at me – spinning it like a stone thrown to bounce on water. The thick card flew past my head. A foot or so to the left and I might have been decapitated. 'That not creativity . . . ' he yelled as the missive hit the wall with a resounding crack, ' . . . that rubbish!' (Not being English he naturally lacked William Hill's eloquence.)

All three clients – and every agency greybeard can relate similar sagas – were unwittingly expressing their attitudes to the client/agency relationship. Not for them the oft-proclaimed, highfalutin view that the agency/client relationship is a professional partnership of business equals. They – and many, many others like them – espoused the twin old-fashioned axioms that he who pays the piper calls the tune, and that advertising agencies are filled to overflowing with young smart-arses which regularly need to be kicked. Who can deny the truth of both?

And for all three clients – and for the many, many others like them – the agency produced effective, workmanlike advertising which presumably met their requirements and had a generally beneficial effect on their sales.

I would merely express the view that if they – and the many, many others like them – dealt with their agencies with more savvy, their advertising would be better: more persuasive, more relevant, more effective. (More savvy is *not* a synonym for more wimpish, as we shall see – but I suppose it does mean, among other things, more civilisedly.)

The question is not how to make the agency work hard; the question is how to make the agency produce its best. Anyone will work hard if you pay them and bully them a little; but for some clients agencies will always go that extra mile. Those are the clients – and I've been fortunate enough to work for quite a few – who capture the high ground.

The underlying dilemma in all agency/client relationships – it was touched on in Andrew Robertson's cogent speech to the Institute of Practitioners in Advertising's seventy-fifth birthday conference – is whether agencies are professional advisers, or whether they are just suppliers. Naturally agencies prefer to see themselves as professional advisers. Most clients nonetheless tend to think of them as suppliers, albeit rather sophisticated suppliers, providing expensive and unmeasurable services. It is a false dichotomy.

Clients should not encourage agency people to dress up as management gurus, to aspire to being other than they are. Creating successful advertising is difficult enough, and admirable enough, and important enough for it to be unnecessary for agencies to pretend to be good at other knitting.

Clients who become close friends of agency people naturally seek their advice, as the evenings wear on and the wine seeps sweetly out of the bottles, on a vast plethora of subjects from marketing plans to marriage plans. But that doesn't turn the agency folk into professional business consultants (or marital guidance counsellors, for that matter).

In addition to such friendly intercourse, clients frequently ask their agencies to get involved with their marketing operations, to act as marketing communications consultants, to provide wide-ranging marketing advice. Agencies love doing all this: it is absorbing, it is challenging, and it is flattering to be asked. But as we saw in the last chapter, agencies no longer employ a surfeit of staff, ready, willing, and able to do such work at the drop of a hint as they did in the past. If a client wants it done, it must be additionally paid for.

Clients are, however, unwise to treat agencies simply as suppliers: at least in the crude way that William Hill – and the many, many others – so often do. The client/agency relationship, when it burgeons and is fruitful, is not quite like any other business relationship. It is – or should be – more like a commercial romance than a continuing buyer-versus-seller haggle. It is unique.

For a start, and contrary to popular belief, client/agency relationships are long-lasting. On average clients stay with their agencies seven years. The biggest (and the most successful) clients stay with their agencies much longer. Over the years the agency and client teams naturally get to know each other exceedingly well. At the junior brand management/account executive level they may speak to each other every day, often several times a day. They eat together, drink together, grumble about their bosses together, cry on each other's shoulders and often become good friends. Several of the closest friends I have today were clients I started working with in my twenties.

At more senior levels client and agency executives may well speak to each other two or three times a week, for years. Again they often become friends. There are not many other business relationships as close.

Naturally, considerable benefits accrue to clients from these long, close relationships. Otherwise clients would doubtless chop and change more often; but only foolish ones do. In the 1960s two celebrated entrepreneurs, John Bloom and Cyril Lord, decided that long-lasting agency relationships were asinine. So neither appointed agencies to handle their business, although both were buying large spaces in newspapers most days of the week.

Instead, each of them held regular tournaments, into which any agency that fancied its chances could enter campaign ideas. The entrepreneur would peruse all the ideas on offer and pick those which took his fancy. The agencies which had created the victorious advertisements would then execute them, run them, and collect the 15% commission. If your campaign struck lucky you made a fast buck. If not, you lost your bet. It was like Russian roulette, with Bloom and Lord spinning the cartridge chambers.

I should mention that although Bloom, a washing-machine wizard, and Lord, a carpet king, played the same game, they were wholly independent of each other.

And they both, independently, went bust.

And in Bloom's case, at least, he took several of the Russian roulette agencies down with him.

Since the 1960s no other advertiser has attempted, to my knowledge, to operate the Bloom/Lord tournament system – though some of the partwork magazine publishers have come close. A tiny number of flaky, fly-by-night advertisers switch agencies whenever they get bored, which is all too often. They are well known in adland, and only desperate agencies ever accept their business. Clients with ants in their pants get the advertising they deserve: off-the-peg, self-service, undistinguished and ill-fitting.

It takes quite a while for client and agency to learn to work together efficiently. For a client, to keep indoctrinating new agencies wastes precious time – it takes much longer than anyone ever expects for a new agency to get the feel of a client's brands and marketplace. Long-term relationships enable agencies to take long-term recruitment and training decisions, which benefit their clients. And agencies usually know a fair amount about their clients' confidential future plans – which may cease to be all that confidential the moment the agency is fired. All of which are excellent, businesslike, unromantic reasons for client fidelity.

However, long-lasting relationships inevitably breed complacency. Agencies, like spouses, all too easily start to take their other halves for granted. People who have been working together for too long grow casual, sloppy, lax. At that point the client must read the agency the riot act, and crack the whip: clearly, sharply, and unequivocally. Otherwise mild irritations fester into dangerous sores.

Wise clients know that good agencies can always be made to pull up their socks; only in the direst cases is it necessary to administer the boot. (As well as being time-consuming, appointing new agencies is by no means a hazardless game.)

Because agencies have comparatively few clients they throw a great deal into each relationship. Most businesses have a large number of customers, even if a handful are dominant. Few agencies have more than forty or fifty clients, most have far fewer. That's why agencies are so especially fearful of losing clients: they don't have many to lose. And this anxiety leads to both the best and the worst in agencies' behaviour. Commitment and involvement on the one hand, cringing and sycophancy on the other. Savvy clients encourage the former and expunge the latter.

Finally, much of the uniqueness of the relationship centres around the odd word 'client'.

When I was in my early thirties I issued an edict in my agency that clients should no longer be called clients; instead they should be called customers. 'Agencies use the word client,' I pontificated, 'to make themselves feel grand and important. It helps them convince themselves they are professionals rather than tradespeople. It is pompous, and it is misleading. Our clients are our customers, nothing more or less. They pay us to do a job of work, we do it. There's no more to it than that.'

Interestingly our clients (sorry, customers) purported to find the change in their nomenclature rather fetching. They felt it to be down-to-earth, hard-nosed, close-to-the-coal-face and all that. But even more interestingly, despite my best endeavours, the idea never stuck. Within a few weeks our clients became clients again.

Today I consider my youthful rubric to have been more than a little pompous and misleading. There is a basic difference between a customer and a client. It involves a measure of expertise, and thus a degree of trust. I know little (or even less) about dentistry, accountancy, law, medicine (and a whole lot of other things, for that matter). So it seems sensible – unavoidable – for me to trust my dentist, accountant, lawyer, doctor; and that in turn makes it sensible for me to have long-lasting relationships with them. (Once I have found good 'uns.)

So it is with advertising. Customers don't always trust their suppliers, but clients must trust their agency. They have no choice. The working relationships interlock so tightly. Trust does not equal unquestioning blind faith. I trust my solicitor, but I disagree with him all the time. (He's not infallible. If he thinks he is, he's wrong again.) Trust is a nebulous concept. It implies having confidence in somebody, having respect for their opinions, but not doing everything they say. Trust, in business, means feeling you are in the same team. Team mates may be competitive, they sometimes jostle each other, but they always unite when it counts.

Whenever an agency presents an idea to a client it is, of logical necessity, just one of an infinite number of possible ideas it could have chosen to present. There is no limit to the number of ideas out there in the ether. Clients who do not trust their agency will never feel the ideas presented are the best possible for the task. They will always worry that something better could have been done.

The products – the ideas – that agencies sell to their clients are, after all, will-o'-the-wisps: insubstantial and unquantifiable. Marks and Spencer can specify the acceptable quality of cotton vests; Sainsbury's can specify the acceptable quality of baked beans; British Airways can specify the acceptable quality of components. Nobody can specify the acceptable quality of an advertisement.

Inevitably, this means that subjective feelings enter strongly into the relationship. Everyone tries to keep them out but willy-nilly they creep back in. That is a key reason why clients must trust their agencies (and agencies trust their clients). Trust enters into so many aspects of the client/agency relationship that if a client cannot trust his agency he had best send them packing. It is one of the rare occasions when this must be done.

It isn't just the big decisions. Every day in every way the client must be able to rely upon – to trust – his agency muckers.

Can the photograph be taken twenty-four hours sooner (it's needed for a showcard)? Can the cost of the commercial be cut by

£7K (we've overshot the budget)? Can the press advertisements be delayed a week (the product isn't ready yet)? Can you nip up and meet me in Wigan tomorrow (yes, I know I said I was coming to your offices, but I can't)? Can you ask your lawyers whether this will be acceptable (I don't want to ask ours – you know what they're like)? Can the forty-second commercials be shortened to thirties (we've overshot the budget, again)?

A welter of such mundane requests flows incessantly between client and agency. And each relies on some small degree of mutual trust.

So wise clients know it is in their own interests to win their agency's trust – just as it is in every leader's interests to win the trust of his followers. You win trust in an agency/client relationship in the same way that you do in any other human relationship. In this respect at least, agency/client relationships are far from unique.

Trust then is at the core of the agency/client relationship. But it is not enough. (As I was taught long ago by my logic tutor: it is necessary but it is not sufficient.) If I were a client my overwhelming objectives would be threefold:

i   to get the very best people in the agency working on my business
ii to make sure they never get spirited away to work on other business
iii to motivate them to excel themselves on my account.

If I could achieve all three I would be confident my advertising was scraping the sky. What is the way to go about it?

First, I would have no qualms about paying the agency generously. Whether commission-based or fee-based, I would ensure that my remuneration package was at least as profitable to the agency as that of any other client. Well, I would say that, wouldn't I?

But there is no rationale for any other decision. Most clients, as we saw in the last chapter, do not nowadays see things this way. They are wrong. And if I were a client, their cheese-paring would offer me a potential competitive advantage. This is why the best and most successful advertisers all pay top dollar. And they are among the biggest spenders, so they would have most to save by salami-slicing.

Almost everyone in the advertising world knows that Unilever espoused this principle publicly, in 1992, after a long and thorough analysis of its agency remuneration arrangements around the world. Unilever may not do absolutely everything right, but they are pretty good at advertising.

In a small or new agency the very best people would probably be the partners, and it would be especially important to get them firmly pinioned to my account, as they are bound to be prey to a lot of competitive distractions. In larger agencies it can be more difficult to identify the best people; but it can always be done with a little effort.

Paying the agency generously would only be the first step towards getting the very best people on my business. Once again it is necessary, but it is not sufficient.

Thereafter I would have regular six-monthly meetings with the agency chairman to remind him of the ungenerous motive for my generosity. (People are so forgetful.) I would remind him that what has gone up might easily come down, and that there is no such thing as a free lunch. I feel sure he would get the message.

And at the same time I would appraise the agency's performance, department by department, and use the opportunity to lock in my second objective: keeping good people on my business once I had found them.

From any agency's perspective, there are never quite enough class acts to go round. When a client grumbles and asks for someone to be replaced by someone better, it may mean annoying one client to please another. And the best people in agencies like to move about a bit, to gain experience across a wide variety of clients and diverse range of markets. If they are not offered this opportunity for diversity, they leave. This puts agency management in a tough spot, when a client grows overenamoured of one of its best staff. So when a client insists that John or Jane must stay on his business he must expect an explanation of the problems and a fight.

But if the client is firm enough and fierce enough he'll win. It is a sad truth, but in these matters those clients who shout loudest (albeit politely) get their way. As an agency boss, I have switched good people away from those clients who I knew would not protest too vociferously, and kept other good people working with other clients because I knew that if I moved them my life would be unliveable. (Not that I would admit any of this publicly, you realise.)

Back to being a client. Having got the agency's best people on my business I now need to motivate them. In large measure this is, admittedly, the agency's job. That is why I am paying them generously. I have neither the time, nor the inclination, nor is it my responsibility to supplant the agency management.

Despite this, it is very much in my interests to be thought to be 'a good client'. I want the agency's best people to want to work, to beg to work, on my business. I want them to want to stay on my business, whether I bully their chairman or not. I want them to work longer, and harder, and more enthusiastically on my advertising than they do on any of the agency's other accounts. I know I will never be able to see, to analyse, to evaluate the results of their greater endeavour. But only fools believe that things which cannot be measured cannot be real. I want my agency team to tell me, confidentially, in a whisper, that the advertising they produce for me is better than they produce for anyone else, that they love working on my account and that they are utterly committed to my business. Naturally I will believe them.

While the results of their efforts will not be measurable, if I motivate the agency team to the best of my ability the outcome can only be beneficial to my bottom line. And to motivate them, five attitudes are paramount:

    i   honesty
    ii toughness
    iii flexibility
    iv consistency
    v   enthusiasm

They overlap a little, but they are distinct. In most cases the best way to see how important they are is by considering their opposites.

How to be a High Ground Client

First honesty – opposite, dishonesty. Dishonesty is one of the most common, and is certainly the most demotivating and demoralising failing among clients. (We're talking petty dishonesty here, not financial skulduggery or fraud or anything truly evil.)

Many clients lie to their agencies repeatedly, mostly about trivial matters, and presumably imagine that the agency people are too daft, dumb and blind to notice.

Junior client executives censure the agency for things they themselves have not done; they impute to their bosses decisions which they have made themselves, but cannot defend; they make the agency carry the can for their own bungles.

Well, we all go in for a smidgeon of transferred blame from time to time: nobody's perfect. But dullards believe that, with an agency to hand, they have a permanent whipping boy, whose main role in life is to be bollocked, and who dare not complain. It's no way to inspire good work.

Honesty overlaps with toughness. And the opposite of toughness is wimpishness. Good clients do not grumble incessantly, but they are lucidly clear when things go wrong and they don't fudge-and-mudge wimpishly about things they dislike.

Many clients seem to find it horrifyingly difficult to tell agency people, face to face, that they dislike – or what they dislike about – a piece of advertising. This is because they are kind – and it's charming, it's lovable, it's well meaning, it's disastrous. I can recall at least a dozen occasions in the last five years when a client has deplored the advertising he has been shown but not had the guts to express his views on the spot. Inevitably things have eventually ended in tears. Tears which need never have occurred had the not-all-that-prickly nettle been grasped instantly.

I can remember only one occasion when a client has failed to express aloud his antipathy to a campaign and I found his behaviour acceptable and excusable. We had created a campaign for Hennessy cognac and presented it to the eponymous Gilles Hennessy of that ilk. The advertisement showed our beloved Queen (we would have needed to use a lookalike) hobnobbing with St Bernards – then the Hennessy mascots – instead of her own beloved Corgis.

For reasons I still fail to understand, these lighthearted advertisements so enraged Gilles that I feared he might suffer an apoplectic seizure. So great was his distaste, so furious his anger, that he was struck dumb. His face changed hue and for a moment he looked as if he might puke. Instead he silently left the room.

You will not be too astonished that the advertisements never ran, nor too astonished that we didn't keep the account for much longer. It occurred to me that perhaps the French get much more emotional about advertisements than we stolid Brits. Or maybe it is that people feel much more passionately about advertisements for brands which carry their great, historic family name. In any event no other campaign I have presented during my career has provoked a similar response.

Normally clients always say something when they are shown new advertisements; and it is best when they tell the truth. Clients, like parents, must be fair but firm.

And flexible. You might think flexibility to be a synonym for wimpishness. Not so. Wimpishness means feeble cowardice; flexibility means the ability to change when it makes sense. The dividing line may be fine but the difference is unmistakable.

Inflexibility is a less heinous, and a less common, sin than dishonesty or wimpishness but for a client it is equally self-destructive. It extinguishes the agency's enthusiasm for new ideas, new initiatives, new ways of looking at old problems. New approaches invariably demand client flexibility. (When I am asked by a stubbornly inflexible client why – if such-and-such is such a good idea – I didn't have it earlier, my answer is that it hardly seems fair to blame Sir Isaac Newton for not having discovered gravity sooner.)

The principle of wise flexibility states: 'Everything can be changed unless there is a very good reason why it can't.' Often there is indeed a very good reason; often there are very many very good reasons. Often there aren't.

Here are a couple of examples of admirable client flexibility.

In the early 1970s International Distillers and Vintners was my agency's largest client, and IDV's marketing director was Tim Ambler (now a senior research fellow at London Business School).

How to be a High Ground Client

Shortly before Christmas 1973 Tim explained to me, firmly and unwimpishly, that he intended to fire my agency because our creative work was not up to scratch. He had discussed the matter at great length with his colleagues and the decision was irrevocable. It was a painful decision, he said, because I and my team were jolly good chaps.

It would be an exaggeration to say there were tears in his eyes, but he was patently telling the truth. He didn't relish firing me. But he was going to.

The next day I phoned and asked if we could be allowed a fortnight – including the Christmas break – in which to persuade him to revoke his decision. No. The decision was taken.

But nothing, I argued, will happen in the next fortnight: you have nothing to lose in allowing us another chance. He did not want to encourage false hopes, he insisted.

I promised him false hopes would be strictly forbidden. Eventually, and flexibly, he agreed to a fortnight's stay of execution.

We worked throughout Christmas. It is the only occasion I can remember being in meetings on Christmas Day, Boxing Day and New Year's Day.

And when we presented our work at the beginning of January it was an instant success. As it happens we then presented, twenty years ago, the start of the Le Piat wine campaign which has run – with its French theme more or less unchanged – for over two decades. It has helped build Le Piat into Britain's most successful wine brand. And it nearly never happened.

Tim Ambler had needed, with his colleagues at IDV, openly to rescind his original recommendation to fire us. That required flexibility. And it won him, and IDV, the agency's undying commitment.

Like Tim Ambler, Amstrad's Alan Sugar is not renowned for wimpishness. He is not even renowned for flexibility; but then reputations are sometimes inaccurate.

Almost fifteen years after the Le Piat saga my agency worked for Amstrad, and we were creating the campaign for the launch of a new personal computer. (I say 'we', but in reality Alan Sugar dealt almost

73

exclusively with my partner Greg Delaney. I occasionally had a small walking-on part.)

It was Friday afternoon and Greg Delaney had gone to Alan Sugar's office to present the campaign. Greg was especially pleased with the work, as were we all. Sugar is not an easy man to please, but everyone in the agency was convinced the campaign idea was spot-on.

Sugar hated it. And like William Hill he is not a man to mince his words. Greg returned to the agency crestfallen. He had never heard more expletives in fewer minutes. He had been mown down by a four-letter Gatling gun.

We all retired for the weekend sharing Greg's disgruntlement. On Monday morning Sugar telephoned. Were we to be fired?

Not at all. He had thought about the campaign over the weekend and had decided he was wrong. He had been too hasty. The campaign ran, and was a phenomenal success. Amstrad sold hundreds of thousands of personal computers in months.

I would never call Alan Sugar, or Amstrad, angelic clients. On the contrary, most of the time they are demons incarnate. But not a lot of businessmen have the panache – in Alan Sugar's case I mean the *chutzpah* – to admit they were wrong after reviling some work. That called for flexibility. And again it paid off.

Consistency, the fourth essential client attribute, again sounds like a contradiction of flexibility. How can you be both consistent and flexible? Easy. Being flexible means being able to change your mind when it is wise to do so; being inconsistent means being haphazard, confused, irrational.

The first important aspect of consistency is the provision to the agency of clear, unambiguous briefs. The importance of the agency's internal creative briefs was stressed in the last chapter. An agency can seldom produce good briefs for itself if it doesn't receive good briefs from its client. I'll say still more about the supreme importance of good briefs in the next chapter. For now all that needs to be emphasised is that clear, unambiguous briefs help clients, later, to offer clear, unambiguous responses to the advertising, when it is presented to them.

Random, idiosyncratic responses to creative ideas – inconsistency – are depressing and demotivating. Lobbing haphazard spanners into the works does not increase the efficiency of the machine. Inconsistent clients destroy an agency's morale. Nobody wants to work on their business.

Last, but definitely not least, enthusiasm. It must be terribly tedious for clients, but agencies need constant stroking and encouragement. Most agency folk are insecure neurotics – even if they have confident smiles. (*Especially* if they have confident smiles.)

A few years ago I attended a dinner at which David Ogilvy, the great Scottish wizard who founded Ogilvy & Mather, was asked what aspect of his career in advertising he had most enjoyed.

'What gave you the idea that I enjoyed any of it?' he replied instantly. 'Most of the time I was petrified of losing clients. I liked the fame for a bit, but after a while even that palled.'

How could someone so successful be so insecure? No problem: David is an adman through and through.

If it is true that clients must be brutal when things go wrong, it is equally true that they must be blatantly enthusiastic when things go right. And they must show it. Enthusiastically.

When Bill Brodie, now retired, was managing director of Premier Beverages he told me that at the end of every telephone call with someone from the agency he hoped that they would rush into one of their colleague's offices and say how much they enjoyed working on his business. It's a tall order – but the objective is flawless. And perhaps it partly explains why the agency has always produced outstanding work for Premier.

In similar vein Hanson director Christopher Collins, when he owned Goya Perfumes, told me that he aimed to ensure that there was something in the post for me from Goya every day of the week – to keep reminding me that they were one of the agency's liveliest – and most important – clients. (He patently had a poor, if accurate, opinion of my memory.)

Honesty, toughness, flexibility, consistency and enthusiasm. They are doubtless desirable in most business relationships. To motivate the agency team in the steamy cauldron of incessant agency/client strain they are crucial.

Keith Holloway of Grand Metropolitan – deputy chairman of the Incorporated Society of British Advertisers, and one of the most experienced admen in the land, who has held top jobs on both sides of the agency/client canyon – is currently promulgating 'partnership sourcing' as a way of improving clients' relationships with agencies. And it looks likely that his proposals will be broadly accepted by both the ISBA and the IPA.

Partnership sourcing – originally a Japanese concept – demands that companies discuss their needs with suppliers, and try to solve problems collaboratively. It demands, to quote Holloway:

> Long-term relationships, openness, information exchange, pooling of experience, shared training and a disciplined interface . . . a commitment by both sides to doing everything they can to improve the quality and reduce the costs of each other's operation.
>
> *ISBA Conference, November 1993*

Partnership sourcing demands, in other words, that companies treat their suppliers as partners. In my view partnership sourcing is a two-word synonym for 'trust'. But let's not quibble about definitions: Keith Holloway's initiative is both welcome and realistic.

However, amid all this chatter of trust and loyalty, there is one important area where Western clients have never felt able to have trust in their agencies: client conflict. Almost without exception, major clients refuse to allow their agencies to handle advertising for their competitors. They feel it would inevitably lead to breaches of confidence and conflicts of interest. (Japanese clients, in Japan, suffer from no such neuroses.)

To some extent agencies should be flattered by this prohibition. It is a further example of the particularity of the client/agency relationship. (Clients do not mind sharing banks, or printers, or accountants – or even hatmakers, as far as I know.) It reflects the importance which advertisers impute to their agency relationships. If the relationships were unimportant client conflicts would be unimportant. However, this refusal to allow agencies to handle competitors' billings has — almost more than any other single factor — shaped and defined the structure of the agency business.

There are some twenty major competitive car clients, so there need to be twenty agencies to handle them; there are about forty major financial clients — building societies, banks and insurance companies — and they too all want their own agencies; the same is true of electrical consumer durables, of confectionery, of computers, of many kinds of food and of some toiletries. The avoidance of client conflict inevitably fragments the agency business.

Nor can the largest agencies and agency groups ever grow significantly bigger. At least not through handling more advertising. Their major clients will not allow them to handle competitors, nor to acquire any other sizeable agency (which is almost bound to have competitive clients). That is largely why they have diversified into other areas of marketing communication. The principal reason there are so many advertising agencies in the world is that clients insist on monogamy.

Whether or not we agency folk are grateful for the implied flattery, whether or not agencies would truly be unable to handle client conflicts, is irrelevant. The world's major clients have made up their minds and are not about to change them. Even Japanese clients are now beginning to follow Western practice, outside of Japan. Agencies have no choice in the matter.

Some international corporations, however, have taken the principle beyond legitimate, or even sensible, bounds. They refuse to allow their agencies to handle advertising for competing corporations, even if there are no competing products involved.

It works — I mean it doesn't work — like this. Because corporation A and corporation B both make matchboxes and compete in Argentina, they will not agree to share an agency in Britain where A only makes wasp-bite creams and B only makes Zimmer frames. (An absurd example to highlight an absurd situation.)

This is not savvy client behaviour. It makes agencies stroppy; it hinders their growth; it benefits nobody.

It's how to be a low ground client.

5

High Ground Creativity

I started out as a copywriter. Half a dozen rejected trade ads later, the charms of expense account lunches and the enchantments of a future company car seduced me into the mundane world of account management and lance-corporal chastisements. My vocational choices have always been based upon far-sighted assessments of career potential and intellectual challenge.

Having made the switch I inevitably wondered from time to time – usually when life as an account manager was just a bowl of prunes – whether I had made the right decision. This of course was a symptom of yet another universal human urge: the grass in the next field is always greener.

So when my colleague Paul Delaney decided to relinquish his creative director's casting couch and take a sabbatical, the opportunity seemed too good to miss. The gate to the next field had fortuitously swung open: I rushed in. I was chairman of the agency so it was a touch difficult for anyone to stop me.

After some twenty years in agency management the attractions of life in the creative department appeared boundless. No more tables of fathomless figures to muddle my mind; no endless trivial decision-making; no interminable meetings organising, reorganising and disorganising the conclusions arrived at previous interminable meetings; an end to hustle, bustle and media muscle. Instead comtemplation, concentration, inspiration and creation. Bliss.

It was not until the day before Paul Delaney was due to leave that terror struck. Suddenly – in less time than it takes to say angels fear to tread – it occurred to me that I hadn't the least idea how to do the job to which I had carelessly appointed myself. Rumour had it that my prospective flock, the copywriters and art directors in the creative department, had greeted the news of my impending leadership with ill-concealed dismay. Rumour also had it that most of them had immediately started searching for alternative employment. I had expected them to be delighted that a sensible and well-balanced chap like myself would henceforth be responsible for their pay, rations and wherewithal. Not so. I was dumbfounded, at the very least. I tore into Paul Delaney's office seeking his advice.

'Being a creative director's easy-peasy,' he said reassuringly. 'It's all a matter of image.'

Having said which, he picked up the creative brief for a new campaign that was lying on his desk, and read it over two or three times with an increasingly furrowed brow, while I stood nervously waiting.

Explosively, without warning, the room shook, rattled and rolled as Paul slammed his fist into his desk, ripped the offending brief into tiny shreds and hurled them at me like useless confetti.

'This brief's a joke,' he bellowed, 'it's rubbish, it's meaningless, it's shite. And you want it done by Wednesday? That's outrageous. The budget's an effing pittance. And you expect us to do great advertising? By Wednesday? Get out of my office you . . . ! Out – before I throw you out!'

As chairman of the agency I was nominally his boss. Nevertheless I had suffered many similar outbursts over the years. I had naïvely, optimistically, hoped that on his penultimate day he would be suffused with nostalgia, sweetness and light. Not so. As his office walls reverberated to the power of his larynx and his fist, I realised that his faithful followers without had gone reverently silent. They knew that their leader, probably for the last time, was exerting his rightful prerogative to throw a full-blooded all-screaming-and-shouting creative tantrum.

Paul himself, however, relaxed and broke into a charming, cheerful, cheeky grin.

'That's the way to be a creative director,' he laughed. 'I told you it's easy-peasy.'

Paul Delaney's splendid histronics reflect the outside world's stereotype of creative directorial behaviour: volatile, unreasonable, hysterical, egotistical and aggressive. How on earth, the world wonders, can anyone deal with people like that?

The answer is that things are not really like that. Well not always.

Anyone who deals with advertising creative people – with copywriters, art directors, designers, TV commercial directors, photographers, and occasionally actors – needs first to answer five questions:

i   How does the creative process differ from other management processes?
ii Are creative people really different from other people?
iii If so, how do they differ?
iv How can they be successfully motivated?
v   How can they be controlled?

Taken together, the answers to these five interlocking questions will help you inspire high ground creativity.

How does the creative process differ from other management processes?

What is creativity?

'Creativity,' said the design historian Stephen Bayley, 'is one of those things that it is much easier to detect than to define.'

There are many such others: beauty, honour, love, truth, wisdom – most, if not all, of the most profound words and concepts we use.

'It isn't creative if it doesn't sell,' said the slogan of advertising agency Benton & Bowles for many years. That is patent hogwash.

Surprisingly, the word 'creativity' only began to appear in British dictionaries during the 1970s. Its first appearance in the Oxford English Dictionary was in a supplement published in 1972. This was the result of a burgeoning of interest in creativity in the 1950s and 1960s, mostly in the USA where they had grown fearful that the Russians were overtaking them, particularly in the space race, because Russian scientists were believed to be more creative.

Although the word creativity is comparatively new, the concept of creation – of bringing things into existence for the first time – has naturally perplexed human beings throughout the ages. The notion that something can, magically as it were, evolve out of nothing is an affront to the rest of our experience, to common sense, to logic. If you want a chair you must start with wood, if you want a car you will need the metal, if you want some milk you must find a cow.

But if you want an idea? An advertising campaign?

Creativity is utterly unlike any other product or service. All other goods and services can be, and are, produced from raw materials, to specifications, often manufactured by robots on production lines. Creativity cannot be mechanically mass-produced. Each and every creative idea comes into existence on a one-off basis in a human mind. That will never change. Despite the wilder fantasies of science fiction, machines – no matter how sophisticated – will never have ideas. So advertising will continue to depend, forever, upon creative individuals. And upon managing them successfully. That is why computerisation – mechanisation of any kind – will never be of great importance.

Even today precious little is known about the nature of creativity, about how ideas come about. In an address in 1950 at Pennsylvania State College the then president of the American Psychological Association chose creativity as his theme, 'with considerable hesitation, for it represents an area in which psychologists generally, whether they be angels or not, have feared to tread.'

And in the broad spectrum of psychologists' interests and preoccupations, creativity is still on the periphery.

Though the French mathematician Henri Poincaré made a stab at it at the beginning of this century, the first determined attempt to provide a realistic theory of creativity must be credited to the great polymath Arthur Koestler who – being both an accomplished novelist and a scientific scholar – was uniquely qualified to analyse the creative process. His seminal work *The Act of Creation* was published just thirty years ago.

Koestler defined the process of creativity as 'bisociation': putting together two unconnected facts or ideas to form a single idea. And he contrasted bisociation with 'association'. Association refers to previously established connections between ideas, while bisociation involves the making of connections where none existed before:

> I have coined the term 'bisociation' in order to make a distinction between the routine skills of thinking on a single 'plane', as it were, and the creative act which, as I shall try to show, always operates on more than one plane. The former may be called single-minded, the latter a double-minded, transitory state of unstable equilibrium where the balance of both thought and emotion is disturbed.

(Note that Koestler believed creativity inevitably involved instability, and the disturbance of both emotion and thought.)

At about the same time that Koestler was developing his theory of bisociation in Britain, two neurosurgeons called Philip Vogel and Joseph Bogen were carrying out pioneering exploratory work in the USA into the workings of the brain. Scientists had long known that the brain is divided into two halves, left and right. But Vogel and Bogen showed that the two halves operate quite differently from each other, and can more realistically be thought of as two independent brains working in harmony than as a single brain divided into two, because each half-brain carries out different functions – functions that the other half-brain has no idea how to perform. In general the left brain handles 'logical' thinking (e.g. mathematics, deductions, analysis, language, logic), the right brain 'creative' thinking (e.g. imagination, colour, music, rhythm, daydreaming).

Further work by a Professor Robert Ornstein, at the University of California, also found that people who were trained to use one side of their brain more or less exclusively grew relatively unable to use the other. It could therefore be postulated that creative people are those who use their right brain intensively, while the rest of us coast along using the left.

More recently a great deal of experimental research has confirmed that the two halves of the brain can and do work independently –

even to the point of continuing to function after they have been surgically severed. However, a researcher named Michael Gazzaniga, who was involved in the original Vogel investigations into split-brain activity, has since debunked the neat left/right division of abilities:

> Special talents can reside in the right brain or the left. What is important is not so much where things are located, but that specific brain systems handle specific tasks.

In other words the creative functions are separate from the logical functions but neither will always be found, in all human beings, to the left or to the right.

Other theorists have developed analyses of creativity which all reflect, in some measure, Koestler's theory of bisociation and the left-versus-right brain division.

Edward de Bono, Britain's leading thinker in this area, has contrasted 'lateral thinking', which consists of sideways leaps of the imagination (right-brain activity), with 'vertical thinking', a continuous progression down a logical chain (left-brain activity). De Bono believes that you can stimulate lateral thinking if you deliberately break up your vertical thinking by 'arranging discontinuity'.

And in another part of this theoretical forest the American William Gordon invented 'synectics' – yet another classical word, this time meaning the joining together of different and apparently irrelevant elements. Gordon, like all the others, believes that the mind's 'natural' processes are ordered and logical while creativity, in contrast, is illogical and haphazard.

The essential conclusion to be drawn from all these analyses is that despite their differences the theorists unanimously agree on one thing: not only are rationality and creativity entirely different mental processes, but they are generally in conflict. At times of creation, logic must make itself scarce.

Whatever creativity is – and nobody yet knows – it is quintessentially irrational. In contrast business management is – or at least aspires to be – rational. And this means that there is an underlying and unavoidable clash of cultures and processes when managers find themselves in control of creativity.

To quote Sir Dennis Forman, the charismatic ex-chairman of Granada Television:

> There is an unbridgeable gap between the logic of business management and the laws of the creative world. The art of managing a creative group is to ensure that the conditions are as conducive to good work as they can be, and only then to apply the rules of efficiency . . . this is a lesson which the McKinseys of the world will not learn, and perhaps cannot learn.

But is the gap really unbridgeable? I think not.

Management is not, and never will be, a predictive science like physics; still less is it like engineering. (Human engineering is a fatuous phrase implying a causality that does not and never will exist.) Creativity being what it is – whatever it is – nobody will ever succeed in managing it unerringly. However some managers are a great deal better at doing so than others. All management is difficult. The management of creativity – of creative people – raises its own particular problems. The more profoundly they are understood, the more effectively they can be mastered.

Are creative people really different from other people? If so, how?

Start any conversation about the nature of creative people and you can safely bet a first folio Shakespeare to a well-thumbed Jeffrey Archer that within five minutes someone will mention either Van Gogh, or Gauguin, or both. Why are they mentioned so frequently? Not because they are typical, but because they are atypical. They epitomise our image of creative people. Yet not a lot of creative folk either amputate their ears or dash off to Polynesia; not a lot destroy their lives in blind, unremitting pursuit of their karma. Most creative people live fairly conventional lives.

A couple of years ago one of London's top advertising art directors threw a typewriter through his window in a fit of pique. I have now heard that story forty or fifty times. The art director simultaneously became the folk hero of most of London's young creative folk, for having displayed his creative integrity so forcefully, and the *bête noire* of agency managements. As with Gauguin and Van Gogh, both sides enjoy recounting the tale because they feel that it epitomises the way creative people like to behave. But the truth is that art directors seldom toss typewriters out of windows. If they did, strolling round Soho and Covent Garden would be even more hazardous than it is.

If the air were thick with orbiting typewriters they would hardly be worth mentioning: the commonplace is dull. It was the rarity of the incident that made it so worth gossiping about.

Every scrap of evidence shows that creativity and mental instability rarely go hand in hand. The fact has been well established since 1904 when Havelock Ellis (better known for his *Studies in the Psychology of Sex*) published a book called *A Study of British Genius*.

Havelock Ellis listed 1,030 'geniuses' among whom only 44 (4.2%) were demonstrably insane. This figure is remarkably low, since Ellis included senile disorders within his definition of insanity; and nowadays one in fifteen of the British population (6.7%) is resident in a mental hospital at some point in their lives. You could deduce from that that geniuses are marginally more sane than the rest of us: perhaps they are.

Much the same point has recently been made, more succinctly, by Professor Carl Hakmiller of Connecticut University:

> The myth of weirdos running around wearing plaid shirts and no socks just isn't true.

However, the myth that creatives are nutters has considerable appeal both to creative people and to managers. To the creatives it is an excuse (not to say an encouragement) to indulge in capricious, selfish, wilful behaviour; to the managers it explains why the creatives are impossible to control and provides them with a heaven-sent excuse for being unable to deal with them. To manage creatives successfully you must obviously twig their personality traits and idiosyncrasies, but you must never treat them as oddballs: understanding yes – concessions no.

Having said all this, it is true that creative people are not quite like the rest of us. (I recognise that we are all creative to some degree but I am talking here, and throughout, about people who earn their living by being creative every day of their lives. To insist that all human beings are equally creative unhelpfully blurs the distinction between my local publican – who draws jolly nice little posters for his pub – and Picasso.)

It is a difficult area to research, but there appear to be clear correlations between creativity and personality. The correlations are not extreme, but they exist. An authoritative study at the School of Art in Chicago showed art students to be more socially aloof, more introspective, more self-sufficient, more radical, more experimental and more nonconformist than the general run of students at large. All these personality traits reflect with reasonable accuracy the popular creative stereotype.

However, the differences between the art students and the others were not vast. If you draw a spectrum with complete conformity at one end and thoroughgoing nonconformity at the other, the bulk of creative people will be found in the shades which veer towards nonconformity. A few will be far out on the extreme edge; most will differ from the norm only marginally.

Researchers who have studied creative people agree that one of their most notable characteristics is independence. They are influenced much more by their own, inner standards than by those of the society to which they belong. In a study of architects, for example, in which the subjects were divided into three groups according to their creativity, the most creative group were principally concerned with meeting standards of excellence which they discovered within themselves; the least creative group were most concerned with conforming to the standards of the architectural profession. From a business point of view such independence breeds several unfortunate by-products. It breeds egotism. It breeds a disdain for gung-ho company loyalty. It breeds combative stubbornness. It breeds a craving for personal fame. It breeds unreasonableness. However, these personality foibles, though substantial, are far from impossible to cope with.

The problem of unreasonableness leads to the frequently questioned relationship between creativity and intelligence. In recent years it has become fashionable among psychologists to dissociate intelligence from creativity completely – to the point where it might be supposed that a high IQ is a bar to originality. But there is no correlation between creativity and IQ. So IQ scores can never be used to predict creativity, one way or t'other.

Here again you can see the seeds of dissension between creativity and management. Managers are trained to respect and respond to logical argument and intellectual abilities. Often lacking these abilities, creative people fall back upon stubbornness, and appear intransigent because they lack analytical debating skills.

The obsession which drives managers to distraction – and causes most management difficulties – is creatives' single-minded preoccupation with their output. As Dr Anthony Storr puts it in *The Dynamics of Creation*, 'The work, rather than the person, becomes the focus of self-esteem.'

Creative people are unique in the way that they are personally associated with the results of their endeavours. (This doesn't just apply to advertising, incidentally; it is equally true of television, the cinema, fashion, journalism, architecture and all other creative businesses.) The vast majority of the world's workers, in the vast majority of jobs, do their work anonymously. Even within their own industries the names of the innumerable managers and executives who keep the wheels of business turning are rarely seen in lights.

In advertising, by contrast, everybody knows which copywriters and which art directors are responsible for which advertisements. That is why the advertising industry so adores awards: awards identify and glorify the creatives. A visiting Martian would rapidly conclude that only dogged determination can save the average advertising creative man from being veritably pelted with statuettes as he wends his weary way from one awards dinner to the next. No other industry devotes quite so much time to patting itself on the back.

Barristers, bus conductors and bricklayers all manage to graft their way through life without endlessly ringing each other's necks with garlands – but advertising creative folk seem to suffer from a psychotic compulsion to keep massaging their egos with silken sashes and rosettes. It is because their work is the focus of their self-esteem.

It makes motivating them fairly easy, and controlling them especially difficult.

How can creative people be successfully motivated?

The single most important word is *challenge*.

Creative people know – consciously or subconsciously – that new things rarely come into existence without a struggle. If there is no challenge there is no struggle – and then creatives instinctively sense that they are not being called upon to create, but to repeat.

One of the paradoxes of creativity is that creatives desperately want to create yet often need to be forced to do so. (This is not such uncommon human behaviour: most sportsmen desperately want to improve their performance yet still need tough trainers to bully them into it.) All creative people know that there are times when they must be pushed, must be made to stretch themselves, even if they will never admit it.

You will never lose the respect of creative people by complaining that the work they have shown you is not sufficiently innovative, or original, or creative – that it is not nearly as innovative, original or creative as you know them to be capable of. They may argue vehemently, they may look crestfallen, but they won't hate you. You will only lose creatives' respect when you say that the work is too radical, too different, that it does not follow established principles and guidelines.

Their work, remember, is the focus of their self-esteem: and there is little self-esteem to be scraped from following established guidelines.

High Ground Creativity

Once they have been challenged, it's time for cuddles: to maximise their motivation it is necessary to massage their egos. As I said in the last chapter, all admen are insecure – and some are even more insecure than others. (Robert Jacoby – then the diminutive but ruthlessly powerful president of Ted Bates Inc., the second largest advertising agency in the world, once quipped to me: 'If people knew how much time I spend massaging people's egos around here they'd think I was crazy.')

Here are ten easy-to-abide-by commandments with which to massage and motivate creatives:

i *Absorb their risks* – you must willingly and publicly take your share of the blame if – I mean when – things go wrong.

ii *Stretch the regulations* – though you cannot disregard rules and policies, you must know when they need to be more honoured in the breach than in the observance.

iii *Be comfortable with half-developed ideas* – it should not be necessary for every 't' to be crossed and every 'i' to be dotted before an idea is given consideration; creatives must have confidence that you can understand and appreciate ideas at an early stage of gestation.

iv *Don't dwell on mistakes* – mistakes are an inherent part of the creative process: to creative people 'I told you so' is a particularly unappealing phrase.

v *Be a good listener* – creative people love to talk about their work, and managers have to learn to love to listen.

vi *Provide lots of feedback* – creatives are always eager for evaluation of their work, and since real results are often long delayed (and even then not necessarily precise) you should provide as much encouraging data, along the way, as you can.

vii *Accept trivial foibles* – we have already seen that creatives are not quite the same as everyone else; allowing them a few innocent quirks will stress your acceptance of their nonconformity.

89

viii *Defend them against attackers* – in all advertising agencies the creatives are subject to frequent, and often unjustified, criticism: you must speak up, and be heard to speak up, loudly and boldly on their behalf.

ix *Praise the praiseworthy* – maybe it is traditional British reticence (Americans don't seem to suffer from the same difficulty) but many managers find it embarrassing to pay compliments when work is well done. When dealing with creatives this is disastrous.

x *Don't overdo it* – if you gush too much and offer praise too often or too easily, you will depreciate its value; nor, as you might hope, will it win you affection. Occasional, enthusiastic praise is infinitely more valuable than incessant and overenthusiastic slaps on the back.

And here are ten drop-dead guaranteed idea squashers:

It's a good idea but . . .
It's all right in theory . . .
I know it won't work . . .
The client won't understand it . . .
It's a bit too clever . . .
We've never done it that way before . . .
They'll never go for it . . .
We've tried it before . . .
Let's think it over for a while . . .
What you're really saying is . . .

You may by now be thinking that in all this talk of motivation I have so far omitted the most fundamental word of all: money. This is not because creatives are not interested in money: far from it.

'No man but a blockhead ever wrote except for money,' quoth the great Dr Samuel Johnson.

And the brilliant American advertising agency chief Howard Gossage quipped:

It is generally thought that artists are interested in art. Nothing could be further from the truth. Artists are interested in money. It's the rest of us who are interested in art.

However there is not, in my experience, any correlation between the money creative people are paid and the resulting quality of their work. Unlike piece-workers they cannot be incentivised to work harder by being paid more. They negotiate, toughly, to get as much as they can – which is often a great deal. Thereafter they get involved in the work, and their self-esteem takes over as quality controller.

Two final points on motivating creative people: first, it is a continuous day-to-day process. You cannot switch it on with a counterfeit smile whenever it happens to cross your mind. Their insecurity ensures that creative people are perpetually suspicious of the men in suits: they can suss out duplicity, and even insincerity, from miles off.

Second, producing great creative work, as well as being painful, should be fun. Laughing and larking about relieve tension, generate enthusiasm, demolish barriers and relax the mind. If by any chance you happen to work in the next room to the creative folk, and you hear laughter, be happy.

How can they be controlled?

Most books and articles on creativity – most books and articles on management in general – concentrate on motivation. The presumption is that encouragement, stimulation, inspiration are all that is required.

Whereas my own experience suggests that it is at least as difficult to control people successfully as to motivate them successfully. And most managers are infinitely worse at controlling people than at encouraging them: they are either too weak or too heavy-handed. Especially when it comes to creative people.

In an army the most essential element in controlling troops is to give clear orders. In dealing with creative people the most important element – as I indicated in the last chapter – is to give a clear brief.

A brief is different from an order in this basic way. An order states precisely how the task should be carried out; a brief states the problem, and the objective, but leaves open the ways in which the objective might be achieved. In advertising, to adapt the old military maxim, time spent on briefing is seldom wasted.

Few things cause more ill-will between creatives and managers – and then more lack of control – than the waste of time, effort, resources and imagination which is the direct and unavoidable consequence of inadequate briefing. Money is lost, tempers are frayed, goodwill dwindles to nil. The managers insist that the creatives failed (or didn't bother to try) to understand the brief, while the creatives insist that the brief was too vague, or incomprehensible, or downright wrong. Inevitably the work has to be done again, and maybe again and again, with great irritation and in great haste.

An advertising brief should, in essence, be the same as a legal brief: this is where we are, this is where we want to get to, please show me the way. The more exactly the initial location can be defined the better. That is why creating creative briefs takes so much time and effort. One of the commonest, and direst briefing mistakes is to believe that a loose, open brief will provide creative people with an open canvas and will enable them to freewheel, to dream dreams, to let their imaginations run riot.

Wrong. To be more accurate, right and wrong.

Their imaginations may well run riot, but riots rarely end productively.

Good briefs are tight briefs. If there are difficulties to be overcome – there always are – make sure they are in the brief from the start: speak now or forever hold your peace. As the remarkably creative Barbara Nokes, creative director of CME/KHBB, puts it:

> The creative process is generally preceded by sheer terror. You're confronted with a blank sheet of paper and a sharp pencil. You start with the brief, and the tighter the brief the easier it is to work out. If you know where the walls are you can travel down that narrow corridor and be completely wild. But if someone says it's an open brief you have no idea where to start.

Those who hope to give the creative imagination free rein by not mentioning constraints and limitations often believe that it is preferable for such constraints and limitations to be introduced into the project at a later stage, when it has achieved more momentum. Very occasionally, this approach succeeds. Far more often it leads to imaginative ideas being mangled when they eventually collide with reality. Never hesitate to brief creatives as fully as you can, warts and all. The limitations and constraints are part of the challenge. The best creative people will respond with originality and vigour.

Briefs should always be written, but they should never be delivered by messenger. As well as being a detailed specification, the brief should inspire, enthuse and intrigue. Pieces of paper delivered by messengers rarely inspire, enthuse and intrigue. In any event the brief will provoke the creative people to question, to seek clarification, to argue, to grumble and let off steam. (As Paul Delaney faked back at the beginning of this chapter.)

Above all, the brief must specify the time available for the job and the money that can be spent on it.

Adhering to time schedules and keeping to budgets are key management functions in any business, but in advertising they are like evil gremlins in every campaign, tinkering with the works, loosening the nuts and bolts so that at any moment everything may career out of control.

Few creative people are good at timekeeping. This explains why they are often believed to be downright idle. The truth is that they – the good ones – continually strive, in their minds, to improve whatever they have already done. So they delay exposing their ideas to others for as long as they can.

Moreover, as Abraham Maslow, one of this century's leading psychologists, has observed.

> The creative person, in the inspirational phase of the creative furore, loses his past and his future and lives only in the moment. He is all there, totally immersed, fascinated and absorbed in the present, in the current situation, in the here and now, with the matter in hand.... The ability to become 'lost in the present' seems to be a *sine qua non* for creativeness of any kind.

(A phenomenon I can modestly confirm in my own small less-than-creative way: time never passes faster than when I'm scribbling away.)

There is no similar, simple, psychological explanation of why creative people are so often lousy at keeping within budgets. I doubt whether a psychological explanation is required. The problem derives from creatives' obsession with their output: they are perfectionists. And perfectionism is expensive. Perfectionism takes time, and demands that anything which is not absolutely perfect be revised, and reworked, and possibly jettisoned if it is still not up to scratch. ('Let's start again, no matter how much it costs.')

In advertising, as in life, there are some jobs which must be done instantly even if this means they cannot be done perfectly; and some jobs which must be done perfectly even if this means they cannot be done instantly. Creative people find it all but impossible to distinguish between the two – and they always veer towards the latter. It is the manager's job to guide them.

Stating the time and money constraints, clearly and unequivocally in the brief, does not of course resolve the problems. It is necessary, but again it is not sufficient. Thereafter, throughout the duration of the job, the creative people will have to be watched, and chivvied, and cajoled, and hectored. The battles must be perpetually fought, and can never be won.

By now you may well be wondering whether all this management effort is really necessary, whether the game is worth the candle. Why bother to cosset these fractious creative creatures?

Are 'creative' advertisements – campaigns which are original and often entertaining, and which win the gongs and gain the esteem and spark the applause of both creative juries and the public – really more sales effective than the rest?

Many advertisers now suspect, understandably, that agency copywriters and art directors are so obsessed with winning *lions d'or* and *prix d'honneurs* that they do not care a cuss whether or not their advertisements achieve their real, commercial objectives. Some advertisers go so far as to believe – it's a commonplace advertising myth – that prize-winning campaigns are *ipso facto* ineffective.

And listening to creative people chatter in their Mayfair pubs and gossip in their Soho clubs would confirm such advertisers' worst fears. Vulgar words like sales and distribution and profits are never to be heard. Glittering words like gold, silver and even bronze are forever on creative lips.

However, the flip side of the medallions is that famous, award-winning campaigns have frequently been outstandingly successful in the marketplace. From the everlasting Brooke Bond PG chimps, through Smirnoff, Heineken, Hamlet, Silk Cut and Benson and Hedges, via Sainsbury's, Levis, Häagen-Dazs and most recently Tango – the last few years have been bespangled with campaigns which have won both ribbons and sales.

Moreover, all advertisers (even the churlishly suspicious ones) agree that advertising agencies' unique contribution to their sales effort is creativity: the ability to conjure ideas out of the air and to express them in persuasive words and images. The ability to create remarkable advertising is, in David Ogilvy's memorable phrase, 'the heart, liver and lights of the advertising business.'

In a praiseworthy attempt to answer the perennial question, 'Are highly creative campaigns more (or less) effective than others?' *Campaign* magazine analysed whether winners of the IPA Advertising Effectiveness Awards were also winners of creative awards.

All of the twenty-eight IPA award-winners appraised had proved their sales effectiveness. But only one of them had picked up a Designers and Art Directors' Gold, the most prestigious creative plum in the UK. Additionally, however, eight had picked up lesser creative trophies.

So almost one-third of the IPA Advertising Effectiveness Award winners won some sort of creative rosette: that must be well above average. On the other hand two-thirds of the IPA winners won no creative prize at all: so creativity and sales results are loosely correlated, at best.

The difficulties involved in establishing a satisfactory correlation derive from the fact that there are two aspects to advertising creativity. First, originality. Second, aesthetics. To blur the problem still further, these overlap. But they are not the same.

Advertisements must strive to be original, because they must strive to be different from other advertisements. They must not strive too hard to be different – to be different for the sake of being different – but they must strive to be *relevantly* different. Being different is one way of maximising the likelihood of being noticed. So originality, or remarkability as David Ogilvy called it, is inherent in successful advertising.

But when it comes to aesthetics things get more uncertain. Aesthetics – style, design, eloquence, appearance, wit – are sometimes important, sometimes not. For some products attractive aesthetics are an essential ingredient in the marketing mix: this is obviously true for fashionwear, for furnishings (especially electronic leisure equipment), for perfume, and for cars; it is also true, if a little less so, for alcoholic drinks, for toiletries, for cigarettes and for certain foods; but it appears to be irrelevant for domestic cleansers, and confectionery, for some retailers and for most popular media. (If you believe *The Sun* and *Hello* are things of beauty and joys forever you have a curious sense of aesthetics. But they are wonderful products.)

Exactly why attractive aesthetics are more important in some product categories than in others is worthy of a thesis in its own right. When the aforementioned Ph.D. student has completed his dissertation on telephones and the holes in Swiss cheese, perhaps he'll turn his mind to it.

All we need note for the moment is that when attractive aesthetics are important in the product they will likewise be important in the advertising; and when they are not they probably won't. That is why certain product categories scoop up most of the creative awards while others win none. (I cannot recall a household cleanser commercial ever winning an advertising Oscar.)

The advertising industry likes, admires and prizes aesthetically attractive advertisements. So do I. So do most of the population. But the cruel fact is that aesthetically attractive advertisements are neither universally correlated nor inversely correlated with sales effectiveness.

Originality on the other hand – relevant originality – is *always* good news. Relevant originality, not aesthetics, is what advertising creativity is all about. Inspiring creative people to be truly original, yet on brief, and on time, and within budget, is what the fuss is about. It isn't easy-peasy.

Inspiring great advertising creativity is not unlike driving a car in a city: bursts of acceleration, frequent braking, unforeseen hazards, numerous changes of direction and a high risk of accident. Rarely is it like driving on a deserted motorway, demanding only attentiveness and a gentle nudge of the wheel from time to time. The causeway to the creative high ground is full of twists and bends.

And while we're still on the subject, I should mention that my attempt to succeed Paul Delaney as creative director was less than triumphant. So it was mercifully brief. I'm glad I had a go. It was a fun diversion. But I won't bother again. Not that anyone would let me.

6

Smart Targeting

While agencies are in the doldrums, the media are in ebullient turmoil. In the 1980s the buzz word in the advertising lexicon was *creativity*. These days it is *media*.

Media fragmentation, media strategy, media research, media muscle, media moguls, media studies, media targeting, media independents, media centralisation, media specialists. The future of media, the power of media, the censorship of media, the ownership of media, the media explosion, interactive media, the new media. The media, as Marshall McLuhan might have said, are the message.

Unquestionably technological developments will radically alter the way everybody uses media – and the way media use everybody – during the next few years. The speed of change has never been speedier. Today's media spew forth endless articles about tomorrow's media. The media, naturally, are frantically interested in the media. A great deal more interested than anyone else.

In the United States they are experimenting with personalised newspapers. The publisher's database knows everything about you – knows your hobbies and the subjects you find a bore, knows your enthusiasms and your antipathies, knows your politics and your passions – and tailors your daily paper to your personal tastes. Do you think anyone will want to read such a tedious organ for more than a few days?

New televisual media developments – interactive television, interactive CDs, cable, digital compression, CD Rom and a host of whizzo, consumer-unfriendly inventions – await us just over the horizon.

What effects will this riot of hyperactivity have on advertising? Not a lot.

History is littered with major communications media which have had little or no impact on advertising — books, telephones and fax machines to name but three.

Interactive television will make home shopping off your TV screen as simple as it has long been simple to shop at home off-the-page or through catalogues. Great Universal Stores, Littlewoods and their competitors have been generating massive mail-order sales for aeons. Their operations have never much impinged on the sales of fast-moving consumer goods, or consumer durables, or any of the other major advertising sectors. Nor — as I stressed in the opening chapter — will interactive television.

QVC Network — America's largest and highest profile home-shopping TV channel — mostly sells jewellery, gifts and clothing. More than half its turnover comes from jewellery. It sells almost nothing that would traditionally have been sold by brand advertising. Nor is televisual home shopping particularly new. Remember K-Tel? Remember Tjaereborg? Televisual home shopping keeps right on coming but never quite arrives. The much heralded interactive television revolution will not happen for many years, and even when it happens nothing much will happen. If you think this prognosis unduly conservative, read what QVC's own chairman emeritus, Joseph Segel, has to say:

> TV should be less costly than direct mail because you don't have the cost of paper, ink and postage — and you may reach many unknown prospects. On the other hand the number of people tuned to a particular channel when your commercial runs is likely to be a small fraction of the number you could reach by direct mail.... Interactive special interest channels will be tested, and some may be successful. I emphasise that this is 'possible', not 'definite', because it has yet to be proven that such specialised channels can be produced profitably. The cost of running a shopping channel is far greater than most people realise.... Some system developers and their software

programmers assume that consumers are itching to be converted from passive to interactive TV viewers. Certainly there are some people who fit that mould. But I venture to say that the great American public prefers just to watch television and let someone else do the work.

Toronto, October 1993

It makes no sense at all to buy most things by mail order. Nor is mail order, as Segel went on to elucidate, a particularly easy, enjoyable or efficient way to shop. Most people like to feel, touch and see with their eyes the goods they purchase. None of which implies that there will not be a lot of money to be made out of interactive television. In the very long run, when all the hype has died down, there may well be. But then over the years a great deal of money has doubtless been made by the makers of rubber bands. In the office equipment pantheon rubber bands have their place, but their place is modest. In the pantheon of marketing communications media, interactive television will have its place, but its place will be modest. In the consumer goods sector it will be a competitor to postal bargains. I suspect it will mostly be used, on a highly specialised basis, by business-to-business advertisers. An interactive farming channel to reach farmers, perhaps, or an interactive medical channel to reach doctors.

The fragmentation of television viewing – narrow casting in media jargon – will make mass audiences a great deal more difficult to reach. That will re-emphasise the crucial importance of targeting, an issue to which we will return in a moment. Simultaneously narrow casting will make a few minority audiences as easy to reach televisually as they have long been easy to reach in print. *Angling Times* may find itself competing with a specialist fishing channel. *Practical Gardening* may find itself competing with a specialist gardening channel. Big deal.

British viewers now spend more time watching the traditional commercial channels – almost two hours per day watching ITV, C4 and TVAM – than ever before. The much-hyped 'new media' are a snare and a delusion. They are taking people's eyes off the ball. The challenge of the next decade will be to buy the old media more cost-effectively.

During recent years most of the emphasis has been on buying media cheaply – the emphasis has been on cost, not value. This has been an understandable reaction to the soaring media rates of the late 1980s. In the five years 1985–89 television advertising costs increased almost 60% faster than inflation. Naturally advertisers grew more than somewhat splenetic. Their reaction has been to gang up into bigger and bigger buying units and then to batter the media into better bargains. This has been the principle impetus behind the explosive growth of media specialists. And – aided by the recession – it has worked. Since 1989 media costs have fallen, in real terms, by almost 10%. But they will not fall further.

The time has come to focus less on costs and more on value, less on tactics and more on strategy, less on pummelling the media and more on targeting the consumer. The vital developments that are taking place are anyway occurring not in the media but in the marketplace. Market segmentation continues to be the name of the high ground game. It is burgeoning market segmentation, not new media technology or buying muscle, which will make media planning and buying increasingly complex, and increasingly sophisticated, during the years to come.

Much tosh is talked about the declining number of brands on retailers' shelves. The reality is precisely the opposite. There was a time, and not so long ago, when cats had to be content, day-after-day, with boiled up fish heads. (I can still remember the acrid smell. It permeated my infancy.) Dogs had to be content with scraps, with the occasional bone as a delectable treat on high days and holy days.

Last weekend I counted the varieties of cat and dog food in my nearby Tesco. There were 159 different varieties of cat foods, from twenty-three different brands (including Tesco's own label). Dogs were offered only – only! – 121 varieties, from twenty-one brands. (But then dogs are less finicky than cats.) The figures do not include different pack sizes, of which there were legion, nor do they include the little treats and sweetmeats which doting pet owners so love to buy. The 280 cat and dog varieties were all foods: cans, boxes, trays, packages – wet, moist and dry. In centuries to come space-age archaeologists may question the collective sanity of a society which felt the need for 280 different varieties of cat and dog food. On the other hand there will probably, by then, be tens of thousands of different petfood delicacies, sold in pet superstores.

As it is with pets, so it most definitely is with humans. There was a time, and not so long ago, when people bought all their worldly goods from their local village store, or in their local High Street. The shops held a narrow range of stock. Today the average supermarket stocks over 15,000 different items. If you are in any doubt at all about the cornucopia of goodies on offer, look at the beer shelves, or the soft drink shelves, or the breakfast cereals, the toiletries, the frozen foods, the wines, the herbs and spices, the breads, the biscuits, the jams.... Having finished counting the cat and dog foods I wandered over to the toilet rolls: including colourways, there were no fewer than thirty-two different varieties on offer. That magnificent miscellany of ways to wipe our bottoms is a hymn to market segmentation.

Nor does market segmentation begin and end in the supermarkets. Cast your eye over the electrical and electronic gadgetry in Dixons and Comet, the do-it-yourself goods in Homebase and Texas, the publications in Smith's and Menzies, the cars in automobile showrooms, the medicaments in Boots and Superdrug. Just choosing a headache remedy is enough to give you a headache.

It is no exaggeration to say that every time somebody makes a purchase they are (subconsciously) choosing from tens of thousands of alternatives. And if they decide not to make a purchase at all, but to save their money, then there are, once again, literally thousands of choices to choose from – insurance policies, building society investments, authorised unit trusts ... there are now more than 1,500 unit trusts, alone.

As the gross national product slowly but steadily increases it slowly but steadily splinters. In 1983 MEAL (now Register MEAL) recorded 15,000 advertised brands. Ten years later that figure has more than doubled, to 32,500. Nor is there any reason to predict that this process is about to stop. In West Germany, for example, the number of advertised brands grew from 32,800 in 1980 to more than 47,300 in 1991 – an increase of 44%. Affluence means diversity. Poverty means uniformity. Visit any Third World country. Then stroll through Harrods. QED.

Above-the-line mass media will continue to be the most cost-effective way to reach this diversity of consumers for years and years to come. One of the maddeningly confusing things about modern advertising is that it uses mass media to communicate with quite small audiences. Targeting those small audiences accurately will increasingly become the key to high ground marketing. No matter how brilliantly creative, how brilliantly persuasive, how brilliantly impactful your campaign may be, it isn't worth a light if it does not reach the right target market, inexpensively. Mass media provide the vehicle. Yet defining the target market is still one of the most underrated parts of the advertising process. Everybody pays it lip service. Few undertake the complex and time-consuming work necessary to do it properly.

A recent study revealed that 35% of major British advertisers were willing to admit they unnecessarily waste money as a result of poor targeting. I'll bet a couple of supermarket trolleys to half a dozen cluster analyses that 35% is a massive underestimate. Because target markets are – or rather should be – far tinier than is commonly supposed. And as a result they can usually be defined far more accurately than is commonly supposed.

Fundamentally this is because the continuing surge of market segmentation over the years has resulted in all brands becoming minority brands. There is no brand in Britain – *no* brand, of any kind – which is bought regularly by more than 50% of the population. Only a tiny handful – Coca Cola, Kellogg's, Andrex – are bought regularly by as many as one-third of the population. (Remember the population includes men as well as women.) For the great majority of brands, the great majority of the population never buy them at all. This is an inevitable consequence of the burgeoning number of brands. And it is nothing to worry about because quite small numbers of people can support very large brands indeed.

Most of the largest brands are bought by only 10%–15% of the population. That means 85%–90% do *not* buy them. And the great majority of brands, tens of thousands of them, are bought regularly only by miniscule minorities. They are the 'heavy users', upon whom every brand is dependent. The huge lager market, for example, whose explosive growth was so much publicised in the 1980s, is dependent on just 6% of the adult population – just 2,500,000 people – who consume 90% of all the lager drunk each year. (The really heavy users, 3% of adults, 1.3 million people, account for 70% alone.) This means that even the most major lager brands are drunk regularly by only a few hundred thousand topers. And the same principle applies to all great brands, as Professor Andrew Ehrenberg demonstrated conclusively in his classic study *Repeat Buying* (1988). Ehrenberg showed that 80% of the sales of any major brand will be purchased by heavy buyers – those who buy six times a year or more. And the heavy buyers are normally 25%–30% of 'ever buyers'. So that in terms of the total population heavy buyers are minorities of minorities. Yet many if not most advertisers determinedly waste money targeting light users and infrequent users.

Here are several ways of establishing the truth of all this for yourself.

Have you ever considered how few advertised brands you buy?

If you visit a supermarket every week you may leave with thirty, forty or perhaps even fifty items on your checkout list. The average number of items of all kinds purchased per visit is currently about twenty.

Many of the items – fruit, vegetables, fresh meat, delicatessen and so on – will not be advertised brands. At a maximum (if you have an exceedingly picky family and several picky pets) you will have bought a couple of dozen advertised brands, out of the 15,000 lines on sale in the store. Over the course of a year your choices will swing out a bit, but you are exceedingly unlikely to buy more than two hundred different advertised brands annually.

If you are a husband you may hardly ever visit a supermarket at all: men are only responsible for about one-third of supermarket purchases. But you probably go to the pub from time to time, since

65% of men go to the pub once a month or more. There, during the course of a year, you may imbibe a dozen or so different brands of booze, but probably far fewer.

Unless you play the stock market, you will make only a small number of investment decisions during the year, and you almost definitely won't change your bank. Consumer durables? Maybe a dozen a year, if you're a consumer durables freak. Cars? In Britain your car may well be supplied by your employer, but if it is not you will probably only buy one every three years. And though it may seem otherwise when you study your wardrobe and your bank balance, you do not buy that many brands of clothes either. Nor will most of them be advertised brands because there is not much advertising of clothes. Even when you throw in confectionery, medicines, hardware, all the services you can think of and the kitchen sink (a new one every decade or so) it is virtually certain that you do not buy more than 400 advertised brands a year.

One day, in the not-too-distant future, it will be possible to get the precise figure, if you are Mr or Mrs Average, from a computer. But for the moment an estimate will do and 400 is indubitably the maximum.

Here's another rough-and-ready way to get at the same figure. Wander around your house and count all the advertised brands. Remember to count all the consumer durables and – if you are horticulturally inclined – to look in the garden shed. You will find you need to make some arbitrary decisions, particularly about retailers' own brands, and about different varieties of the same brand. But exactitude is not called for. A few more or a few less will not make much difference.

I have done this several times, and always reach a figure of between 140 and 150 advertised brands. Yesterday it was 149.

Obviously, once again, my own and my family's brand choices change during the course of each year. And we buy certain branded services – financial, travel, holidays and the like which cannot be kept in the larder.

But on the basis of this rigorously scientific piece of research, a purchase level of 400 brands a year again looks like the maximum.

Compare that with the 32,500 branded goods and services that are currently advertised in Britain each year. Or even ignore the 23,000 or so which spend less than £50,000 on advertising, and concentrate on the 9,500 which spend more than £50,000 according to Register MEAL.* Mr and Mrs Average will buy only 400 of the 9,500 brands being advertised. Admittedly not every one of those 9,500 brands is being aimed at them, but the majority are.

Remember that we are being generous about that 400 figure. It is probably fewer. Remember, too, that by no means all of those 400 brands will have been bought because of their advertising. Far from it. Some will have been bought because of word-of-mouth recommendation, others because the packaging looked appealing, others because they were a bargain offer, still others simply on whim. Even without a Ph.D. in economics it is easy to see that Mr and Mrs Average have been influenced, *at the very maximum*, by only 400 of the 9,500 brand campaigns. That's about 4%.

Yet we also know that Mr and Mrs Average are bombarded by a veritable welter of advertisements, every day of the week every week of the year.

Does that mean that all those millions and millions of advertisements which failed to persuade them were money down the drain?

It's another yes and no.

Waste is inherent in the use of all marketing communications. The notion that every reader of a publication, or every viewer of a commercial break, or every recipient of a direct mail shot, might immediately dash out and buy the product advertised is palpably dotty.

But the fact that only a minority respond to any advertising does not mean advertising is not cost-effective. Millions and millions of advertisers, since Aesclyptoe and before, have repeatedly proved its power. Advertising communicates with large numbers of people in

---

* Register MEAL recently increased its baseline expenditure from £50,000 to £150,000, and as a result now individually lists only 7,000-plus brands, as against 9,500 previously (2,500 brands which spent between £50,000 and £150,000 have been delisted). Obviously this minor change in Register MEAL's analytical procedure in no way affects the argument.

order to reach the relevant minority – because the advertiser cannot know, in advance, exactly which individuals will respond to his blandishments. The single, simple reason why media advertising works is that, despite its much-publicised expense, it is still an astonishingly cheap means of mass communication. That fine old phrase 'cost per thousand' is still the crux, the very essence of media advertising.

A national peak-time thirty-second spot on ITV will reach 1,000 people for about £4. If you buy off-peak, you can reach them still cheaper – much cheaper. To reach 1,000 people by direct mail, in contrast, will cost more than £200. If you use a costly mailing shot it will cost more – much more. For £200 the television advertiser will net 50,000 people, a fair number of whom will be customers and potential customers. So the advertising can encompass waste and still deliver results economically and cost-effectively.

Nonetheless all waste is gruesome. The art of targeting is to minimise waste by increasing the percentage of readers or viewers who will respond. It's a pure numbers game. The advertiser will never know, in advance, *precisely* who will respond to his messages. But then not even the most accurate and finely tuned direct mail shot can ever achieve 100% response. Not even the most silver-tongued salesman will win with every prospect. You are more likely to find fairies at the bottom of your garden than to achieve 100% success when you are selling.

Naturally the objective is to strike the highest success rate possible. The reality is that the figure is unlikely ever to exceed a few percent, at the very most. (Even the most tightly targeted, sharply focused and carefully personalised direct mail shots rarely generate as much as 10% response.)

But generating a response level of a few percent is not to be sneezed at. In the mass marketing of consumer goods any advertising which achieves a response level of 2% is stupendously successful. Two percent of the adult population is almost 1,000,000 people. If 1,000,000 people spend just £2 a month on an FMCG brand, that's £24,000,000 a year. There is no marketing director in the land who would not break open the champagne (we're talking Dom Perignon here) if his advertising campaign generated £24,000,000 additional sales.

Any consumer durables manufacturer who sold 1,000,000 units as the result of his advertising would find his production director in tears (of joy and frenzy).

Any political party whose advertising delivered an extra 1,000,000 votes would almost certainly sweep to power.

There is no product, nor brand, nor service, of any kind in Britain that would not sing hosannas, sound the trumpets and paint the town red if it won another 1,000,000 purchasers. Yet 1,000,000 purchasers is still just over 2% of the adult population. That is why targeting is so crucial.

The reason we can picture, in our mind's eye, the users of most brands is that most brands are used regularly by only small percentages of the adult population. That is why we can describe the types of people who use different brands with almost amazing clarity when asked to do so by market researchers. If brands were universal they would have no character. This is the flip side of the fact that – as I showed earlier – none of us uses all that many brands in the first place.

Even the different washing powder and detergent brands – than which few different brands are less different – are used by dissimilar groups of people. Dissimilar, that is, in what they want from their washing powders and detergents. And that is why – to return to a point made briefly in Chapter 1 – it is no longer straightforward to define the meaning of 'best' in consumer goods markets. Different people demand different qualities from their brands. That is the essence of market segmentation.

People who choose the same brand, or the same shop, or the same service as each other are to some degree like each other: to the degree, at least, that out of the abundance of brands and shops and services available they select the same ones.

We are all half-conscious that this is the case, all the time. We talk about Sainsbury shoppers and have a loose image of them being rather alike – just as Volvo drivers are all the same (well, more or less), and men who wear Marks & Spencer suits are making a bit of a statement about themselves, as are people who drink Martini or Mateus Rosé or serve OK sauce or Bird's Eye fish fingers or Mr Kipling cakes, or drive BMWs or smoke Marlboro, or walk around with a Walkman . . . all of which bears witness to the potency of brands in today's world, and to their grip on our perceptions and imaginations. Similarly it bears witness to the fine nuances of market segmentation which brands now exemplify.

High ground targeting involves finding out as much as is humanly possible about those people who choose the same brand – your brand – and making sure the advertising reaches them, and is right for them. The widely accepted management dictum 'Keep Close to the Customer' does not say 'Keep Close to the Non-Customer', nor even 'Keep Close to the Potential Customer'.

It is wise to keep close to the customer because keeping close to the customer is highly profitable. To quote from a recent *Harvard Business Review*:

> Customer defections have a surprisingly powerful impact on the bottom line. They can have more to do with a company's profit than size, market size, unit costs, and many other factors usually associated with competitive advantage. As a customer's relationship with the brand lengthens, profits rise. And not just by a little. Companies can boost profits by almost 100% by retaining just 5% more of their customers.

Little wonder then that *customer loyalty* is currently the groovy phrase in chic marketing circles.

But if you want to win new customers – and winning new customers is indubitably A Good Thing – how can it make sense to target existing customers? Surely, logic seemingly dictates, non-users cannot be that similar to existing users or they would already *be* users. By definition non-customers must be different from customers.

No contest. But *prospective* customers are more like existing customers than they are like the rest of non-customers. So that advertising targeted at existing customers will also be targeted at prospective customers, willy-nilly.

This can be proved by infant school arithmetic. Let us take a major brand, being purchased regularly by 10% of the population – that's 4,000,000 adults. To achieve a 10% sales increase it will be necessary to convert an additional 1% of the population to regular consumption – another 400,000 customers. (This is a simplistic picture, but it clarifies the principles.)

Is that additional 1% more likely to be similar to the 10% already buying? Or to the 89% who will continue not to buy?

Attempting to grapple with the problem, market researchers have desperately searched for ways of winnowing down the 90%, so that the 1% among them can be identified. Naturally they have been unsuccessful. The task is impossible. Intention-to-buy questionnaires are notoriously unreliable. There are no techniques which can accurately identify prospective purchasers. The best that anybody can do is weed out those who – for whatever reason – have categorically decided not to buy.

Sometimes that will be for practical reasons (people without cats are unlikely to buy Whiskas); sometimes it will be for reasons of taste (people who hate bacon are unlikely to buy Danepak); sometimes it will be for economic reasons (people without dosh are unlikely to buy Ferraris); sometimes it will be for style reasons (people who want to look modish are unlikely to buy their clothes at Littlewoods); sometimes it will be for unpredictable, irrational, idiosyncratic reasons.

But the weeding out of definite non-purchasers, useful though it can be, is a million miles from the identification of prospective purchasers. As we'll see in the next chapter, no research, or database, or media can possibly identify prospective customers. But fortunately, accurately targeted campaigns can whittle down the wastage, and provide prospective customers with the opportunity to identify themselves, to spot the advertising addressed to them and respond. That is exactly what high ground campaigns achieve. And it is an increasingly complex task. It is increasingly complex because while target markets are growing ever more segmented the media available to reach them are likewise growing ever more segmented.

The number of newspapers and freesheets in Britain grew from

550 to over 1,000 in the decade between 1981 and 1991. The number of consumer magazines increased from 1,367 to 2,300 in the same period. Television and radio channels are breeding so rapidly it is all but impossible to keep pace: already there are thirty-eight UK television channels and over 150 commercial radio stations. Matching the media to the target market today calls for sophisticated computer literacy.

Ever since the first major media surveys – the pioneering Hulton Readership Survey was launched in 1947 – one of the many holy grails for which the advertising industry has searched is the relationship between media consumption and brand purchase. Until the 1980s almost all media surveys aimed to correlate media consumption with brand purchase via demographic characteristics. The underlying assumption was that people of the same age, and social class, and sex are likely to behave similarly to each other. Or anyway more similarly than people of different ages, social classes and sexes.

Nobody believed the correlations to be perfect, but they were the sharpest in the marketing toolbox. Unfortunately as society has grown more affluent, and brand choices more diverse, those tools have grown blunter.

In the 1970s several research companies and advertising agencies began to explore new systems for classifying the population which, it was hoped, would provide greater precision. They worked on the hypothesis that people could be categorised by personality (as well as by demography) and that personality groupings would be better able to predict brand usage than simple demographic groupings.

Probably the most famous of these new systems was VALS (Values And Life Styles), which was invented by the research institute SRI International in California. VALS claimed to distinguish nine psychographic groups which shared 'cross-cultural consumer characteristics', or CCCCs. Those groups were, it was claimed, universal – being based on universal human behaviour and attitudes. (No room for *globus confusingus* here then.)

The nine groups were given catchy names: Survivors, Sustainers, Belongers, Emulators, Achievers, I-Am-Me's, Experientials, Societally Conscious, Integrateds.

And the VALS system achieved worldwide notoriety in May 1987 when it caused Margaret Thatcher to scupper her election campaign. Apparently the Belongers were deserting her in droves. This petrifying news provoked her famous Wobbly Thursday, during which she ditched the Tories' campaign strategy and everything else she could lay her hands on and as a result won the election. Or so the story goes.

Despite its apparent success in the service of Lady Thatcher the VALS system, and several others like it, have fallen into gentle desuetude over recent years. The notion that the entire world, or even the entire British population, could be split into nine personality groups has taken a lot of stick. And rightly so. It is clearly cock-eyed. (The recession caused much of the destruction. I-Am-Me's suddenly metamorphosed into unemployed yuppies, Belongers were transmuted into Survivors and everyone's CCCCs got frightfully muddled up.)

Because there are no psychographic clusters which embrace the entire populace, advertising people got bored with the whole idea and, as my mum used to say, threw the baby out with the bath water. Mistake.

Though it isn't possible to parcel everyone into a few neat, universal, psychographic bundles the same does not apply to individual markets – where personality-based groupings correlate closely with consumers' behaviour. That is the logic of market segmentation: different groups of people want marginally different products (brands) to fulfil marginally different needs. Their varying brand preferences reflect their personality similarities, and their differences. That is why people who regularly buy the same brand as each other are, to that extent, similar to each other.

The error made by VALS and its lookalikes was to search for personality characteristics that would apply across all markets. Common sense should have predicted that this would be far too simple to make sense. ('There is a ready solution to every problem,' wrote the American humorist H. L. Mencken, 'it's simple, neat – and wrong.')

Each market, and each brand, must be analysed individually. (This is difficult, messy – and right.) There are personality clusterings operating in every product field, but they cannot be aggregated or consolidated. The personality clusters which apply to cars don't apply to coffee, the personality clusters which apply to breakfast cereals don't apply to building societies, the personality clusters which apply to cosmetics don't apply to confectionery. It now seems astonishing that anybody could ever have thought otherwise.

Methodically analysing the personality and lifestyle traits operative for each brand, in each market, and then relating this information to readership and television viewing data moves advertising a great deal closer to the holy grail of precision targeting.* It provides identikit portraits of a brand's users, to help the copywriters and art directors understand them far better than the old demographic definitions could ever do. That makes for high ground creativity. It maximises response levels and minimises wastage. It makes it possible to predict the very programmes they watch, and to track their channel switching during an evening's viewing. That makes for high ground media planning.

Moreover, with the data derived from his psychological cluster analyses the media buyer is in a powerful position to negotiate with the publications and television contractors. Demographic data is commonplace. Each of the media knows how many female ABC1s or 25–39s living in East Anglia they can reach and how that matches your brand's profile. And they know how their competitors stack up on the same measurements. They will be ready to negotiate on the basis of these demographic figures, confident that they can offer a deal that at least approximates to good value.

But they will not have, they cannot have, the relevant psychographic analyses – and in media-buying, as in all negotiations, knowledge is power. With the identity of his target consumers to hand, the adept media buyer will be able to manoeuvre good deals for his clients all along the way. In order to buy media sharply in

---

* For certain advertisers – retailers of all kinds, particularly – geodemographic cluster analyses can be used in conjunction with lifestyle cluster analyses to refine and sharpen targeting still further. In my agency we have combined geodemographic and lifestyle analyses for our clients Greene King (pubs) and Chrysler Jeep (automobile showrooms) with notable success.

today's fearsomely competitive marketplace, detailed psychographic targeting data is essential.

None of which – as I said earlier – is intended to decry the potency of muscle power. In media buying as elsewhere, right is now firmly on the side of might. For years I baulked at the power of bulk. For years I was sceptical, for years I argued that buying and selling media was unlike buying and selling foodstuffs or raw materials. I argued that it was against the media's own interests to sell their space and time more cheaply to the big buyers because it would slash their revenue. I was wrong.

The predictable truth is that in order to maximise their turnover the media aim to negotiate big-bucks deals with major advertisers, and major media buyers, and then top up their take with smaller deals at more lucrative rates. (As Damon Runyon put it: 'The race is not always to the swift, nor the battle to the strong, but that's the way to bet.')

That is not to say that small advertisers never get good deals. They do. As we have seen, the media marketplace is exceptionally fragmented, and in some ways is truly unlike most other markets. There is always a profuse diversity of 'products' on sale. A peak-time spot in London is as different from an afternoon spot in Scotland as a full page in the *Financial Times* is different from a quarter page in *Woman's Own*. The media buyer has a massive multiplicity of alternatives from which to select, and he can nearly always get good deals if he twists and turns, ducks and dives, manoeuvres and manipulates full-bloodedly. Nor do many minor advertisers want or need to buy into major media – with specialised products they can use specialised publications, or specify television and radio slots which specifically reach their target audience.

The media marketplace is unbelievably complex. The terrain is maze-like and uneven. But if you are looking for the high ground, it will generally be where the big battalions are encamped. And this will become increasingly true in future. The spread of multinational televisual media will be slow – *globus confusingus* will see to that – but it will be relentless. At the same time, national television audiences will splinter as more and more channels come on-stream.

None of this will pose insoluble problems for advertising – though you would certainly think otherwise if you believed all the guff in the endless torrent of features on fragmentation and narrow-casting. Even when British television is shattered into a thousand tiny stations – which will not be for many decades to come, if ever – it will still be far simpler to buy, and less fractured, than the press and magazines. And it will still be far, far simpler to buy than television in the USA, where each local area has its own mélange of innumerable transmissions. There there are over 2,000 terrestrial television stations, plus 200 or so satellite stations. Most US towns now offer a choice of 130-plus channels, and this figure is widely forecast to leap to about 500 by the end of the century. How will viewers – let alone advertising time buyers – cope?

In comparison, purchasing broadcast advertising time in Britain will remain, as it has always been, difficult but straightforward. It will inevitably become a great deal more intricate than it was in the good old simple days of ITV and Channel 4. That is why smart targeting is growing increasingly vital. That is why there will be an increasing concentration of buying power into those operations with the resources and the know-how to exert their muscle in the market; and it is why media specialists have become – and will continue to be – an independent force to be reckoned with in British advertising.

The old order is changing, yielding place to new. The only constant, as Karl Marx quipped, is change. But the pace of change is steady. 'Never prophesize, especially about the future,' aphorised the late movie mogul Sam Goldwyn, but I'll risk it: changes are a daily occurence in the media but cataclysmic changes – despite the hype – are not on the agenda.

7

Testing, Shmesting

In 1923, Claude Hopkins, the greatest copywriter of his day, wrote:

> The time has come when advertising has, in some hands, reached the status of a science. It is based on fixed principles and is reasonably exact. The causes and effects have been analysed until they are well understood. The correct methods of procedure have been proved and established. We know what is most effective and we act on basic laws. Advertising, once a gamble, has thus become, under able direction, one of the safest business ventures. Certainly no other enterprise with comparable possibilities need involve so little risk.

Hopkins specialised in direct-response, off-the-page advertising, whose results have always been less elusive than those of brand advertising. But even for direct-response advertising his claims are OTT. I hesitate to call him a fibber but he was patently an optimist. He called his most acclaimed book: *Scientific Advertising*. Despite the developments in media targeting, there is no such thing.

Following gingerly in Hopkins' footsteps the great advertising and research men of the 1950s and 1960s – David Ogilvy, Rosser Reeves, Norman B. Norman, Ernest Dichter, Horace Schwerin and chums – all sought to postulate correct methods of procedure which have been 'proven and established'.

That was an era when hardly a month passed without a new advertising rule book being published, each packed with seemingly immutable maxims:

NEW is the most powerful word in the English language.... YOU is the most powerful word in the English language.... Humorous advertising never works because people don't buy from clowns ... no billboard should contain more than 14 words ... magazine headlines should always be between 6 and 12 words in length ... every advertisement must contain a Unique Sales Proposition ... coupons should always be in the bottom right-hand corner ... the pack must always appear within the first 7 seconds of a 30-second commercial ... people do not read reversed-out type ... people do not read sans-serif type ... TRUE is the most powerful word in the English language ... WHO? is the most powerful word in the English language ... 'FLU is the most powerful word ...

Greenhorns like me were required to read, mark, learn and inwardly digest such bromides as though they were Newtonian laws. The advertising world loved them, and clung to them, because they offered certainty in an uncertain world. They seemed to prove that, in Claude Hopkins' words, 'Advertising has, in some hands, reached the status of a science.'

Today nobody who knows anything about advertising bothers to search for such quasi-scientific laws, let alone believes them. This has partly come about because television has become the dominant medium for consumer goods advertising, and it has proved a great deal harder to promulgate plausible rules for TV commercials than it seemed to be for print advertisements. But mostly it is because the vast quantities of research that have been carried out over recent decades have taught the advertising industry that there are no universal, infallible rules. But is that research itself infallible?

In other words, if advertising itself is still not – despite Claude Hopkins' optimism – a science, can advertising research be a science? Well, it depends what you mean by a science.

Advertising research – testing advertisements before they appear – most definitely isn't a science in the way that physics and chemistry are sciences. It isn't reliably predictive, its results can seldom be replicated, its findings are liable to widely varying interpretations.

Like the other relatively new behavioural sciences which seek to apply the methods of physics to the study of humanity – economics, psychology, sociology – advertising research swiftly trips over its shoelaces when it promises too much. Seeking to measure and understand human beings cannot (and never will be) infallible in the way that the sciences of inanimate objects can be. However much market research techniques are improved and refined, that will not change.

At best, advertising research is a science like weather forecasting. (If you consider weather forecasting a science.) Like weather forecasting it is an applied science, and aims to be predictive, but dealing with ever-changing, unpredictable forces its results cannot be guaranteed. If practised cautiously and cleverly advertising research – like weather forecasting – is possibly slightly more often right than wrong, slightly more often helpful than unhelpful, and can prolong active commercial life. A little.

Charles Raymond's words, from the first issue of *The Journal of Advertising Research* more than thirty years ago, are altogether more realistic than those of Claude Hopkins:

> An advertising problem is not attacked, but painfully translated into a set of answerable questions. There are no breakthroughs, only small decreases in the unexplained variance. Instead of final conquest there will simply be better advertising decisions, measurably better.

That sounds modest and unexceptionable, if hardly stirring. But hang on: even here there has been some sleight of hand. How do we know the advertising decisions will be better, let alone measurably better? Has there ever been irrefutable confirmation of advertising research findings in the marketplace? No. Have there been well-known campaigns which researched like a dream yet failed to move even a Free Trial Pack off the shelf? Yes. Hasn't every advertising agency in the world created campaigns that it knew in its bones would be effective and then seen them tested to destruction? Yes, yes, yes.

Everyone knows the existing techniques are inadequate – like weather forecasting – and that the results are unverifiable. Everyone ignores, or tries forcibly to demolish, findings that are not to their liking. Everyone has pet stories of advertising that researched appallingly yet succeeded brilliantly in the marketplace – Heineken's 'Refreshes The Parts' campaign, Benson & Hedges' surreal pack campaign and the American Avis 'We Try Harder' campaign are most people's favourite examples.

For many years researchers put their faith in mechanical aids, hoping that technology would succeed where the human brain had so signally failed. Eye-movement cameras, psycho galvanometers, corneal reflectors, tachistoscopes, polygraph machines, pupil dilation recorders, electrode eye measurers – would you believe that there are human beings innocently trusting enough to let market researchers fix electrodes to their eyeballs? – and a heap of other Emmett-like apparatus has been used in the attempt to correlate people's unconscious physical responses with advertising effectiveness. It has all been in vain. None of the contraptions have worked, none have added much to the sum of human knowledge. To quote one of the classic textbooks on the subject, *Assessing the Effectiveness of Advertising*, by Jack Potter and Mark Lovell:

> We have ploughed unrewarding furrows in this particular field and are unimpressed by any of the techniques on offer.

In addition to the innate capriciousness of human behaviour, there are several other reasons why advertising research is chock-full of pitfalls:

i   Samples are rarely defined precisely enough.
ii Researchers inadvertently influence the results.
iii Too much reliance is placed on wonky data.

Defining the Sample

The last chapter stressed the importance of targeting in media selection. The same applies to advertising research, with knobs on.

Market research is an economical way of obtaining data which could always be obtained more accurately at greater cost. Because advertising testing is widely known to be inadequate, most advertisers cannot be bothered to spend much money on it. So it starts imperfect and gets worse. If a thing's worth doing, as the old mantra goes, it's worth doing well. If advertising testing is going to be done at all, it must be done properly. This means, above all, that it must be carried out on the correct people – and finding them will almost always be expensive.

Some data is better than no data – the thesis upon which most advertisement testing is today carried out – is a blatant fallacy. In theory, dubious data is neither better nor worse than no data. In practice, dubious data is always worse. It allows idle people to act thoughtlessly, and daft people to parrot nonsense facts. If the research sample is not accurately drawn, the test results will not be merely useless: they will probably be misleading. People who are not truly in the market for a product will not be interested in its features. To a non-purchaser, product details are irrelevant. And boring. We might reasonably expect the opposite to be true for purchasers.

That is why advertising tests *never* work for off-the-page, direct-response advertisements. (Claude Hopkins, incidentally, was in no way interested in the kind of test carried out nowadays.) The percentage of the readers of any publication who will respond to any direct-response advertisement is miniscule – seldom as much as 1%. Finding these people, and exposing them to advertisements in a test situation, is impossible. Experienced direct-response advertisers rarely even try. Novices regularly have a go, and get burned.

For example, every piece of research on unit trust advertising 'proves' that the advertisements are overfull of long, unread and unreadable stuff and nonsense. The reality is that anyone willing to cut out a coupon and post it with a cheque for hundreds or even thousands of pounds will want to read everything they can. Those people – the real prospective purchasers – cannot be identified, isolated, and researched in advance. They normally constitute a few hundred, at most a few thousand – a drop in the ocean of any national newspaper's readership.

Testing, Shmesting

Precisely the same principles apply to brand advertising.

If you do not own a cat (76% of the population do not), if you do not drink lager (about 80% of the population do not), if you do not intend to buy a microwave this year (95% will not), then you will not be in the least interested in the cat food's ingredients, the lager's taste, or the microwave's bells and whistles. So the less the advertisements tell you about the products, the more acceptable they will be to you. Moreover you will say so volubly in market research.

No matter how much it costs – and no matter how illogical it may sound – it always pays to test new advertising on existing users of the brand. If they respond well, prospective users will likewise respond well. As the last chapter showed, trying to find prospective users is like looking for needles in a haystack. But worse. At least needles don't look much like hay; prospective users look just like prospective non-users (or should that be non-prospective users?). And it is useless asking them to identify themselves, as researchers so often do – 'Are you likely to buy X at some time in the future?' – because the truth is that most of the time people cannot truthfully answer.

The most authoritative study to date of all the known techniques of predicting purchase behaviour, carried out by the lively and iconoclastic Department of Marketing at Massey University in New Zealand, showed that even for entire product categories – let alone individual brands – predicted purchase rates are subject to exceedingly wide margins of error: margins so wide as to make the predictions uselessly unreliable. This is doubtless because few people themselves have any idea whether or not they are likely to change their purchasing behaviour in the future, so when market researchers ask them to make such artificial decisions they are understandably flummoxed. (As political opinion polling regularly proves.)

To get the sample right, keep keeping close to the customers – and you will never go far wrong.*

---

* I have been focusing here on existing brands. Launching new brands, which by definition have no existing customers, is manifestly a different ball game. I am convinced the high failure rate among new brands is, in large measure, due to the difficulty of finding precisely the right sample on which to test them. I have seen it occur dozens of times. And the same is true of the re-launch of failing brands. In my experience few failing brands are ever successfully relaunched. It is a phenomenon much talked about, and often attempted, but rarely achieved.

How Researchers Influence the Results

Some years ago the learned, authoritative and intellectual *Journal of the Market Research Society* published a paper showing that different researchers often produce diametrically opposite test results from the same advertising material. The author, a lecturer in marketing, then went on to suggest seditiously that many researchers become so integrated and involved with their client's problems that in the end they 'deliver results which fit the client's expectations and for which the client will be pleased to pay.'

Worse yet, the learned, authoritative and intellectual editors of the *Journal of the Market Research Society* endorsed this heretical thesis, and described as 'particularly pleasing' the lecturer's comment that: 'Researchers have been found to possess chameleon-like qualities, quickly adapting to the changing demands of clients as well as of respondents.'

Naturally these calumnies sent the market research world into a dizzy tizzy. Letters – probably writs – whizzed in all directions. It was proposed that the learned, authoritative and intellectual editors of the *Journal* should be summarily dismissed. (They weren't.) Market Research Society functionaries sought to dowse the flames by reminding everyone of what a truly tricky problem it all is. To obfuscate the issue as thoroughly as possible one published letter contained a fifty-nine-word sentence of magnificent impenetrability.

Most of the altercation concerned qualitative research: focus group discussions and/or depth interviews. These are small-scale, statistically invalid projects, involving fewer than a hundred – often fewer than twenty – respondents. That is the way that well over 90% of campaigns are currently tested in Britain. A tiny minority of advertisers employ larger-scale, quantitative methods – which have their own considerable defects – but nowadays qualitative testing is *à la mode*. And the *Journal of the Market Research Society*'s allegations have never been effectively rebutted.

It is not suggested – at least I myself have never suggested – that the researchers consciously and deliberately rig the results. Most researchers are too honest, and too sensible, even to try. But qualitative researchers can hardly avoid communicating their attitudes to the respondents, unwittingly and unconsciously, by body language and tone of voice. The same has been shown to be true in drug efficacy tests, which is why doctors are now never told which is the drug being tested and which the placebo. Drug tests are now always 'double blind' – neither the doctor nor the patient knows what is being tested. The same cannot be achieved in advertising tests. During advertising tests the researcher is the respondents' centre of attention throughout the process. And researchers – they tend to be well-educated, middle-class graduates – have their own predelictions, in addition to being well aware of which results will 'fit their client's expectations and for which the client will be pleased to pay.' The researchers themselves mostly prefer clever advertisements, and dislike 'hard sell' advertisements. Their influence on British advertising can hardly be overstated.

And this explains a paradox which puzzled me for ages. How can it come about, I wondered, if almost every new campaign is pre-tested, (which is the case) that some succeed and others fail? (This must, by definition, be the case.) The answer is that the researchers always tell their clients that *their* advertising is spiffing.

The influence of the researcher cannot be eradicated. It is reminiscent of Heisenberg's famous uncertainty principle, in physics: in subatomic experimentation the investigation and measurement of the results inevitably interferes with the results themselves – shining light on to the process itself changes the process.

To ameliorate the inherent weaknesses of the system, the best you can do is:

i   Use hard-bitten experienced researchers (even if this costs more).
ii Use researchers who are as distant as possible from the advertising process, and change them as soon as they get too involved.
iii Send observers (a-k-a-spies) to watch over the proceedings.

Put Not Your Trust in Wonky Data

It is often said that many marketing people nowadays use research in the same way that a drunk uses a lamp post: for support rather than illumination.

But I've never seen much wrong in using a lamp post for support when support is what you need. Likewise I am strongly in favour of using market research for support when it is support that is needed. When the findings of an advertising test corroborate my opinions, that's great. When the findings of an advertising test confute my opinions two explanations present themselves:

i The research is wrong.
ii I am wrong.

We have already established that advertising testing is far from infallible. A long and bewildering career in advertising has, sadly, convinced me that I too am far from infallible. So is everyone else. (That is probably the only truth about advertising which is scientifically proven.)

A negative advertising test result therefore demands close scrutiny and an investigation of probabilities.

Is it more likely that the test is wrong, or more likely that I am wrong? There is no justifiable reason for thinking that either of us will invariably be wrong – or invariably be right. I guess the statistical likelihood is that we will both be right about 50% of the time. So I regularly challenge research results with which I disagree – or rather, which disagree with me.

This puzzles (not to say irritates) my clients, who allege that I embrace those advertising tests, however ropy, which support me but tear apart those which do not. That, they claim, is inconsistency. Heaven forbid! If you start as I do – as everyone does – from the premise that advertising testing is not a reliable and predictive science, then it makes complete sense to accept those results which confirm your views and to question closely those which do not. In my book, that is consistency: having consistent views and standing by them until they can be *proved* to be wrong.

Sometimes – well anyway occasionally – advertising tests throw up results which, though antipathetic, make sense. Fine. In that event it would be mulishly churlish to reject them. But if the results sabotage common sense, they are probably wrong.

So far we have been examining pre-tests: tests carried out before the advertising has appeared.

The second means of advertisement evaluation is post-testing: tests carried out after the campaign has run, or while it is running.

It might be wondered what the purpose would be of researching campaigns after the weighty costs of producing them have been incurred. There are two standard answers.

First, the cost of producing a campaign is generally a small proportion, 10% or so, of the media costs for space and time. So if the advertising is definitely a dodo it is better to ditch it than to continue pouring away money. Second, post-testing helps the advertiser and agency to refashion the advertising as the campaign progresses, to hone and polish future commercials and advertisements.

The simplest, most mundane form of post-testing is twenty-four recall. Twenty-four hours after a new commercial is screened for the first time, a representative panel of respondents is telephoned, asked whether they watched television the previous night and quizzed about their memories of the commercial in question, if any. By accumulating data for a raft of commercials over the years, it has become possible to identify whether each new commercial is more, or less, memorable than its predecessors and to jettison the duds. A different version of the twenty-four-hour recall test is the 'Reel-of-Ten' – in which respondents are shown a reel of ten commercials of which nine are standard, and constant, and the tenth is the commercial being tested.

Twenty-four-hour recall and Reel-of-Ten tests have been around for at least thirty years, and a few advertisers swear by them. Most agencies swear *at* them, because they generate formulaic, easy-to-grasp-at-first-glance commercials. But advertising is more complicated than that. It builds its effectiveness over time, via repetition. And formulaic, easy-to-grasp-at-first-glance commercials frequently become exceedingly irritating at the second, third, fourth ... and tenth glance. Tests have consistently shown, less than surprisingly, that twenty-four recall and Reel-of-Ten measurements greatly underrate all emotional and image campaigns. To quote David Ogilvy: 'It is open to question whether recall tests even measure recall. They measure the viewer's ability to articulate what he/she recalled, which is a different thing.'

More sophisticated than the twenty-four-hour recall and Reel-of-Ten tests, and nowadays used by many more major advertisers, are advertising awareness tracking studies. These involve interviewing, during the course of the campaign and thereafter, appropriate samples of respondents, so that their awareness of and attitudes to the advertising can be tracked over time. This technique provides much more robust data than twenty-four-hour recall testing – but it likewise has many failings.

Throughout advertising history innumerable campaigns have been highly memorable but produced scanty sales. Oldies will remember the launch of Strand cigarettes as one of the most notorious. Strand was launched shortly after I began in advertising, and I was both thrilled and astonished by the campaign's massive impact. It was, and probably still is, one of the most famous campaigns ever. Awareness of the advertising reached 90% of the population within weeks, everybody talked about it, television comedians parodied it, and media gurus analysed it. Strand sold hardly a pack and in less time than it takes to strike a light was withdrawn.

There have been many similar – though few quite so full-throated – high-awareness failures since. To quote the most thoroughgoing study yet carried out into the correlation between advertising awareness and sales, written by Simon Broadbent and S. Coleman in 1986, there is 'little or no association between campaigns' short-term sales effectiveness and their awareness effectiveness.'

This is perfectly understandable. Think of all the brands of which you are aware, but which you will never buy. Think of all the commercials and posters you see and remember, for products you will never buy. Tracking the public's awareness of campaigns trips over many of the hurdles I have previously stressed: advertising persuades comparatively small percentages of the population at any one time to act and switch brands – very rarely more than hundreds of thousands. But awareness tracking is not and cannot be that accurate, that fine. So it measures the impact of the advertising among the mass of the population – the mass of whom are utterly irrelevant, in sales terms.

It is often argued that this does little harm because widespread awareness always has value. I am not so sure. The quest for awareness leads advertisers and their agencies to seek 'famous' advertising which may or may not be precisely targeted. And worse still, to quote a celebrated paper by Paul Feldwick and Chris Baker:

> There is an insidious 'logic' that can creep into any area of advertising evaluation. This 'logic' runs as follows: first, measure whatever can easily be measured; next, presume that which cannot easily be measured to be unimportant; finally, act as if that which cannot easily be measured does not exist.

Paul Feldwick has also stated:

> We [BMP/DDB Needham] know of a number of campaigns with high scores for advertising effectiveness which have not achieved their sales objectives, and campaigns with low-awareness scores which have proved very effective in the market place.

I'll drink to that. So will every direct-response advertiser.

Consumer goods advertisers chase after research data in much the same way that greyhounds chase after electric rabbits: they may not be real but they are all that's on offer. And awareness, being all that's on offer, and comparatively easy to measure, has become the almost universal yardstick of advertising effectiveness. The yardstick has its uses, but they they are limited.

All of which explains why those seeking the advertising high ground will not find it in the area of advertising research. An ounce of judgement is worth tons of questionable research.

My own scepticism about market research was born when I was a toddler. An interviewer knocked on our door and asked my mother which paper she read. '*The Times*,' she replied unhesitatingly. 'But Mum,' I said as the door slammed, 'you don't read *The Times*.' 'Maybe not, but it's no business of hers,' she silenced me haughtily.

Quite apart from newspaper reading, about which my mum seems to have been peculiarly sensitive, there are many subjects which prompt respondents to fib to market researchers. Not surprisingly, few people are willing to tell the unvarnished truth about their alcohol and cigarette consumption. And their fabrications will be especially gross if the interview takes place in front of another member of their family. If I imbibe a bottle of hooch a day I'll admit a few doubles to the interviewer unless my spouse is within earshot, in which case I hardly ever touch the stuff.

Market researchers have long been aware of respondents' proclivity to massage such embarrassing facts. But at the 1993 Market Research Society Conference – attended by over 800 research pundits – a bright young researcher called Stephen Chinn, from Saatchi's, lobbed a grenade into the proceedings when he revealed that many respondents are nowadays going much further. They are no longer simply being parsimonious with the truth. They are deliberately and consciously manipulating the market researchers. So if advertising research has always been dubious, it will become still more dubious in future.

Chinn carried out a pioneering study which showed that many interviewees now understand the researchers' methods all too well. As one young Nottingham lager drinker put it:

> What you don't seem to realise is how much we know about what you're doing, and what role you need us to play. You think what you're doing is clever and remote, but we understand it. Had it occurred to you that we probably know more about you than you know about us?

Some respondents in Chinn's study went further still. They scorned the apparent ignorance of the companies who sponsor the market surveys. Surely, they said, these big businesses ought to know the answers already, or anyway be able to work them out for themselves? Some respondents cheerfully admitted to playing games with the researchers, viz.: 'I don't want to have adverts that make me buy things . . . I just want adverts to be dead funny!'

And the notion that the manufacturers carry out surveys in order to be able to understand their customers' needs was thought laughable. The respondents were well aware that they were being interviewed to help the manufacturers keep their production lines flowing and their profits growing.

Maybe none of this should come as a surprise. Market research is a well-established industry worth over £400 million a year. Opinion polls and surveys are published in newspapers daily. Everyone by now knows roughly how they work – and as the 1992 general election irrefutably established, by no means everyone responds to them truthfully. The fifty-three pre-election polls were, when averaged out, 8.5% adrift from the actual result. Nor was this result, incidentally, as atypical as the pollsters like to claim. The pollsters have predicted wrongly the results of four out of the last seven general elections. Professor Ivor Crewe, of Essex University, has suggested that many voters may be manipulating opinion polls in the same way that they manipulate by-elections – to register disapproval and let politicians know how they feel. Living proof of Stephen Chinn's thesis. Does it seem even likely that people would invariably tell the truth, the whole truth and nothing but the truth to interviewers?

In a world which aspires to political correctness, most people prefer to be seen – even by interviewers – as socially responsible rather than selfish. Many claim they would be willing to pay higher taxes *pro bono publico* (and then change their minds in the polling booth); many claim to be neurotically anxious about environmental pollution (but buy the same old detergents as they always have); many claim that safety is much more important to them than speed (and then buy the zippiest motor they can afford). Or like my mum, they simply upgrade themselves a bit, and shop at Harrods rather than C&A. Not everyone lies. But if a fair proportion do (8.5% for example), that will be more than sufficient to skew the results into uselessness. Psychologists have developed a battery of questions which help them identify habitual liars. These questions are never used in market research. Market researchers never even attempt to weed out habitual liars from their samples. Chinn's most important finding – which is less than astonishing as soon as you think about it – is that respondents' level of sophistication, and hence their tendency to fib, is growing apace. If Chinn is right, the opinion polls' failure to predict accurately the results of the UK and US elections is a harbinger of things to come. The consequences for advertising and marketing research will be immense.

Focus groups, depth interviews, twenty-four-hour recall, Reel-of-Ten, awareness tracking – as well as attitudinal data, propensity-to-purchase measurements and the entire gamut of advertising testing techniques – each and all throw pencils of light on the advertising process. None illuminates more than one small corner of the tangle of ways in which advertising works. None measures advertising effectiveness with any accuracy. A detailed IRI/Behaviourscan study in the USA in 1991, which tracked advertising and actual *sales* data, showed there to be *no* correlation between advertising test scores and sales achievements. The test scores measured both recall and persuasion – but did not correctly predict results.

The most reliable measurements of advertising effectiveness are area tests and, where relevant, coupon responses. And even these must be treated with caution. All experienced direct-response advertisers will affirm that their results are frequently freakish and inexplicable. The same is true, as Nielson analyses have shown, of area tests. To those who want advertising to be precisely measurable – finance directors and other bean-counters especially – it is all a beastly pain in the butt.

Naturally I understand advertisers' need to believe in testing. It is like a sick person's need to believe in patent medicines. Neither patent medicines nor weather forecasts are useless – but both have a tendency to overclaim. For my part, I have no desire for advertising to become a science – any more than fashion or architecture, music or movies, publishing or entertainment could become sciences. I am no Luddite: I have been a committed member of the Market Research Society since my twenties. But market research is informative, not predictive. Had I wished to be a scientist I'd have become an engineer. Instinct, intuition, sensitivity, taste and style are what it is all about – and ever more shall be so.

8
Launching a High Ground Agency

Launching your own advertising agency is not for the faint-hearted. It's fun, it's exhilarating, it's satisfying, it's rewarding, but having launched two I would not start another for all the tea in Typhoo. Flatteringly, during recent years, several teeny-bopper agencies have suggested I might join them, as some kind of geriatric ballast. No way: two has been company, three would be a crowd.

Many in advertising believe that before setting up an agency you must first spot a gap in the market. Hogwash. There are no gaps in the market. Not in the sense that the phrase is used in consumer goods marketing. There are well over three hundred agencies in Britain and between them they cover the waterfront – some brilliantly, some badly, most indifferently. To set up a successful agency you simply need to be certain you can do the same things your competitors do – only better.

So the first and most momentous decision to be made in setting up an agency is the selection of your partners. Agency founders set about selecting their partners in different ways, employing different criteria, espousing different theories. John Bartle, Nigel Bogle and John Hegarty had previously worked together for several years and so knew themselves to be compatible. David Abbott, Peter Mead and Adrian Vickers had never worked together and appear to have shared little but a passion for soccer. Both triumvirates have built excellent, successful agencies and their partnerships have endured. Few agency collaborations achieve such longevity. There are no available statistics, but I would guess most partnerships prematurely ejaculate at least one of the partners within a couple of years. It rarely proves fatal.

For my part I have always tried to team up with the very best people in town who could do the things that I could not. That gave me plenty of scope. It has certainly meant finding people with remarkable creative talent; and when I was younger it meant finding someone with sufficient gravitas to butter-up the bank manager. Whether or not I knew the people beforehand was, to me, immaterial. And the structures of my two agencies reflected precisely the eras in which they were launched.

Just over a decade elapsed between the founding of my first agency in 1974, and the founding of Delaney Fletcher Delaney (now DFSD Bozell) in 1985. During that decade, the advertising agency business mutated. In 1974 it was essential, from the beginning, to have sufficient capital to buy media space and time. In my case that meant offering my home to the bank as security for a loan. So it was essential to employ a finance director capable of eluding bankruptcy, and an experienced media buyer. Because, as it happened, one of our founder clients in 1974 was Spanish Olives, we also employed a home economist and a press relations lady; because chart-making computer software had not yet been invented we employed a chart-sketcher; because so many activities needed to be co-ordinated we employed a traffic man. My principle partners were Sir William Shelton, then a Member of Parliament, who was chairman and uncommonly good with bank managers, and Paul Delaney, who was creative director and uncommonly good with advertisements. Happily, in 1974 all our founder clients paid us 15% commission on their media billings – often plus a few bob more – so we were able to employ our small battalion of helpmates and still make a modest profit from the start.

By 1985 the mould had been broken. Delaney Fletcher Delaney began with seven people – four of them creatives. We worked with independent media specialists, so employed no media buyer. There was no need for a finance director, other than me, plus a part-time book keeper. A secretary, a telephonist/receptionist and a production manager completed our happy band. We would probably have employed still fewer, but for the fact that the agency grew out of the chrysalis of Barry and Greg Delaney's creative consultancy (Delaney & Delaney), and as a result we had a few clients right from the beginning. Barry and Greg are brothers of my previous creative partner Paul.

Delaney Fletcher Delaney's first few weeks were petrifying, exhausting and richly comic in turns. I had left Ted Bates, where I had been chairman and chief executive on a remuneration package of about £140,000: by no means a bad screw in 1985. I joined Barry and Greg Delaney on a remuneration package of nil. Returning to a comparatively impecunious lifestyle is the second momentous decision that anyone launching their own agency must face, as my bank manager forcibly pointed out to me at the time. Goodbye company car, goodbye chauffeur, goodbye lavish expenses, goodbye posh restaurants, goodbye Glyndebourne and Concorde, goodbye all first-class travel, goodbye little perks – telephone bills, health insurance, TV licence, taxis – goodbye full-time secretary and nice army of subalterns waiting and willing to do my bidding at the drop of a layout pad. Goodbye to all that – and hello to a poorer but purer life. (For five years after leaving Ted Bates, unless I was in a tearing hurry, when driving I coasted downhill to save petrol. A fruitless exercise, but it kept me in mind of the pennies.)

Nearly everyone who sets up an agency has previously achieved some level of eminence in advertising – otherwise they would be unable to open their own shop. The foolish ones continue to pay themselves too generously, being unable or unwilling to face the reality of their straitened circumstances. This immediately puts strains on their baby agency's cashflow, on their ability to recruit additional good people, and on their profitability. It was one of the few mistakes Delaney Fletcher Delaney did not make.

One of the less momentous decisions every new agency makes is its choice of name. Agency names are an unending source of entertainment to the outside world. People seem to find monikers like Still, Court, Price, Twivy and de Souza, or BMP DDB Needham, or Bartle Bogle Hegarty – or even, astonishingly, Delaney Fletcher Slaymaker Delaney and Bozell – hilarious. Top businesspersons endlessly rib agency folk about their ineptitude at choosing brand names for themselves. Journalists and television commentators chortle merrily at their ludicrous prolixity.

Why on earth, they all ask, can't agencies have sensible trade names, like other organisations? The answer is that they can, and quite often do. (How about Alliance, Arc, Cogent, Euro, Lansdowne, Lintas, Primary Contact, Portland and Zenith?) But agencies are personal service businesses. They are more akin to solicitors, accountants and architects (all of which have similarly risible names) than they are to manufacturing companies. When an agency starts up, clients buy into the talents and abilities of the founding partners. That is why it makes sense for the founding partners to put their names on the door. (So it is nothing at all to do with our egos.)

When we set up Delaney Fletcher Delaney it took us all of three minutes to decide the name. Other things were more problematical. Realising that if everything went ruinously wrong I might one day, in a pauperised dotage, look back on leaving Ted Bates as one of my nuttier decisions, I briefly kept a shorthand notebook diary for the only time in my career. Therein I wrote:

> Doubtless I will miss the prestige, the glamour, the comforts, the challenge of management, the access to data and to personal help, maybe the fame (maybe not), my standing in the advertising industry and the high life.
>
> On the other hand, I'll enjoy the freedom, the creativity, building the business, the puritanism and maybe getting rich again (if DFD makes it).

I had quit Ted Bates, as my diary noted, partly for the excitement of building a new agency; partly because I could not face the prospect of working for the same agency, in the same job, for a further thirteen years until I retired; partly because the only possible promotion I could hope for would involve living in New York; and partly because the roisterous goings-on at Ted Bates HQ on Broadway seemed to me to be eerily reminiscent of the fall of the

Roman Empire. Ted Bates' president, Robert Jacoby, had adopted a management style that was Nero-esque but without the compassion. It was not a congenial place to work. As Jacoby was fond of saying, 'You don't think we pay you all this money to enjoy yourself, do you?' Cliques, cabals and conspiracies were rife. Sexual and alcoholic athleticism were rampant. Bates employed an unusually large number of bright, talented people, most of who disliked each other warmly. The agency was a time-bomb waiting to explode. Persuading Saatchi and Saatchi to cough up $450,000,000 for his shaky empire, as he did twelve months later, was Jacoby's greatest triumph.

Though my basic remuneration at Delaney Fletcher Delaney was nil, I was to receive a commission on all new business won. More importantly, Greg and Barry Delaney sold me 30% of their shares at a rock-bottom price. In 1985 advertising agencies were going public at absurdly high price/earnings ratios. Stock market flotation P/Es of 30/40 were not uncommon. With heart-warming faith in their own future, and with a projected pre-tax profit in 1985 of about £100,000, Barry and Greg cheerfully, if optimistically, put a top-dollar value on their creative consultancy (for negotiating purposes at least). I did not do the arithmetic in quite the same way they did, but nonetheless – being equally optimistic – I was happy with the deal.

In the event all our calculations were for the birds. We launched the agency on 7 May 1985. Ten days later, Friday 17 May, we were to be visited by the managing director of our largest client Hillard's, the Midlands supermarket chain, since swallowed up by Tesco. The purpose of the meeting was to discuss Hillard's future advertising plans, and it would simultaneously be a serendipitous opportunity for me to meet Bob Dowds, the managing director. Dowds was due to arrive at noon, and we would then go off to lunch.

The choice of which restaurant to patronise – always difficult – is especially tricky for new agencies, and double so when certain kinds of tough-minded client (such as Midlands supermarket chiefs) are to be fed. As a new agency you cannot afford anywhere too lavish, nor do you wish to look poor. Entertaining tough-minded clients you must anyway never appear too rich, or they will squeeze your fee, nor dare you insult them by taking them somewhere too cheap. Nor should you choose somewhere too far away, requiring the costly and time-wasting use of taxis. All these niceties must be carefully weighed and balanced.

Eventually, after inordinate debate, Barry, Greg and I selected a nearby new *nouvelle cuisine* eatery which would be perfect. Dowds duly arrived at noon. He wasted no time in getting to the point. Hillards, he announced, would not be running any advertising during the following two years. Instead they would be spending their total marketing budget on price cuts and sales promotions. Delaney Fletcher Delaney had therefore lost the account. To be more precise, DFD had not lost the account, there no longer being an account to lose. No other agency would be appointed. Hillards had, Dowds added graciously, greatly enjoyed working with Delaney and Delaney, as was, and had been looking forward to working with Delaney Fletcher Delaney in the future. Should Hillards decide to recommence advertising in 1987 they would most certainly return to us.

'I hope you don't have this effect on all Barry and Greg's clients,' Dowds drolly said to me as he stood up to leave. 'Now I must be off.'

It was 12.04 p.m.

'Won't you stay to lunch?' Barry asked, remembering the much-debated restaurant.

'Not much point', Dowds replied. 'And it wouldn't be fair. And I honestly don't have the time.'

By 12.10 p.m. he had left, taking his no-longer-existent account with him. I have since learned that Barry and Greg Delaney seldom drink at lunchtime. That day the three of us went to the new *nouvelle cuisine* restaurant and got gently blotto.

At about £150,000 a year, Hillard's fees had contributed over one-third of the agency's income. That weekend I recalculated our newborn agency's revenue and our running costs. My diary for Sunday 19 May reads:

> Estimated revenue £180,000. Estimated costs £303,000. Projected loss £123,000. Little sleep.

The next morning, in our shared office, I revealed my dire prognostications to my two partners. 'We've never done projections that way before,' Greg responded. 'In a creative consultancy, business comes and goes. You get used to it. Don't worry.'

My optimism wasn't that elastic.

'If I were still working at Ted Bates,' I replied, 'by now a telex would be winging its way across the Atlantic on which would be typed just two little words: CUT COSTS.'

'I like it,' Barry responded. 'Good idea. We should cut costs. How?'

'We can't cut costs much,' I mumbled, 'because more than 90% comprise the rent on these new offices we've leased, together with the overheads, plus the minimal salaries we're paying the staff and the two of you. We can possibly save £20,000 or £30,000, that's maximum.'

'Don't worry,' Greg repeated, 'clients come, clients go. That's the way it is.'

Luckily Greg was wrong. During the subsequent years clients came, but rarely went. Despite the Hillard's débâcle we made a small profit in 1985, and three years later – the last year before we were acquired by Bozell – we hit pre-tax profits of £791,000. Nonetheless during 1985 the words 'little sleep' appear in my diary repeatedly. I had forgotten how stressful it is to launch an agency – even if one has done it before.

Nor did the clients materialise out of the blue, as though by magic, without effort on our part, as advertising fairy tales imply. Even before leaving Ted Bates I had written a list of every client and prospective client whom I knew personally, and with whom I could make immediate contact. The list was circumscribed by my Bates contract of employment, which forbade me to poach any of their clients for two years. Nevertheless, after two decades in advertising I was disconcerted by how few clients appeared on my list. It ran out at about two dozen. Without thinking much about it, I had imagined there would be hundreds. I thought I knew virtually everybody. The reality was that I knew scarcely anybody. Yet I am sure I knew far more than most people do when they set up an agency. From which you can safely deduce that anyone thinking of setting up an agency cannot rely upon personal contacts alone. Many beginners imagine they can do so. Not so.

Naturally I contacted all those on my list, and was fortunate enough to win business from several – though never without fighting for it, usually via a competitive pitch. The days when clients handed their chums chunky slices of business, on a plate, are long since past. Only very occasionally, in very exceptional circumstances, do accounts – usually small accounts – nowadays move from agency to agency without competitive presentations taking place. In my view this is good news. In contrast to most of my agency competitors I approve of competitive pitches. Competitive pitches open up the business. (And we win more than our fair share.)

It is apparent from my diary that, from the beginning, I was obsessed with gaining publicity for Delaney Fletcher Delaney. It is naturally essential for a pipsqueak agency to emerge from obscurity, but I am now stupefied by the extent to which winning – or not winning – publicity lifted or depressed me during those early days. It seems to have been much more important to me than winning business. Here are a few entries:

> Won Panasonic. Total cockup re publicity. V depressing.... Good PR lined up for next week, re Capital Transport Campaign, in *Sunday Times*, on BBC, also *Options* magazine for article re Greene King.... Capital Transport Publicity bombed – took it for granted, stupidly ... on LBC commenting on Mrs T's cabinet ... drafted feature for *Guardian* on sex in advertisements – there isn't much, so doubt if they'll publish ... furious letter to *Campaign* because *Time Out* win not clearly announced, they promise to correct next week ... long article in *Campaign* on creativity, seems to have sunk without trace ... piece on political advertising in *Marketing Week*: doesn't anyone read the trade press? ... *Guardian* accepted sexless piece, goodie ... broadcast on Capital Radio re SDP infuriated Barry ... on Radio Glasgow, waste of time but good practice ...

... and on and on. Never a week went by without me and/or the agency appearing somewhere, somehow, in something. Publicity is the life-blood of a new agency.

Not that my obsession with publicity was unique. Many young agency founders badger – harass – the trade press even more incessantly. I could name four agency bosses who cold-bloodedly started affairs with *Campaign* journalists specifically and deliberately to generate publicity for their agencies. Cheeringly, in each case the fickle finger of fate intervened and the agency boss fell sweetly in love with the journalist. The road to heaven is paved with bad intentions.

In contrast advertising – advertising the agency itself – is relatively unimportant. This is one of the apparent paradoxes of the agency business. Novitiate journalists frequently notice how infrequently agencies advertise themselves, and gleefully pounce upon this as positive proof that (in their hearts) agencies know advertising does not work. If agencies believe in advertising why do they so rarely put their money where their mouth is? the journalists ask disingenuously.

There are several answers. First, in order to build its awareness and its reputation an agency needs consistent publicity, week by week, for months and years. To achieve this by way of media advertising would be exorbitantly expensive, and wasteful, since it can be achieved for almost nothing by way of editorial publicity. (The same is not true of most consumer goods – though it similarly applies, in large measure, to fashion, to books, to records, to restaurants and to the theatre.)

Second, agencies find it embarrassingly difficult to be modestly immodest about themselves. Over the years a handful of agencies – Saatchi & Saatchi and the young Abbot Mead Vickers in particular – have succeeded in producing truly excellent advertising for themselves. But they are the exceptions. (And even they got it wrong at least as often as they got it right.) Agencies are far better at, and far less self-conscious about, promoting other people's products.

Third, in order to reach the tightly defined and tiny market that most agencies wish to reach, direct mail is a more cost-effective means of communication than media advertising. There are only about 1,500 relevant individuals involved on the marketing departments of companies spending more than £500,000 a year on advertising. You can write to them all for less than £1,000.

So we employed direct mail from the start. We did not do it as well as it could have been done, nor did we do it sufficiently frequently. But we did it adequately. Each mailing produced about a hundred responses. The majority would nicely tell us to get stuffed. A few would accept our invitation to come and see the agency's work. Anybody who tells you clients do not respond to agency mailings is talking through his database: I have bulging files of responses which prove the contrary.

And the same is true of telephone selling. Until recently I refused to believe that clients could be inveigled into agencies by cold calls. No doubt this was largely because I myself am hopeless at cold calling. I seldom get past haughty secretaries. When I do, I forget what to say. I get tongue-tied, I sound nervous. (I am nervous!) I know all the official tricks of the trade – phone when the secretary is likely to be out, prepare your speech carefully, anticipate objections, smile when you are speaking. I even dedicated a chapter in one of my books to the subject. But I cannot do it. Nor can the bosses of most other agencies, if I am to believe what they tell me (and I do, I do).

Maurice Saatchi claims* he used to make twenty-five cold calls a day when Saatchi's began in 1970, but I wonder whether he would be much cop at the job now. Not that he would need to be. Saatchi & Saatchi have employed marvellous computer-aided telephone salesmen for ages, as we ourselves now do. I wish we had started telephone selling much earlier. It works. And a strategically planned combination of direct mailing plus telephone selling works best of all

Despite missing out on telephone selling, Delaney Fletcher Delaney achieved a steady strike rate of just over one introductory presentation per week – almost sixty a year – and we worked our way on to a fair number of good-quality pitch lists in the first few months, including Panasonic, Thomas Cook, Tuborg Lager, the

* In *The Brothers: The Rise and Rise of Saatchi & Saatchi,* by Ivan Fallon.

Halifax, Wiggins Teape, Fujifilms, the TUC, *Time Out* and Liberty shops. Of those we won about a third. Any agency which wins three or four major bits of business a year (and holds on to them) is doing pretty good.

From the beginning I kept exact records of what happened to each and every prospective client contact, analysing at which point (if any) we lost the scent and detailing the reason. This did not always help us to do the right thing, but at least it stopped us mending unbroken clocks. For example, because agencies see their own presentations so often – sixty per year is almost up to repertory theatre level – they have a recurrent yearning to keep altering them, to stop themselves growing bored. By carefully tracking clients' responses it is easily possible to see whether change is, or is not, a smart idea.

As an agency grows the nature of the challenges it faces changes rapidly. When we began we occupied a small suite of rooms in a dingy Victorian office block overlooking Covent Garden piazza. Most mornings the doorway was decorated with sundry detritus – grotty fag packs, used lager cans, used lager, and a condom or two.

I suspected – I may have been wrong – that this less than pulchritudinous panorama would not enhance our desired image as a dynamic, go-go agency. So on those early mornings when we were presenting to prospective clients before the Covent Garden road sweepers got going, I would scramble downstairs and sweep away the previous night's debris, leaving the entrance spick and span. This activity much perturbed Barry Delaney, who felt that any prospective client arriving earlier than his appointed hour would be even less impressed by the spectacle of the agency chairman sweeping the doorway than by a few well-worn condoms. We disputed this issue frequently but failed to reach agreement. Eventually we resolved the argument by moving to more salubrious offices.

Other teething troubles included the loss of one prospective client, who failed to see our nameplate on the ground floor and so failed to find his way into the agency at all; the lack of lighting in the boardroom – the ultra-chic Milanese lights we had ordered failed to materialise for several months, making late-evening meetings a bit of a trial; and the cacophony of the bands playing in the Covent Garden piazza which, during the summer, made conversation, or even thought, an unwinnable struggle — and turned new-client presentations into a nightmare. As we grew, such tribulations passed into agency mythology and we started to grapple with (even) more fundamental issues. The most important was — as it has always been, now and forever shall be — the selection and recruitment of the brightest and the best.

The importance of recruiting the best people had been imbued in me since my novitiate days at the Robert Sharp agency. The Robert Sharp founding partners were fanatical about it — and unusually good at it. As a result a succession of highly talented people passed through what was quite a small agency. Ex-Robert Sharp employees include Len Deighton, Salman Rushdie, Fay Maschler, David (*Sunday Sport*) Sullivan, Rupert Gavin and — still in advertising — Martin Boase, Adrian Vickers, Robin Wight, David Reich and Tony Vickers among many others. Regrettably, the agency failed to hold on to most of the bright people it recruited — the principle reason it failed to grow. In their early years Charles and Maurice Saatchi were equally good at spotting talented novices, and successfully held on to them much longer.

It is a cliché of the agency business that the assets go down in the lift and home each night, but being a cliché does not make it untrue. Agencies can, and do, invent philosophies, and methodologies, and organisational systems, but what counts is the people. Salaries and associated costs amount to between 50% and 60% of every well-managed agency's outgoings. Even the greatest agencies, with the highest of reputations, quickly come to grief if the quality of their people falters. It has happened to many a once-fine agency. It is happening right now to several in London.

There is no known way of selecting good people that is 100%, or even 70%, reliable. I have studied just about every system yet invented, tried many of them, and have returned to the old, fallible, guaranteed unreliable interview. Spotting people with talent is itself a talent. I do not believe it can be learned: you've either got it or you ain't. And even if you have, you will still make loads of blunders.

To minimise your blunder rate you can, you must, check whenever possible with previous employers. Typed references are hardly worth the paper they are photocopied on. Naturally you cannot speak to the interviewee's present employers, but within the advertising village it is almost always possible to make contact with an earlier boss or two. What they don't say is always as important as what they do say. When asked for a personal reference people rarely like to denigrate, but nor do they like to lie. Perhaps surprisingly, to the best of my knowledge no competitor has ever tried to foist a dud on me. Maybe that says something nice about the advertising business, maybe it is simply enlightened self-interest. They recognise that next week the boot will be on the other foot.

Having recruited the brightest and the best it is naturally essential to motivate them, and to keep them. So many books have been written and so many theories advanced about people management that it is pointless to attempt to do justice to the subject here. However, it is worth spotlighting half a dozen management problems which are especially problematical in advertising agencies:

i	*Meetings*	Agencies are full of people and people adore meetings. Resist them: communicate quickly, informally, spontaneously. Keep in mind Sir Barnett Cocks' dictum: 'A committee is a cul de sac down which ideas are lured and then quietly strangled.'
ii	*Success*	Good people always want to work for successful companies, and in advertising success is particularly transparent. The people who scour the trade press most avidly for news about the agency are the agency staff.
iii	*Hierarchies*	Good advertising people are instinctively radical; they dislike hierarchies, deplore pomposity, detest people who give them uncompromising orders. From a senior to a junior, 'Would you please do this' will be much more effective than 'Do this!'

iv *Delegation* Advertising people are notoriously bad at delegation, they either delegate far too little or far too much. Neither a meddler nor an idler be.

v *Office Politics* Unhappy agencies are breeding grounds for office politics, and agency bosses frequently exacerbate the situation by criticising each other publicly (albeit behind closed doors!). Office politics can never be eradicated but they can be minimised, if the directors resolutely refuse to play ball.

vi *Leadership* Agencies being hyper-active roller coasters, almost everybody is manic-depressive. Agency bosses must shoulder the blame when things go wrong and lavish congratulations when things go right – not the other way round, as most do.

(How I wish I always achieved all the above.)

There is little doubt that agencies are at their pleasantest, as places to work, when the staff level reaches sixty-ish. At that point the operation is large enough to be fully resourced and fully professional, yet small enough for everybody to know everybody. There is a strong camaraderie, there is little hierarchy, there are few office politics, it is unnecessary to send memos to let people know what is going on, bosses can leave their doors open, everyone shares the glory of victories, everyone shares the bitterness of defeats.

Biological research shows that primates congregate in groups of different sizes, and the size of group is related to the size of their neocortex, the thin outer layer of the brain which is responsible for much of our conscious thought. The most effective size of human groups, it has been found, is about 140 (the size of an army company). Nonetheless I am certain that advertising people work best in groups of sixty or so – the same size of group that chimps (with significantly smaller neocortexes) generally prefer. Maybe agency folk resemble chimps more than they resemble other human beings.

As an agency succeeds, and grows, the general euphoria invariably prompts the agency panjandrums to wonder whether it is worth growing still bigger. David Ogilvy reports that when the staff of Ogilvy & Mather numbered fewer than a hundred he considered putting a stop to further expansion, but was dissuaded by his partners. His partners were right. It is impossible, tempting though it may seem, to put an artificial brake on an agency's growth – and still to build a high ground agency.

If an agency ceases to grow then young Turks cannot be promoted – they have nowhere to go but out of the door.... If an agency ceases to win clients it will be seen to be unsuccessful – and even its existing clients will start to feel unsettled.... If an agency loses the habit of winning clients it will not easily be able to pick up new business when eventually, as sure as God made little pitches, it loses an account or two.... If an agency ceases to win business it will cease to win publicity.... If an agency ceases to win business it will miss the adrenalin-pumping, neurosis-generating, personality-clashing excitement of competitive presentations.... By now you will have got the message. Unappealing though it is in many respects, growth cannot be escaped. Except by failure.

In addition to euphoria, there is nowadays another reason for trying to limit an agency's size to sixty or so employees. If any agency grows beyond that size it will, unavoidably, need to handle international clients. One or two agencies – Bartle Bogle Hegarty is the most celebrated – are trying to handle multinational business without a multinational network. I do not believe this can work, for long. The great majority of multinational advertisers (99.9% or more) wish to work with multinational agencies.

So successful British agencies eventually need multinational partners. And that will inevitably involve relinquishing some, or all, of the agency's equity to the multinational agency – a prospect that young, growing agencies find less than entrancing. But it need not be too painful. I have, again, done it twice. On each occasion my founding partners and I judged that we had reached the size – or were about to reach the size – when we could no longer go it alone.

The first sale was much encouraged by the Ayatollah Khomeini, who for a time became closely involved in our business. We had handled Iran Air's advertising since the agency began, and Paul Delaney's brilliant campaigns had, over the years, scooped up stacks of creative gongs around the world. The advertising positioned Iran Air as a modern, technologically sophisticated, fully fledged international carrier – differentiating it from the trumped-up pipsqueak airlines run by most newly emerging nations.

The Shah himself, we were told, thought our advertising simply spiffing – which was less than surprising as it indirectly boosted and praised Iran's forward-looking image. However, the Shah, it will be remembered, was suddenly turfed out one afternoon in 1979 and replaced by the Ayatollah. The Ayatollah did not think our campaign spiffing: it reflected everything he detested about the Shah's Iran.

Indeed the Ayatollah wasn't too happy with the airline at all. So he sent one of his henchmen to see its boss – a rather nice and honest Iranian general, but unfortunately a Sunni Moslem: the wrong kind, from the Ayatollah's point of view. The henchman told the general that the new regime had incontrovertible proof of malpractice and corruption within the airline, for which he would be publicly tried and executed. Alternatively, the henchman went on, slipping the general a revolver, matters could be sorted out more neatly and simply. The general shot himself.

The Ayatollah, or anyway his blokes, then declared (among other things) that they would not be paying for any of our advertising. It had been, they claimed, personal puffery for the Shah, not advertising for the airline at all.

Iran Air was easily the agency's largest account. They had always been slow payers, but the general had invariably coughed up in the end. We handled their advertising in the UK and throughout Europe and at the time they owed us nearly £1,000,000 – equal to more than £2,000,000 today. We had no significant insurance cover. Like the foreign office, the CIA and the Kremlin we had not foreseen the Shah's precipitate overthrow, and insuring foreign governments is anyway all but impossible. If the Ayatollah refused to pay we would be bankrupt.

The fate of the general ensured that our other chums at Iran Air – the chaps we had worked with closely for years – were now far from chummy. They were not about to authorise the payment of our invoices. They didn't answer our telexes, or our letters, or take telephone calls, or acknowledge our claims in any way. Advertising invoices? What advertising invoices?

For weeks we tried, with growing desperation, to get our money. Finally we resorted to the law. There is ancient British legislation which enables a British company to take possession of a visiting merchant ship when it enters a British port, in payment for outstanding debts. Our lawyers believed that law would apply in this case.

We went to court on a Friday. Iran Air made no appearance, entered no defence. The Ayatollah clearly thought British courts too trivial to trifle with. The sitting judge – how I hated him – said he had never before been involved in a case concerning so large a sum which had not been contested. He therefore intended to go through the papers himself as though he were Iran Air's counsel, and would announce his decision the following Monday morning. This admirable manifestation of British justice ensured that Bill Shelton, Paul Delaney, the other partners and I all suffered a further frightening seventy-two hours.

On Monday, as promised, the judge gave judgement. He awarded us the next Iran Air plane to arrive at Heathrow. It touched down at around lunchtime. We took possession. Heathrow air traffic control were instructed not to allow the aircraft to leave British soil. We were – almost certainly the only advertising agency in history – the proud possessors of a Boeing 747 SP. Full of Iranians.

The jumbo was on its way to New York. For the first time Iran Air woke up to the gravity of the situation. It consulted its UK lawyers. Meanwhile the aircraft, and its passengers, sat on the Heathrow tarmac. At the agency we popped a bottle of champagne. Too soon. Around six o'clock the airline's lawyers contacted our own. They had found a small legalistic gaffe in our deposition. This would enable them, the next morning, to get our court order revoked. At the same time they would sue us for costs. The costs of holding a 747 SP at Heathrow overnight, the costs of lodging several hundred waiting passengers in a New York hotel, the ensuing costs caused by the delay . . . the costs might easily run to millions.

Alternatively, Iran Air's lawyers promised, if we surrendered the plane immediately, representatives of the airline would come to London within three days and pay the invoices. We knew they wouldn't, of course. For about an hour we debated the issue. Then we let the plane go, assured by our lawyers that if Iran Air again defaulted we could return to court, with the legalistic gaffe corrected, and take possession of another jumbo.

It was a week before the Iran Air people arrived. They began to go through the invoices one by one. Several months' advertising, in a host of publications, in eight different countries, including production costs; every item without exception was contested. After a particularly unpleasant dispute concerning some photography which they claimed we had not been authorised to undertake, we were solemnly warned that if we continued to be so intransigent we would be fired, and they would move their prestigious account to another agency.

Slowly the money began to trickle in, until the predictable – the inevitable – happened. They refused to pay £60,000 worth of invoices still in dispute. They knew we would be unable to go to court again. If we did, having learned their lesson, they would fight us tooth and claw. We would incur massive legal costs, and might not win our full £60,000 claim. Again we despaired.

Fortunately the airline's kindly finance department came to our rescue. They paid one batch of invoices, totalling almost £80,000, twice. We pocketed the extra £20,000. The boot was now on the other foot. Iran Air threatened legal action. Go ahead, we encouraged them. After a few weeks' quibbling they gave up. Then, formally and in writing, we resigned the account and closed the books.

It had all been too much for my partner Sir William Shelton. If we had been declared bankrupt he would have been forced to resign as a Member of Parliament: not a prospect he relished. So we decided to expedite our long-planned sale of the agency. Even without Iran Air we were doing pretty well: we were regularly courted by multinational suitors.

We sold to Ted Bates, then the world's second-largest agency. It was an initial success, but subsequently floundered. Happily, my second attempt at selling to a major multinational has so far proved an unequivocal boon and blessing. Four years ago, when Delaney Fletcher Delaney was acquired by Bozell, multinational business constituted 3% of our income. Next year it will account for almost 40%. And this growth has been achieved steadily, without histronics or bellicose transatlantic argy-bargy.

Not that I have any cast-iron recommendations on how to pick a multinational partner. It seems to be as hazardous, and as fortuitous, as marriage. Lots of British agencies have had several goes at it, before finding and settling down with their heart's desire. The only hint I can proffer to a British agency being courted by a multinational is that – as with marriage – love will find a way. If the multinational agency thinks your agency sufficiently delectable it will pay almost any price, agree to almost any contractual terms. Negotiate hard. If the multinational cries off, it was not in love in the first place. Better to discover that before the marriage than afterwards.

In the light of all the uncertainties, of the fissures and the stresses and the strains, if I could put myself in a time machine and start all over again, would I hang out my shingle and launch my own agency, as I did in the past? Probably not. Times have changed.

It is, admittedly, the inalienable right of all ambitious young admen to set up their own shop. That is the way it has always been. While their elders are in their clubs planning secret mergers, the young ones are in the pubs planning secret breakaways. And over recent years new shops have been spawned faster than baby bunnies at a rabbit orgy. In the past decade, there have been more than fifty. Even during the recent dispiriting recession, at least half a dozen toddlers burst lustily into the cruel world.

What is it that drives so many fledglings to fly away from highly paid and secure nests in big agencies in order to face risk and ruin building their own? They want to do things their own way, to escape the heavy-handed management of bigger operations, as I did. And of

LAUNCHING A HIGH GROUND AGENCY

course not the least of their reasons, however sweetly they may deny it, is the hope of eventually making loadsamoney.

For agency builders to bag their crocks of gold it is necessary for them to sell all or part of their shop, one day, to somebody else. But who will they sell to in the future? The London stock market is unlikely ever again to greet agency flotations with the exuberance it did in the 1980s. The other traditional route, selling to a foreign multinational agency seeking to muscle in on the UK market, is better, but is no easier. All the major multinationals are already spoken for, with well-established London offices. From time to time, in the future as in the past, multinationals will come shopping for hot British shops when they need to fire up a comatose local office. But the remote possibility of a merger, at some unspecified time in the future, with the moribund local office of a multinational agency, would be far too uncertain to inspire me to launch my own shop today.

So if you launch an agency in the 1990s, maybe you must accept the fact that it will never be easy to sell it at a handsome profit. Perhaps the only way out will be to pass it on eventually to your successors, or even to leave it to your children, as they did in days gone by. (Old fogeys will remember Royds. And Vernons. And Brunnings. And Osbornes. All of them passed from father to son. None of them any longer exists.)

In any event, unless your ambitions are modest and you just want to be a boutique, even leaving your agency to your heirs now raises problems. As we have already seen, by AD 2001 up to 50% of all British advertising will be handled internationally. There will always be a place for local shops, just as there is a place for regional shops (and for corner shops). But their potential will be limited. Excluded from multinational pitches, their growth will be severely curtailed.

Nor will it be possible for future British agencies to nip round the globe, as Saatchi's did in the 1970s and 1980s, building up their own international networks. All the good international networks, and most of the good agencies throughout the world, either have been bought or cannot be bought. Even the mighty Japanese agency Dentsu is encountering difficulties building up its international operation; and it was principally the cost of trying to build its own European network that finally bankrupted Yellowhammer Plc. It would now be as difficult to build a new multinational agency as to start a new mass-production automobile company. The hot-rods are out on the track, and the gates have shut.

It is still the inalienable right of all ambitious young agency men to set up their own shop. But for those who brave it, as many young agencies are even now discovering, the outlook is distinctly hazy. And depressing though it is to say so, the outlook is hazier still for women.

Perceptive readers will by now have noticed that when generalising about the advertising business I have consistently used the masculine gender: advertising *men* and so forth. This is not due to male chauvinism, idleness, or even a desire for grammatical simplicity. It is a reflection of the unhappy fact that an industry which prides itself on its open-mindedness and lack of prejudice is still male-dominated.

No woman has her name on the door of any of the top fifty agencies; just one of the top fifty agencies is run by a woman; there is only one female creative supremo among the top fifty; the boards of all the major agencies are still enclaves of masculinity; and even among the new, young, radical agencies female partners are few and far between, as rare as poster sites in the Antarctic. One of the new agencies launched in 1993 was founded by a woman – the first and only to date.

In a country led by a queen, until recently governed by a lady prime minister, which has a female boss of MI5, this backwardness in a supposedly forward-looking industry is hard to explain – and must be even harder for women to stomach. The classic excuses – women cannot devote themselves wholeheartedly to the business, they have their careers fractured by children – do not bear much examination. There are exceptionally successful women in other spheres of work.

In any event such excuses are confounded by the fact that there is one area of advertising and marketing where women succeed at least as well as men: planning. Many of the planning directors in agencies are female, and their jobs are as all-embracing, as demanding, as time-consuming as any one else's. So what is the explanation? Before she left to sail round the world, Saatchi & Saatchi's own sagacious planning director Marilyn Baxter investigated the issue for the Institute of Practitioners in Advertising. Her report reached three clear conclusions.

First, she blamed history. For a woman to be at the top now she should have started in advertising fifteen or twenty years ago. But twenty years ago only 19% of graduate entrants into advertising were women. Nowadays the figure is almost 50%. So in another couple of decades everything should come right. She dubbed this her 'cohort' theory.

Second, she blamed clients' prejudices and, more importantly, agencies' preconceptions about clients' prejudices. Agency managements insist that many male clients, and even some female clients, prefer to deal with men – especially on so-called macho accounts: beer and cars in particular. Stuff and nonsense.

Third, she blamed women's lack of confidence, especially in the creative department. Because creative ideas are so fragile, and their validity so unprovable, copywriters and art directors often need to fight for their work, to defend it strongly, to promote it determinedly and, like Paul Delaney, with vehemence. Few women have the confidence to do so. That is why so very few top creative people are women. (In contrast, most disputes in planning concern objective data – rather than subjective opinions. Having mastered the data it is easy for women to excel in argument. And they do.)

Let us hope Marilyn Baxter's cohort theory proves correct. Otherwise advertising will slip behind even the other regressive, stick-in-the-mud sectors of British industry, and tomorrow's brightest and best females will shun advertising agencies, and rightly so.

And that would not be a high ground future.

9
How to Make Clients Happy

During my first few months in advertising, one of the many things that puzzled me was why on earth our clients stayed with us. Wet behind the ears though I was, I knew there were dozens of good agencies in town – I had unsuccessfully applied to most of them for jobs – and I could not suss why any client should choose our agency rather than one of the others. Perusing the billboards, reading the advertisements, watching the commercials, it seemed obvious that while few of the campaigns were splendiferous, most were proficient – and equally obvious that they were produced by a host of different agencies each of which must, on the evidence, also be proficient. It was several years before I conceitedly became confident I could do better.

My youthful perplexity was exacerbated by the marketing director of one of our largest clients – one of Britain's largest toiletries companies – who casually remarked to me that there were at least half a dozen excellent agencies in London, and he preferred to work with the one which took him to lunch at the Ritz most often. (Ah, the decadent 1960s.) But ritzy entertaining apart, how can any agency differentiate itself from the three hundred or so others which jostle it in the marketplace race?

Most attempt to do so by inventing something they dub an 'agency philosophy'. Agency philosophies do not make clients happy, or for that matter unhappy. Indeed clients seldom give a toss about agency philosophies. When clients are asked why they appointed agency A, B or Z they never say, 'Because of its philosophy.' None of the founding fathers of the agency business maundered on about their philosophies. David Ogilvy, in particular, went out of his way to deny having one, and the word cannot be found anywhere in his 1960s classic *Confessions of an Advertising Man* (still probably the best book on advertising ever written). Nonetheless, most agencies suffer from a strange, psychotic craving to have a philosophy. Maybe it is an occupational disease like dermatitis.

Philosophy, the Oxford English Dictionary says, is the love, study or pursuit of wisdom. It is something you *do*, like advertising, not something you *have*, like measles. Nobody expects dentists, or solicitors, or tinkers, tailors, beggermen and thieves to have philosophies. They are required to be good at fillings, at soliciting, at tinkering, tailoring, begging and thieving. When you are writhing under the drill or purchasing a new suit the last thing you require is a sagacious sermon on Spinoza or Sartre, or on some such elegant theological conundrum as *Does Charles Saatchi Really Exist?*

Likewise clients want their agencies to be good at advertising. Correction: they want them to be better at advertising than other agencies. That is the secret of making clients happy. It's not that profound.

Agencies have no need for philosophies – except to make themselves feel important. When Capablanca, the great 1920s world champion chess master, was asked to define the philosophic principles of his game he replied (in Cuban): 'I have none. Every time it is my go I just make the best move.'

The craving of agencies for philosophies is, in my view, mildly unhealthy and leads to grandiose propositions which are either so broad as to be trite or so narrow as to be dangerous. I have read innumerable so-called agency philosophies over the years and I have yet to see one to which those strictures do not apply.

When the philosophies are merely trite – 'We believe in advertising that sells' 'We believe in understanding the consumer' and all the rest of the bland placebos to which agencies supposedly pay obeisance – they are relatively harmless. In practice they do not interfere with the creation of excellent advertising. Indeed nobody takes the least bit of notice of them, day to day.

Agency philosophies which succeed in doing more than stating the obvious, however, are lethal. They act as straitjackets, fettering truly radical thought. Such philosophies squeeze all an agency's campaigns into the same mould, and result in advertisements for the agency (the curse of 1960s advertising) rather than advertisements for the client.

In the 1960s several agencies promulgated credos so specific and so narrow that they might indeed have been dubbed 'philosophies'. The most famous was the Ted Bates agency's dogmatic espousal of the USP (Unique Sales Proposition) philosophy. The USP is a perfect example of an agency's attempt to make all advertisements fit a formula. It was largely the attempt to impose the USP on all its clients, on every campaign – together with Robert Jacoby's management style – which eventually castrated Bates. The USP approach was developed for packaged goods clients in the 1950s and 1960s. For those clients, at that time, it appears to have worked like a dream. Then, like all other constraining agency philosophies, it grew dated. But Bates was publicly locked into it. So the agency was muscle-bound – the inescapable end-result of a truly powerful 'agency philosophy'.

Phooey to agency philosophies. Agencies certainly have their own cultures, their own ways of working. Not being zombies, they have their own opinions, attitudes, talents, specialisations, and distinct points of view which differentiate them from other agencies. So do dentists, solicitors, tinkers, tailors and their mates. Some agencies are unquestionably better at some things than others (ditto dentists . . .). Some agencies are unquestionably better than others in many ways (ditto dentists . . .). That is all that matters. To keep their clients happy every agency's mission statement is, or should be, precisely the same: 'To produce campaigns for our clients which are more effective and more cost-effective than those produced by competitors.'

The ways in which individual agencies will set about achieving this objective will vary but the objective itself must be unwavering. In DFSD Bozell, for the reasons explained earlier, we put massive emphasis on targeting: getting under the skins of our clients' target customers. It seems to have paid off. Over recent years all our major clients have asked us to handle additional assignments – the surest test of whether or not an agency is performing. For CPC Foods, for example, we initially handled their Napolina Italian range – and they then appointed us to Hellman's Mayonnaise and Ambrosia (their largest brand). Similarly Premier Beverages first gave us Cadbury's Chocolate Break, then successively added Marvel, Cadbury's Drinking Chocolate, London Herb & Spice Teas, Cadbury's Highlights and finally Ty-phoo. In several cases where we began by sharing an account with other agencies, our clients have fired the other agencies and appointed us to handle all their business. Presumably they felt we were doing something right.

Certainly targeting has been part of it. But an agency's service to its clients works at many levels – despite the simplification of the role and function of agencies over recent years. I used to claim that it should be possible to summarise every industry's contribution to the world in a single word. For the computer industry the word was *speed*, for the tourist industry *pleasure*, for the food industry *taste*, for the do-it-yourself industry *saving*, for the financial industry (industry?) *return*, and so on. In truth the game does not really work. It is not possible to sum up entire industries so simply and succinctly. Nonetheless the search for a single word focuses the mind on the essential attributes of any product or service, and dispenses with inessential distractions. For advertising agencies the word is *ideas*. And I think that word works.

To produce campaigns which are more effective and more cost-effective than competitors', agencies must continually generate ideas. To motivate their employees and galvanise their enthusiasm, agencies must continually encourage them to have ideas. Ideas for new ways to solve old problems, ideas for new ways to solve new problems, ideas for new ways to use media, ideas for new ways to position clients' brands, ideas for new strategies, ideas – above all – for new advertisements and sometimes for entirely new campaigns. Not all ideas are good ideas: but ideas are what the agency business is all about. Ideas make clients happy. Really great ideas – admittedly a rarity – put them on cloud nine. (And that's very high ground indeed.)

Nowadays the tightening focus on advertising pure and simple, rather than on peripheral activities which used to confuse matters, has spotlit the most important interface between client and agency: the presentation and selling of new creative ideas. Every agency's future now hangs by two threads: its ability to create remarkable advertisements and its ability to persuade clients of their validity. The ability to create remarkable advertisements is worthless if clients cannot be persuaded to run them; the ability to persuade clients to run unremarkable advertisements is worthless, full stop.

Ex-Avis president Robert Townsend in his rumbustions bestseller *Up The Organisation*, and David Ogilvy in his *Confessions of an Advertising Man* both promote the thesis that clients should only amend or reject campaigns insofar as they are factually inaccurate. The Townsend/Ogilvy argument runs: an agency must be responsible for producing the advertisements without let or hindrance. Subject to factual and legal vetting the campaign will then be run as produced. If it works – fine. It if doesn't – fired.

Robert Townsend, who, when he was president of Avis, sired the great 'We try harder – we're only No. 2' campaign, forbade his staff to try to alter in any way the advertisements their agency (Doyle Dane Bernbach) submitted. Similarly, David Ogilvy only agreed to handle the then minuscule Hathaway shirt account after he had extracted from the client a promise: Hathaway would always accept his copy without changing a word. The resulting 'Man in the Hathaway shirt' black eye-patch campaign made advertising history.

Such tales reflect every agency man's fantasies. We dream nightly of being appointed by extraordinarily perspicacious clients who have the good sense and good taste to see that all our creative work is utterly perfect, who greet every presentation with the most beautiful words in the agency man's lexicon: 'Gosh that's wonderful, let's go for it.'

If only life were so simple. Sadly most clients are unwilling to delegate total responsibility for their advertising to their agency. (I'm unwilling to delegate total responsibility for my diet to Sainsbury's, come to that, though I unhesitatingly admit they know a great deal more about food than I do.) So inevitably there comes a piquant moment in every client/agency *affaire de coeur* when, after a fanfare of trumpets and a symphony of sales spiel the campaign is unveiled and the client – like Gilles Hennessy – reacts miserably. At this point battle is joined.

Contrary to agency mythology, I do not believe advertisements are often rejected because they are too creative. It is undeniable that some clients lack imagination and reject all types of communication except the most crude and blatant. But in Britain at least, the majority of clients spur their agencies on to be as original, as creative as possible.

With a few notable exceptions almost every advertisement that ever wins a creative award is palpably excellent, and is recognised as such immediately by (a) the public (b) all agency people and (c) the majority of clients. Van Gogh, James Joyce and Stockhausen are bad analogies. Excellent creativity in advertising is not that difficult to recognise. By definition it could not be: advertisements cannot wait to be appreciated, first by a handful of cognoscenti, and only after decades by the public at large. The very notion is ridiculous.

There are two common reasons why clients reject advertisements, and neither has much to do with creativity. The first and most frequent is because the communications strategy is wrong. That is why I have made such a song and dance about getting the creative brief right in previous chapters.

Clients tend to be more concerned about strategy than about execution, more concerned with content than with style. Agencies tend to be more concerned about execution than about strategy, more concerned with style than with content. When agencies comfort themselves that their ideas have been spurned because they were too creative for the client, it usually means that either they misunderstood the brief, or they interpreted it badly. Naturally the creatives are blamed, because it is their work which has been rubbished. They in turn blame the client service executives for having failed to sell the advertisements with sufficient passion. The truth, nine times out of ten, is that the advertisements were turned down because they were on the wrong track. Creativity, style, wit, execution do not matter a fig if the advertisements say the wrong thing.

The second common reason for advertisements being blackballed is because the client does not feel comfortable with them. The language is too crude, maybe, or the joke to jokey, or the tone too cynical. Agencies find these types of reason for rejection especially unpalatable, wimpish, gutless. Sometimes they are. But every client company – like every agency – has its own personality, its own self-image. It will not be willing to change unless and until it has made a conscious decision to do so. Only the dimmest of agencies thinks it can change its client's culture to suit itself.

Having said this, although clients are customers they are by no means always right. Few human beings warm instantly to new ideas presented to them in a form which is, of necessity, unfinished. While almost everybody reacts positively to good advertising when it appears, its virtues will not always be apparent at script or story board stage. (This is one of the many reasons it is so crucial for clients to trust their agencies.)

How far should an agency go in defence of its work, how stubborn should it be? Such questions are unanswerable, but certain principles are clear:

i   If an agency has the strategy wrong, it should immediately withdraw: don't attempt to defend the indefensible.
ii If the client raises a genuine and valid point, which the agency has not previously considered, it should be analysed openly rather than rejected mindlessly.
iii If the client is simply exploring possible problems, the agency should aid the process.
iv If the problems might be resolved by market research, the agency should press for it to be undertaken, at its own cost if the idea eventually fails (but see Chapter 7).
v   If the client has not fully grasped the way the advertisements will be executed, the agency should volunteer to proceed a stage further, again at its own cost if the idea eventually fails.
vi If different members of the client team react differently, the agency should keep on fighting.

vii If every member of the client team agrees, the battle will be unwinnable.

These principles open up a key management issue for agencies in the 1990s – an issue that is not new, but is now especially salient. Should creative work be presented to clients by the creative people themselves? Or by the client service executives? Which will make the client happier? Which will be more successful?

The issue has become especially salient as a consequence of agencies' own focus on creativity as their prime area of expertise. A recurrent current agency whinge is that clients are paying less and less, while simultaneously demanding more and more top creative attention. And when creative people are occupied in client meetings they cannot be creating clients' campaigns. (Ideas for advertisements which occur in meetings are never much cop.)

Creative people believe most client service executives to be hopeless at selling new ideas because they are too terrified of clients to fight fiercely and fearlessly for the work. Client service people believe that most creatives are hopeless at dealing with clients, and that they handle tricky situations with all the delicacy of rampaging hippopotami. They also know clients who feel they cannot speak openly and criticise freely if the creatives are present; and they worry that creatives who get too close to clients inevitably end up producing work to please them whether or not it is right. (Like market researchers.) Worst of all, creatives quickly grow bored in meetings and it shows. (Pitching against us for part of Kimberley Clark's account some years ago, our competitor's creative director fell asleep during his agency's presentation. The Kimberley Clark team found this endearing. But we won the business.)

Some agencies insist that creative people meet clients at every possible opportunity; others view their attendance at meetings as about as welcome as lukewarm office Nescafé. Whether or not creative people should attend client meetings is another question without a universal answer. Some clients are good with creative people, some are ghastly. Some creative people are marvellous with clients, some are maddening. If the relationship clicks, it bonds the client/agency relationship powerfully. If the relationship fails it undermines the relationship catastrophically. The decision falls squarely in the agency management's lap: the buck stops there.

Because the presentation of creative work inevitably causes battles from time to time, I get concerned when my agency's relationship with one of our clients seems to be running too smoothly for too long. In any successful client/agency relationship there will occasionally be little tiffs. If there are no such problems, that's probably a problem.

Naturally there are healthy problems and unhealthy problems. Healthy problems occur primarily when an agency urges a client to do something he does not want to do. Arguments over communications strategies, creative executions and production estimates are – or usually are – perfectly healthy. The agency may be urging the client to take a risk or – though this is especially dangerous – urging the client to be cautious. (When a client is yearning for revolution and is balked by the agency, the agency inevitably appears idle, unimaginative or defensive – or all three.)

Nevertheless, so long as the agency is not being idle, unimaginative or defensive, whether or not things should be changed is a subject for healthy argument, and wise clients know it. It may sound paradoxical but sometimes the right idea, the difficult idea, is to do nothing.

What then are unhealthy arguments? In client/agency relationships, as in the rest of life, the most unhealthy disputes are about something other than they purport to be about. When clients are unhappy about the campaign they may show their displeasure by nit-picking invoices, or complaining about colour reproduction, or grumbling when agency people cannot attend meetings at the drop of a fax. If the client is avoiding a bigger dispute by creating little ones, that is manifestly unhealthy.

Equally unhealthy are problems which arise out of power struggles within the client's organisation. Wise agencies do their utmost to avoid getting sucked into clients' internal politics. When clients impersonate the Borgias, the agency usually gets knifed.

To return to the problem of no problem. If there are no healthy disputes between client and agency then either this is a symptom of client weakness, which will eventually lead to problems. Or it is a symptom of a lack of originality, of dynamism, of ideas emanating from the agency, which will eventually lead to problems. Or is it a symptom of the client having stopped even bothering to argue with the agency, which is most definitely a problem already. The sound of such silences should be deafening.

There is one other, quite different type of reason for a lack of client v. agency sparring. Many agency people – too many agency people – are scared of confrontations with clients. They may indeed be scared of confrontations with anybody. Lots of people are. I am not advocating fisticuffs, or screaming matches, or throwing personal insults, or deplorably aggressive behaviour. But just as agencies do not respect wimpish behaviour on the part of their clients (Chapter 4), clients do not respect wimpish behaviour in their agencies. As Peter Glynn-Jones, managing director of Smith Kline Beecham Consumer Healthcare insists: 'I want agencies that will tell me what is right, not what I want to hear.'

At Ted Bates, one of our brightest trainees, having endured all of three months' torture at the agency, handed in his notice. Life for trainees at Bates was not, admittedly, always a bowl of cherries. Nevertheless those few kneepant tycoons who were offered the enviable opportunity to achieve fame and fortune under our wing did not generally develop an antipathy to our corporate BO quite so quickly. I enquired what had led him to his momentous and – so far as I was concerned – exceedingly inconvenient decision. 'Sycophancy,' he replied.

I had expected a more mercenary answer. J. Walter Thompson might have offered him a lifetime's free Kellogg's All Bran, perhaps, or Saatchi & Saatchi might have offered him a billion British Airways Air Miles. But none of that.

'I've decided,' he continued, 'that the agency business is not my bag. I cannot be sufficiently sycophantic to clients. I simply can't be a creep.' (He only just stopped himself adding 'like you'.)

As Jeeves may well on occasion have mumbled under his breath in the Croft Sherry commercials, a fellow could be excused for being more than a trifle miffed by such jolly bloody-boiling remarks. Overreacting an itsy-bit, I reassuringly pointed out to the lad that among the agency's account management team were some of the most obnoxious people he was ever likely to meet. It was to no avail. We were all cast immutably as grovelling toads, and that was the end of it. (I hope he's ended up a door-to-door salesman.)

Remembering things past, the incident called to mind my own first interview, two decades earlier, with Michael English, who by coincidence later became my predecessor as chairman of Ted Bates. Facing Mike English in the interview room I too asked, with undergraduate effrontery, whether having to be a sycophant didn't sometimes get him down. He responded less then deferentially. But unfortunately sycophancy is one of the world's most deeply ingrained images of the adman. And during the recent recession, with jobs and billings as scarce as wit in a detergent commercial, the problem has been much aggravated. Sycophancy is bad news.

The other side of the sycophancy coin – and even more unpleasant than the sycophancy itself – is that the worst agency creeps, in order to reclaim a little self-esteem, incessantly slag off their clients. Some clients may be fine drinking companions, in their eyes, but none is worth a milligram of respect. It is a myth of the agency business which dies hard. To quote again from David Ogilvy's *Confessions*:

> Frank Hummert, copy chief of Lord & Thomas, once told me: 'All clients are pigs. You may start by thinking otherwise but you will change your mind!'

Ogilvy goes on to protest: 'I have encountered a handful of pigs and I have resigned them. With a very few exceptions, I have loved my clients.'

With humble deference to the great eye-patch inventor, I believe that his reaction is almost as irrelevant as Hummert's. As I mentioned earlier, I have become friends with many of my clients. But clients are not there to be loved or hated, or even to be friends. They are there to be worked for.

Unhappily, many advertising people find it difficult to establish a satisfactory relationship with those they work for. Clever people of independent spirit often find it hard to be underlings. They react by becoming either sycophantic or surly. The client is either always right or always wrong. Neither response makes shrewd clients happy. Shrewd clients do not want those who work for them to be servile, but they do want them to remember who is in charge. They know how agencies feel because they feel much the same towards their major retail customers. All of us, at different times and with different hats on, are alternatively buyers and sellers.

It is not necessary for agency folk to love their clients, but it certainly makes life easier if they like them. It is not necessary to hold clients in reverential awe, but taking orders from them will be a lot more acceptable if you respect them. It is not even necessary to be especially friendly with clients but it is essential – if you want to make them happy people – to convince them you're doing the job they want you to do, supremely well. And there is no mystery about the job they want you to do: have good ideas and execute them efficiently.

It may sound trite, but it is also essential to entertain clients. (I find the word entertain, in this context, profoundly embarrassing: it makes the process sound like a comedy turn.) It never ceases to bemuse me that in an industry famous for its back-slapping-party-loving-hail-fellow-well-met gregariousness, so many of the top people find socialising a painful strain. Charles Saatchi's reclusiveness is notorious, but he is far from alone. Many agency bosses – I would hazard a guess at *most* agency bosses – dislike entertaining any but a few longstanding cronies. Yet there are numerous benefits to be gained, by both client and agency. That is why, whatever the Inland Revenue may suppose, business entertainment is really work, albeit pleasant work.

This isn't the 1960s. The Ritz may be off the menu. It isn't necessary to gormandise. Younger clients in particular rarely go in for mammoth binges. But tucking in together has, since primitive times, been a symbol of friendship. Few people find it easy to take a meal with those they dislike. Nor – again whatever the Inland Revenue may suppose – is it a particularly commercial phenomenon.

Politicians and civil servants, royalty and churchmen, Chinese communists and South African tribesmen all eat communally, formally and informally, in pursuit of that elusive prize: brotherly love and goodwill.

There is no doubt that some business transactions can be handled better over a meal than over an office desk. A business lunch or dinner will allow both sides to glean more about the other's operations than could possibly be achieved in less relaxed circumstances. Each will pick up subtleties and innuendos, prejudices and trivia, company politics and family problems, current anxieties and future threats – knowledge and insights which make the wheels of collaboration run more smoothly and more efficiently.

Moreover while purists (and economists) prefer to believe that all business relationships are built upon logical assessments of needs and value, the reality is that we all prefer to deal with people and companies we like. Agency folk who entertain entertainingly indubitably enhance their relations with their clients. It isn't all that easy, and here are three tips which may help:

i *Ponder how much to spend.* This is one of the most difficult decisions associated with entertaining (see Bob Dowds, p. 136) And it has been made much more difficult during and since the recession. Spend too profligately and you can cause embarrassment, or persuade your client you are rolling in (his) money; be too stingy and you can provoke resentment. Some clients do not notice such niceties, others most definitely do. Time spent pondering the problem is seldom wasted.

ii *Keep it constant, keep it coming.* When younger I kept a chart of my client entertaining. Now, ludicrously, I rely on my memory. Doubtless I could employ a personal computer, if I were sufficiently clever. Whatever the system the aim is the same. Neither allow long intervals to elapse between social events, nor crowd too many events helter-skelter on top of each other.

iii *Don't assume they will buy any old ads after a few noggins.*

Many, if not most, people get more critical and certainly more aggressive after they have had a few, and can be more difficult to sell to than ever.

Finally on the subject of entertaining, here is a small but perfectly formed lunching tip which I picked up from Jeremy Bullmore, ex-chairman of J. Walter Thomson and now a director of WPP Plc. If you have arranged to lunch with a client in order to raise a specific point do not leave it – as most people do – until the coffee, believing that by then the client will be feeling contented and relaxed. Raise the point immediately you sit down, or anyway as quickly as you can. Leaving it until the end of the meal will result in one of several eventualities:

i   the client will dash off before you have raised it at all, or
ii there will not be time to discuss it sufficiently, which will irritate both of you, or
iii worst of all, it will lead to a dispute, and there will not be time to smooth the client's ruffled feathers.

Many a time and oft, Bullmore's Law has proved invaluable.

However diligently agencies work to keep their clients happy, clients occasionally get itchy feet and decide to move on, or at least to scout around and inspect what's on offer elsewhere before deciding whether to move or to stay. The cliché has it that this most often occurs when new management personnel arrive on the scene – and again the cliché is absolutely correct.

Because I work hard at keeping them happy, only a handful of clients have deserted me over the years. When it happens I take it as a personal slight. I am unable to adopt my ex-partner Sir William Shelton's relaxed doctrine, which Greg Delaney used to share, that clients come and clients go. I abhor losing clients. It upsets me physically. I console myself that just about every time it has happened it has been as a direct consequence of the arrival of new client management. The first time it occurred I idiotically aggravated the situation by regularly pointing out to the new management that the old management, of whom I had been much enamoured, would not have agreed with what they were doing. The new management put up with this nonsense for a few weeks and then asked that I be removed from their account. I was twenty-seven years old at the time. I was more than a bit bruised. But it was my own stupid fault and I knew it. New management must never be taken for granted (let alone insulted!). It may be mildly irritating, but their commitment and confidence must be fought for and won.

When clients grow rather unhappy, but not appallingly unhappy, they usually offer the agency the opportunity to re-pitch, to give them a chance to hold on to the business. Inevitably the agency's knee-jerk reaction is to refuse. Re-pitching to an existing client is dire – painful, ominous and stressful, like trying to persuade a departing lover to stay. Unreliable statistics, frequently quoted on these occasions, suggest that only about one-fifth of re-pitches succeed. (I suspect the figure is a bit higher – maybe one-third.)

The client invariably tells the incumbent agency that he has a completely open mind, that it will be a level playing field, that he will judge all the competitive presentations fairly and objectively, that he would be delighted to stay if things turn out that way. Often, for good measure, he adds that he himself doesn't want to review the agency's appointment at all, but has been forced to do so by his new boss, or by some spurious company regulation ('We review all suppliers' contracts every thirteen years – that's company policy!'). Naturally the agency doesn't believe a word of it. The agency believes that dark and devious forces must be at work. Why else would the client have failed to perceive their diligence, their creativity, their undying commitment to his business?

The strangest re-pitch I have attended occurred when I had just left Robert Sharp & Partners and joined a little-known and short-lived agency called MCR. The agency's largest account was Olivetti, which billed nearly £500,000 (equivalent to at least £3 million today). It accounted for almost 40% of the agency's revenue. A new Italian managing director – let's call him Signor Francobolli – had arrived from Milan and immediately ordered an agency review. The account was far too important to resign. MCR had no alternative but to re-pitch.

The boss and majority owner of the agency – the M in MCR – was a chap called Peter Muttlebury. Muttlebury had borrowed heavily to set up MCR (he had bought a couple of small agencies and merged them) and, though I was unaware of it, he had recently been under immense financial, personal and emotional strain.

The truth, as Peter Muttlebury well recognised, was that the advertisements MCR had been creating for Olivetti had not been wonderful. The explanation favoured by Muttlebury and everyone else in the agency (I was still a new boy) was that our creative work was being hammered by Olivetti's UK advertising manager, let's call him Bert. Bert was not unlike the aforementioned lance-corporal: by no means the soul of sensitivity. Agency mythology had it that each time we presented brilliant creative ideas Bert stamped on them.

At every re-pitch the underlying dilemma is the same. The agency must either defend its previous work, and recommend continuing along the same lines, which has obvious dangers; or ditch its previous work and recommend something entirely new, which has obvious dangers; or search for a compromise, which has obvious dangers. Muttlebury opted for his own particular version of the third option.

The day of the re-pitch arrived. Peter Muttlebury was palpably, understandably agitated. Agency presentations are stressful at the best of times. Re-pitching to keep 40% of your business intact, when you are heavily borrowed, would freak out even the thickest-skinned and most complacent of blokes. Peter was neither thick-skinned nor complacent. Though it was a cold morning he was sweating. Though not a smoker, he was chain-smoking.

We began the presentation by showing Signor Francobolli and Bert some of the advertising we had recently produced for other clients. We had just launched, with considerable success, a part work called *Birds of the World*. Signor Francobolli was notably impressed. We then ran through the advertisements we had created for Olivetti. Signor Francobolli was notably unimpressed.

'I do not understand, Mr Muttlebury,' he said, 'why you do such good work for other clients, but not Olivetti.'

There was a silence. Then Muttlebury saw his chance, both to defend the agency's record and to justify the need for change. He would tell Francobolli the truth.

'Mr Francobolli,' he began quickly, nervously, 'I am going to level with you. A good agency must be honest with its clients. That's the only way. We have a joint problem, here, between us, Olivetti and the agency. And the result is the advertising we have run for Olivetti has been crap, sheer crap . . .'.

He hesitated, wondering for an instant how to explain that it was all Bert's fault, with Bert present in the room. He never completed the sentence because Signor Francobolli stopped him.

'Mr Muttlebury, I don't think I 'eard you correctly. Did you say crap?'

'Crap,' Peter replied, with vigorous emphasis.

'Mr Muttlebury,' Signor Francobolli stood up, 'in the last year my company has spent – how much? – £500,000 on advertising with your company. Now you tell me your company has just done crap. I sue you for £500,000. I put the matter with my solicitors in the morning.'

Naturally he didn't. He couldn't wait that long. He fired us that afternoon.

As I said, re-pitching can be painful, ignominious and stressful. To build a high ground agency it is vital to keep your existing clients happy, and to keep winning additional assignments from them. It ain't half hard, mum.

10
How Advertising Works

I have a collection of about three hundred old advertising books. They help me stay moderately sane in a business where everything switchbacks from hour to hour. The sense of constant flux is exacerbated by the advertising trade media which – like all media – are permanently on the look-out for red-hot, here-and-now, breathtaking new developments and mouthwatering new trends. They know the headline 'Things aren't much different, things are much the same' won't sell many copies. (Though the *Neue Zürcher Zeitung* once headlined its front page '100 Years of Electric Light in Switzerland'.)

The reality is that all advertising history – maybe all history – can be divided into those facts and incidents which establish conclusively that there is Nothing New Under The Sun, and those facts and incidents which Change The Course of History. In advertising in the 1990s it is more than usually difficult to disentangle the former from the latter, to distinguish between those changes which are transitory and those which are structural. That has been one of the underlying themes of this book.

The oldest tome I own is called *The History of Advertising*, by Henry Sampson, published in 1874. Sampson was much exercised by the growth of advertising clutter caused by the explosion of newsprint during the nineteenth century. That is one reason I refuse to get too neurotic about the growth of advertising clutter today. Another splendid oldie, *Advertising and Progress*, by E. S. Hole and John Hart, published in 1914, explores and rebuts the claims that advertising was growing too powerful, and that it manipulated an innocent, gullible public into buying goods they could not afford and did not need. Nearly eighty years later one of advertising's most perceptive spokesmen recently felt it necessary to write:

> The critics of advertising know that consumers can be *made* to consume in ever-increasing quantities. Advertisers *want* consumers to consume in every-increasing quantities. Agencies do their best to *persuade* consumers to consume in ever-increasing quantities. And yet, all too often, they *don't*.
>
> The blame then lies inescapably at the foot of the consumer. I'm afraid it has to be said: the consumer of today is quite frequently guilty of gross irresponsibility. 'Look here,' I sometimes feel like saying to them, 'you're a consumer, aren't you? Then why the hell aren't you out there consuming?'
>
> *Jeremy Bullmore*, Behind The Scenes in Advertising (*1992*)

Plus ça change.

Many, if not most, of my old books contain a chapter entitled 'How Advertising Works' or something very similar. So it seems a trifle surprising, not to say a trifle dispiriting, to find myself marching down this well-trodden path. (The first advertising book I ever reviewed, and it was excellent, was called *What Advertising Is*, in 1972.) If gurus have been maundering on about how advertising works for over a century, can there still be anything left to say?

Perhaps. Over recent years there has been a vast burgeoning of new data, from a hotchpotch of sources, relating to advertising's effects. To quote Colin McDonald (who in 1992 published a fine book called *How Advertising Works!*):

> We now have in many respects more and better-quality data to study, although it may be argued that we do not yet invest enough in studying it. All in all, compared with even twenty years ago, we understand more about the complexity of what we are dealing with; at the same time, we have been comforted by being able to prove to ourselves the possibility that, when the

circumstances are right, advertising does work, because we can see and measure it.

The key word in that quotation is 'complexity'. Much of our recent learning has been derived from the Institute of Practitioners in Advertising's bi-annual Advertising Effectiveness Awards, launched in 1980 by Simon Broadbent of the Leo Burnett agency. Nearly five hundred case histories have now been entered for the IPA Advertising Effectiveness Awards, and almost a hundred of them have won gongs.

In aggregate they constitute far and away the most comprehensive and authoritative investigation into the many different ways in which advertising works ever published, anywhere. And that is exactly what they have established: advertising works in many different ways. That is why most previous attempts to explain how advertising works fell at the first ditch. Advertising is not a homogeneous entity. It cannot be unified or simplified. Personal column classifieds and detergent commercials are as dissimilar (though they are both called advertisements) as tiddleywinks and rugger (though they are both called games). To attempt to squeeze all types of advertising into the same mould is as futile as it would be to try to win at Twickenham with little plastic counters.

Consumers react to advertisements in an infinite variety of ways and each new advertisement generates fractionally different responses from its innumerable predecessors. The mere fact that there have been innumerable predecessors inevitably and in turn influences consumers' responses to each new advertisement. This is something that talented, experienced copywriters and art directors know instinctively.

The average thirty-five-year-old British adult will have seen some 150,000 different commercials, most of them half a dozen times or more. New commercials do not fall on virgin soil. They are received by seasoned, sceptical advertising-literate minds. Minds which, as Saatchi's Stephen Chinn has pointed out, now understand almost too well the ways in which advertising operates.

Many advertisements persuade people to spend, while lots

persuade them to save. Some advertisements sell people things they don't know about, while many sell them things they know about already. Some aim to reinforce their existing loyalties, others to make them unfaithful. Many make them laugh but some bring tears to their eyes. Some may make them question their political beliefs, others may persuade them to change their jobs, their houses, their drinking habits, their sexual activities or even their very lives.

Yet most advertisements are of no interest to most people most of the time. As we saw earlier we buy only 400 or so brands each year, from the 9,500 that spend more than £50,000 a year on advertising. I am not in the least bit interested in buying most of the things I see advertised. Indeed I won't buy them. Nor will you. Nobody is influenced by most of the advertisements they see. A few individual advertisements benefit each of us, every day of the week – and that is quite sufficient to make advertising cost-effective – but the great majority of advertisements are irrelevant to us.

The best way to think about how advertising works is to imagine a crowded street. Each time you walk down a crowded street you see hundreds, maybe thousands, of people and almost every single one of them passes by unnoticed. You won't remember the majority of them thirty seconds – let alone thirty minutes or thirty days – later. It is much the same with advertisements.

A few of the people you pass, a tiny handful, make some impact on you. Why do you notice those you notice? Why do you remember those you remember? Naturally you tend to notice people who are unusual, people who (by definition) stand out in the crowd.

Perhaps they stand out because they are inherently, physically different from other people. They may be strikingly beautiful, or ugly, or look funny, or charming, or especially aggressive.

Perhaps they stand out because they have made themselves seem different. They may be dressed stylishly, or eccentrically, or be made up garishly; or they may be shouting, or singing, or moving strangely.

And of course they may be both physically different *and* dressed unusually. The one does not preclude the other.

Perhaps, on the other hand, they do not stand out for other people at all. To other people they look quite ordinary, but you notice them because something about them has particular relevance for you, personally.

Perhaps they are wearing something that especially interests you, maybe something you have been searching for, or something you particularly like. Maybe you know them already, or they remind you of somebody else. Or maybe you seem to keep seeing them, and they are beginning to impinge on your consciousness.

And there is another occasion when you will pick out a face in the crowd: when it is a face you are looking for. When you are searching for someone in a throng it often seems as though you can see everyone else but them. In reality your eyes are rapidly skimming across dozens and dozens of faces, without taking them in, until finally they alight on the correct one – if it is there to be found.

These interactions and relationships are exactly replicated in people's reactions to advertisements. And they reveal that there are four, and only four, basic reasons why people notice and remember advertisements.

    i   When the product is itself inherently different.
    ii When the advertisement itself is sufficiently unusual.
    iii When the advertisement has some particular, personal relevance (they may even have been searching for it).
    iv When they seem to keep seeing it, and eventually it penetrates their consciousness.

As with faces in the crowd, these are not mutually exclusive. High ground campaigns will blend and dovetail all four.

The campaigns which somehow or other get through to you penetrate the barrier of your *selective perception*.

Selective perception is the extraordinary mechanism by which our eyes, in concert with our brains, pick out and notice particular items from the morass of visual data which assails them at every waking moment. It is the mechanism underlying the four factors which make some advertisements noticeable and memorable, while most are neither.

Selective perception is the protective mechanism *homo sapiens* has developed because it could never cope with all the sense data – let alone all the advertising – which bombards it from morning to night. Selective perception is the mechanism which sorts out all the clutter, negating its capacity to overwhelm and confuse us.

Selective perception is still hardly understood by psychologists, the intractable difficulty being that people can only report those perceptions they know they have had, and can remember, and are aware of – not those perceptions they do not know they have had, and cannot remember, and so are unaware of.

Selective perception is of immense importance in advertising. It is simultaneously advertising's best friend and worst enemy. It is the reason why we notice advertisements, no matter how small, if they include messages of personal relevance to us. But it is also the barrier high ground campaigns must constantly strive to break through in order to get their messages across to people who have not made a conscious decision to ignore them – it is not as deliberate as that – but whose minds are protecting themselves against information overload.

(Perhaps, in some remote prehistoric era, a species existed which tried to process and remember every single titbit it ever saw and heard and smelt and tasted. No wonder the species failed to survive. It must have gone stark raving barmy.)

To overcome the barrier of selective perception most advertisements need to squeeze their messages into people's already junk-laden minds and memories. They need to have impact, to build awareness, to be able, in current jargon, to 'cut through'. They need to intrude. By no means all advertisements, however, need to intrude. And in some respects the unintrusive advertisements are much more important to people than the intrusive advertisements. Unintrusive advertisements are those people search for; intrusive advertisements are those which search for people.

About a quarter of all the money spent on advertising goes on classifieds. Classifieds are the epitome of unintrusive advertising. Every day hundreds of thousands, maybe millions of classified advertisements appear. Nobody knows the exact number – but there must be at least a hundred times more, and quite possibly a thousand times more, classified than display advertisements. There cannot be a single literate adult who has not at some time responded to a classified advertisement, and indeed very few who have not placed one for themselves.

That is one reason why Mr and Mrs Average understand advertising far better than they are often given credit for. Everyone has occasionally sold a second-hand stuffed camel in their local free-sheet – or maybe sought a compatible lonely heart.

Indeed lonely hearts classifieds reveal a great deal about some of the key ways in which advertising works. If you are in the market for a prospective partner, you will require a fair amount of information. The advertiser (your suitor) knows this, and because advertising space is not free, he or she will aim to select the most relevant information and communicate it to you as succinctly as possible.

The single most important fact about them, their availability, is self-evident from their presence in the lonely hearts column. The fact that they are hoping that you (or somebody) will take action as a result of their advertisement is also self-evident because they have spent their money on advertising. Both those bits of information are implicit, and are important, in every kind of advertising. (When I was helping the ill-fated SDP party with its political advertising our market research repeatedly showed that the electorate believed the SDP did not truly want their votes because it did not advertise for them. The depressing truth was that we had no money and so *could not* advertise for them.)

Back to the lonely hearts. The prospective respondent will naturally wish to know the advertiser's sex, age, tastes and interests. Those are all more or less objective facts. The prospective respondent will also require information which is much more subjective in nature: the advertiser's looks, their character, their style.

There would be little point in the advertiser lying about the objective facts. But don't people have an incentive to lie about the subjective data? To describe themselves, for example, as much better looking than they are?

Only slightly.

If you are in any doubt, study the lonely hearts columns yourself. The advertisers – like all advertisers – know the truth will be discovered by anyone who responds to their advertising (buys their products). They know there is no point in claiming they look like Robert Redford or Glenn Close, if they do not. Indeed an analysis of lonely hearts advertisers in *Time Out* magazine showed that only 36% claimed themselves to be either good-looking or attractive. A modicum of self-enhancement is acceptable, and is expected. Too much would be counterproductive, and indeed wasteful – the wrong people would respond to the advertising, hoping to meet a Redford or Close lookalike, and would be disappointed.

All of which applies, universally, to every kind of advertising. However, lonely hearts advertisements are unlike most consumer advertising in that they are not intrusive. As with all classifieds, the reader seeks them out.

Other types of classified include advertisements for jobs, homes, holidays, entertainments, births, marriages, deaths (and Valentines). Of these, job advertising is much the largest sector, by value, accounting for about one-third of the total, and thus about 10% of all advertising.

And there are few things more important to most of us than our jobs, our homes, our holidays, and our entertainments – not to mention births, marriages, deaths (and Valentines). However important we judge our choice of deodorant or detergent to be, it hardly compares with our choice of a new job or a new house.

Even the large display advertisements for houses in magazines like *Country Life* are not truly intrusive. They are all bunched together so people will know where to find them. (I have often wondered why television and radio stations don't carry similar 'classified' sections, at well-publicised times on specific days, when the job ads, or house ads, or lonely hearts ads could be bundled together and those who are interested could watch out for them.)

Nor are classifieds the only advertisements people seek out. Much price-and-line retailer advertising is built upon the premise that lots of people will be looking for particular items, and searching for the lowest prices. Whether it be butter or bitter, a three-piece suite or a VCR, those who scan retail advertisements generally have a fair idea of what they are looking for, in advance; or alternatively they may not know precisely which product they want, and they may just be looking for a bargain or two.

Either way it is the shopper who does most of the work, not the advertisement.

Beyond communicating quickly that it contains loads of bargains, the advertisement hardly needs to intrude. The shopper is a willing accomplice. Unfortunately not one advertising person in a hundred seem to understand this.

And a further group of advertisements which people look out for, when they are relevant to them, are financial offers. If you happen to have some cash which you are contemplating investing – a windfall perhaps, or hard-won savings – then you will scour the personal finance pages for the best offer on offer. If you are desperate for a mortgage or other kind of loan, you will do the same.

Such advertisements do not need to intrude. They simply need to flag those who are looking for them. But if you are not thinking of a new mortgage, or a loan, the financial advertisement will need to tap you on your shoulder and bring itself to your attention. It will need to make you think about all the wonderful things you could do if you borrowed some more lolly. So some financial advertisements can be small and undemonstrative, while others have to be bigger and noisier. It depends on the objective, and on the target market.

Yet another group of advertisements which hardly intrude are those in hobby publications. Advertisements for photographic equipment in *Amateur Photographer*, fishing tackle in *Angling Times*, DIY materials in *Practical Householder* and the like. Everybody agrees – even the editors – that people buy such publications as much for the advertisements as for the editorial. The products advertised reflect the hobbyists' interests, their commitment to their leisure and pleasure. So the advertisements are important to them.

As are many industrial, business-to-business advertisements in trade and technical publications. These often provide news and information which industrial purchasers are looking for and find useful. That is the principle reason why industrial advertising was always permissible in the Communist bloc countries. It was deemed to be useful rather than persuasive (as though such neat dividing lines could be drawn!).

If you add together all classified advertising, including recruitment, some of the retail advertising, some of the financial advertising, hobby advertising, and some business-to-business advertising, then it can be no exaggeration to say that in total 40–50% of all advertising is non-intrusive. They are all advertisments which people patently want. People look for them of their own volition.

And you might tack on another group of small ads, classic patent medicine advertisements. You know the type. They flag the sufferer with such succulent headlines as 'Acne?' or 'Piles?' or 'Embarrassing Irritation?' They are perfect examples of selective perception at work.

These small medicine advertisements spotlight the borderline between intrusion and self-interest. They depend upon readers' consciousness of their ailments. To some extent the readers are subconsciously on the look-out for a remedy. But the advertisements also need to penetrate the reader's mind, because the reader may not be consciously searching for a remedy at that precise moment. To an individual who is suffering, treating his ailment may be quite as important to him as finding a new job or house. That is why small medicine advertisements are not unlike classifieds. The advertiser can rely on the reader's selective perception doing much of the work.

The less work the reader is willing to do, the more intrusive the advertising must be.

Many things that are advertised are not of immense importance to us, and unless they are drawn to our attention we won't bother to watch out for them. In fact we don't bother to think much about them at all. Not many people would peruse the classifieds for a toothpaste advertisement in the way they will do for a holiday or a home. Houses and holidays are worthy of considerable attention and effort; nowadays toiletries, by and large, are not – though in days gone by toiletries were probably pretty engrossing too.

Not long ago my agency carried out research on some immensely witty but immensely wordy deodorant advertisements. Despite the fact that they regularly use the product, the housewives who were shown the campaign were not amused. 'Who could expect us to read so much stuff about a mere deodorant?' they asked irritably. 'It's not worth the trouble. It's quicker to go buy it and find out for yourself.' This response is well known to market researchers, and crops up repeatedly when advertising campaigns for inexpensive consumer goods are being tested. I believe, incidentally, that this explains why the most commonly used time-length for commercials is thirty seconds. Thirty seconds is quite long enough to communicate everything most people wish to know about most consumer goods.

But surely if the consumers really wanted something they should be willing to search for its advertising? Why can't all advertisements be tiny classifieds, activated by people who are genuinely interested in them, rather than big jobs produced by people who want to foist their messages on to other people – people who apparently don't want to receive them? This is the underlying basis of most criticisms of advertising.

And the answer is that nowadays there is too little time, and there are too many products. People frequently do not know whether or not they are interested in a particular product, or service, or warning, or whatever, until an advertisement knocks on their mind's door and tells them about it. And often they need to be told again and again before they take any notice. The need for intrusion and repetition in advertising is, I think, widely misunderstood.

If you are driving south-west from Paris, on the Autoroute 11, you will spot a sign saying *Visitez Chartres*. It is not a directional road sign: you can tell that because it is a distinguished brown, not blue, and because it includes a sketch of the great cathedral. It is a discreet advertisement.

Although it is restrained and simple, the sign, like all road signs, is visual clutter. It is deliberately placed in a position where you can hardly avoid noticing it. It is intrusive. It sullies *la belle France*.

Let us assume that before spotting it you had not the least intention of visiting Chartres. The sign makes you think of doing something you had not previously intended to do. Something you may well enjoy. Just as commercials make you think of doing things you had not previously intended to do. Things you may well enjoy. The notion that human beings know precisely what they want, at all times, is patently idiotic. Nobody knows, in advance, exactly how they wish to spend all their time, or exactly what they wish to spend most of their money on. Advertisements offer persuasive suggestions.

For the *Visitez Chartres* sign to get its simple message across, it is necessary for it to intrude. The sign must jut itself into your mind as you drive past. But the power of intrusion should not be exaggerated. The sign cannot force you to visit Chartres. The sign cannot pick you up by the scruff of the neck, twist your arm behind your back or put a pistol to your head. It does not even employ deep, psychological witchcraft to put across its message. Nor can advertisements – real advertisements – force people to do things they do not want to do. (Nor do the rules allow advertisements to frighten people into doing things they do not want to do, except in cases where appeals to fear can clearly be justified – like road safety, or AIDS.)

The *Visitez Chartres* sign, like real advertisements, is far more likely to work it if falls on fertile ground. It is far more likely to work if it is seen by flying-buttress fanciers, or stained-glass lovers, for example. Indeed they will probably welcome the intrusion. And it will intrude on their consciousness far more easily than it will penetrate the consciousness of those passing drivers to whom visiting old cathedrals would be about as much fun as watching lavatory cleanser commercials for hours on end without a break. *They* will not welcome the intrusion at all. They may even wonder why Chartres has been permitted to litter the French countryside with its unnecessary publicity.

In other words, the intrusion will be welcomed by some and disliked by others. That is a general truth about all intrusive advertising. And it has had profound consequences on the way advertising, particularly television advertising, has developed over recent years. It has encouraged advertisers to wrap their sales messages in wit, and charm, and elegant photography.

Back on the Autoroute 11 you've seen the discreet sign, but you cannot nip off for a cathedral visit today because the kids are caterwauling and are desperate to reach sea, sand and sun. So you forget about it. At least you think you have forgotten. But in subsequent years you pass the sign again. It keeps on intruding. Eventually you give in. To open the mind's door it is often necessary to keep on knocking. But the cathedral-haters will never give in. To them the intrusive road sign could easily become increasingly irritating – like a commercial for a product you do not want.

For the purpose of this little scenario you were in the target market. Indeed you were a keen member of the target market, profoundly interested in Gothic cathedrals and suchlike. That is why you were willing to respond to a bland sign lacking any persuasive copy. Others would take more convincing. If the wily wizards in Chartres' marketing department were given a free hand with the design of the sign they could almost certainly increase the number of visitors. Some witty words about the flying buttresses and stained glass would doubtless work wonders.

Yet still only a tiny proportion of those who saw the sign would nip off the motorway and into the nave. In this respect the *Visitez Chartres* sign works just like the advertising for all other famous brands – if it isn't sacrilegious to call Chartres cathedral a brand. (Not a fast-moving packaged good, admittedly. More of a consumer durable.)

The *Visitez Chartres* sign also helps answer another famous advertising conundrum: does advertising generate its results immediately or in the long term? It might have worked immediately. Alternatively, if it lingers in your memory, it may influence your behaviour weeks, months or even years after you last noticed it. It may oft, when on your couch you lie, in vacant or in pensive mood, flash upon that inward eye that is the bliss of solitude and make you leave sufficient time for a detour to Chartres on your next trip to France.

In other words advertising works both immediately and residually. Any advertiser who has ever put any kind of response mechanism into his advertising – from a freephone number to a write-in cookbook – will know that response is quick and tails off thereafter. Retailers see it happen every Friday.

This is hardly astonishing: it reflects the way in which people's memories work. I may not remember all that many of the faces I saw on the street yesterday, but I'll remember a great deal fewer from six months ago. To justify itself economically advertising needs to find the right people and persuade most of them to take action. Now. Or at the very least, very soon.

No advertisers can afford to wait years for their advertising to take effect. Nor should they. Advertising must generate responses both today and tomorrow. It is treated as a revenue-cost by accountants and by balance sheets, rather than as an investment, because it *is* a revenue-cost (though it also provides long-term benefits). It may take years to pay for itself, but it must start to pay for itself forthwith if not sooner.

Not that short-term results and long-term benefits are mutually incompatible. Indeed it is one of the greatest benefits of advertising, as compared to all other means of marketing communication, that it works both quickly and slowly. Perhaps that explains why the endless debate over whether advertising is a short-term cost or a long-term investment has rumbled on for so many years. It is neither. It is both. But unless short-term results are achieved the long-term benefits will never materialise. Advertising could not possibly work in the future if it did not work in the present. Its immediate effects may not be measurable, but that is a different matter.

Having said which, some advertisements work – and are intended to work – much more speedily than others. (Another example of the heterogeneity of advertising.) Brand-image advertising tends to work more slowly, and for longer, than sales promotion, or retail, or direct-response advertising. In the case of direct-response advertising the purchase is made *while* the advertisement is being read: the order form is an inclusive part of the advertisement. Memory is irrelevant.

Television, radio and billboards could hardly work more differently. Memory is all-important. (Tesco tends to frown on customers who arrive carrying forty-eight-sheet billboards.) This is why theories derived from direct-response advertising – the theories espoused by Claude Hopkins and his disciples – rarely apply to broadcast advertising, or to shop-bought goods generally. Most advertising depends upon memory; direct-response advertising does not. That is about as fundamental a difference as you can get.

All of this may seem to be light years away from the traditional analysis of how advertising works – analyses like AIDA: Attention, Interest, Desire, Action. Such analyses are either wrong, because they are too simplistic; or self-fulfilling, because they can be bent to fit any facts you fancy.

The traditional analyses are built – either explicitly or implicitly – upon the premise that advertising is something powerful firms do to powerless (though sometimes stubborn) consumers. That is not the case. Advertising works because consumers want it to work. And when consumers want it to work. If the consumers did not want advertising to work they would reject or ignore all its messages, and it would fail. They do, individually, reject most of its messages, as we have seen – which proves that advertising is far from irresistibly powerful. But they do not reject *all* its messages because they know advertising benefits them in more ways than they've had frozen dinners.

Advertising introduces people to useful new products and reminds them of old products they had almost forgotten.

Advertising tells people where they can buy goods at low prices and where they can invest their savings at advantageous rates.

Advertising informs people where they can go to be entertained and what they can do to alleviate their pains and sufferings.

Advertising lets people know how to use products in ways they had not previously thought of and how to improve themselves in ways they had not previously dreamed of.

Advertising warns people against behaving dangerously and encourages them to behave responsibly.

Advertising adds extra dimensions – of consistency, of glamour, of quality, of reassurance, of value – to the things people buy.

Advertising saves people time by providing them with neatly encapsulated, easily absorbed information.

Advertising helps people find new jobs, new homes, new holidays, new second-hand knickknacks and even, occasionally, new spouses.

To quote from an excellent recent paper by Evan Davis, Professor John Kay and Jonathan Star:

> [For consumers] advertising is quite consistent with the usual tenets of economic behaviour – it is self-interested and in the long-term rational.
>
> *'Is advertising rational?'* Business Strategy Review, *Autumn 1991*

To confound the confusions about the ways in which advertising works, most people find it exceptionally difficult to distinguish between the deliberate, intended effects of advertisements and their incidental, often accidental, by-products.

Some of the by-products are exceedingly beneficial, others perhaps less so. The most significant by-product is the immense diversity of media with which we are blessed – almost all of them supported by advertising. It is not the purpose of advertising to provide society with a superabundance of lively, informative, entertaining and above all independent media – but it is a magnificent by-product.

On the other hand advertising arguably encourages people to be more materialistic than they would otherwise have been. I am unconvinced by this hypothesis, as I have yet to hear of any society, of any era, anywhere in the world, that was not materialistic. Individuals and religions may eschew – or even deplore – material wealth. But entire societies? Never. It was not advertising that persuaded humanity to develop sharp flint tools and hunting spears; nor advertising which persuaded kings and chieftains to dress more prestigiously than lowlier folk. But whether advertising – as a by-product – encourages people to be *more* materialistic is another of those unanswerable questions. How could one tell?

Advertising's by-products, perhaps predictably, provoke unanswerable questions especially often. (Evaluating the intended, desired effects of advertising is difficult enough; evaluating its unintended effects can be utterly baffling.)

Here's another example. Most advertising – not all, as we have seen, but in financial terms probably most – is designed to sell individual brands. The advertiser and his agency may decide that in order to achieve its aim the advertisement ought to be witty, or pretty, or clamorous, or glamorous. Those qualities are incidental to the advertisement's main purpose: they are means to an end – by-products. However, they lead people to wonder whether witty or pretty or clamorous or glamorous advertisements are, or are not, generally more effective than others. Another impenetrable question.

The most that can be hypothesised is that different types of product are more (or less) amenable to different types of treatment. Housewives find domestic cleaning a serious chore, and so do not appreciate advertisers joking about it. Pub-goers find beer drinking cheering and entertaining, and so expect the advertisements to reflect those qualities.

This is yet another way in which advertisements are heterogeneous.

And it leads to a key question associated with the mechanics of advertising which I have not tried to answer and would not be able to answer if I tried. It is comparatively easy to understand why people buy brands with functional benefits, which advertisements explain to them. But why do they buy so-called image brands – brands whose benefits are purely psychological?

The reason the question is unanswerable is that it is not really a question about advertising at all. Why do we choose to dress in attractive gear, why do we like splendid buildings, why do we enjoy lovely gardens, why do we prefer to listen to music in gorgeous surroundings like Covent Garden or the Royal Albert Hall? Who knows? Clothes, buildings, gardens could all be purely functional and – in theory at least – *Tosca* would sound as good in a sewer as in La Scala. We like the imagery. But all that has nothing, fundamentally, to do with advertising.

Some advertising – not a lot, but the most intriguing – associates its brands with success, glamour and fashion. And to people who aspire to be successful, glamorous and fashionable – most of us – that helps make those brands appealing. So it always has been, at all times, in all societies. Heaven knows why: there's nowt so queer as folk.

The same confusion – between intention and possible by-product – also arises in the distinction between brands and markets. Advertisements for brands sometimes increase the size of the market. In their early days at least, the Smirnoff campaign doubtless grew the vodka market and the Heineken campaign doubtless grew the lager market. It should not have been the intention of Smirnoff and Heineken to grow the vodka and lager markets. That was an unavoidable, and from their point of view somewhat undesirable, by-product of their own brand growth. It occurred because, at that time, the markets for vodka and lager were very new, and very small. Neither the Smirnoff nor the Heineken campaign grew the total alcoholic drinks markets. That was because the market for alcoholic drinks is very old, and very big.

This is true of brand campaigns in all markets. Indubitably brand advertising can help new market sectors to expand. Equally indubitably brand advertising has no effect at all on well-established, mature markets. This is as true of toilet soaps as of alcohol, as true of petrol as of pet food, as true of cars as of confectionery. It is likewise true of cigarettes, though the banners will never be so persuaded.

The fact that campaigns for Lux, for Johnny Walker, for Esso, for Whiskas, for Jeep, for Black Magic and for Benson and Hedges do not increase the sales, respectively, of soaps, alcohol, petrol, cat food, cars, chocolate and cigarettes does not prove that the advertising is ineffective. In each case the advertising was never intended to expand the entire market. It was intended to sell the brand – and may or may not have succeeded.

Perhaps the final reason why it has proved so difficult to untangle the advertising web is that most people – protagonists and antagonists alike – tend either grossly to overestimate or grievously to underestimate its powers. And advertising people – who prefer things to be black or white – always like to say that this campaign has failed, that one succeeded.

At the Hype, Hope and Bamboozlem agency, where they have rather a witty way with words, they nimbly divide advertisements into two groups: 'All our ads are great,' they say succinctly, 'all yours are crap.' Advertisers too, if a little less pungently, will say that advertisement A was effective, advertisement B was not.

But the truth is that advertising is a spectral business, best analysed not in blacks and whites but in shades of grey. Almost all advertising achieves something. The eternal question is, how much?

Consider this example.

You have grown a surfeit of apples in your garden and you take some advertisements to sell them. You may get one customer, or two, or half a dozen, or dozens. If you receive no response at all, the advertisements will have failed; but in the marketplace that eventuality is rare. Most commonly, the response will vary from dreadful to excellent.

If you wish, you can set yourself a goal, a self-imposed target by which you can judge the advertisements' performance.

Obviously you will want to sell sufficient apples to cover the campaign's cost and maybe make a respectable profit. So that could be your goal. Or you could ask everyone you know whether or not they have seen your advertisements and if, say, 50% have done so you will reckon your little campaign has done everything that could reasonably be expected of it. So that could be your goal.

Setting a goal, however, will not affect the advertisements' effectiveness. Goals suggest some campaigns succeed, outright, while others fail, outright. That is not the case. Setting goals is a desirable management discipline. It is not a reflection of the way advertising works. It is like saying all males over six feet are tall, all males under six feet are short. But men come in an infinite number of varied heights. And advertising campaigns achieve an infinite variation in levels of effectiveness.

It is not necessary to know how advertising works to be good at advertising – any more than it is necessary to know how a car works to be a good driver. Many successful advertisers, and agency people, are good at advertising instinctively. But to reach the highest ground – to be a Juan Fangio or a Nigel Mansell – you need to have more than a cursory knowledge of what's what. You need to know how the powerful and complicated machine over which you have control operates. Then you can safely push it to its maximum power.

11

Your Brilliant Career

The best young advertising people are natural rebels (albeit without much cause) and rarely heed the counsel of geriatrics. When I was a weenybopper some senile buffer had only to start a sentence 'In my experience . . . ' for me to reach for my mental magic markers and colour him grey all over.

So I would not have the temerity to suggest that my untidy career might be an example to anyone else. I drifted into advertising fortuitously and have since rather enjoyed myself hoofing it. To have launched two agencies is palpably idiosyncratic. (Though far from unique: George Lois in New York was forever starting new agencies – and excellent some of them were, too.) To have appointed myself, in mid-career, a creative director, with no experience and even less aptitude for the job, was manifestly manic. To have relinquished the chairmanship of one of the UK's top ten shops, almost on whim, is hardly evidence of perspicacious, purposeful planning.

Nonetheless, I think I have learned at least a little about how to climb the greasy pole. Most of my learning has been negative rather than positive: by falling into elephant traps I have discovered where they are. So when I am reincarnated as a trainee adman my progress should be dazzling.

Here then are thirteen lucky lessons which may help those contemplating a life sentence in this bewildering business to reach their own high ground. Some are unique to advertising, most may not be:

    i   Be a phoenix

ii   Beware of ultimata
iii Haughty is naughty
iv   Get a little famous
v   Give back a smidgeon
vi   Don't worry about marrying the job
vii Choose the right DNA
viii Be blameworthy
ix   Conferences, si!
x   Nettle-grasping
xi   It's not only retail that's detail
xii Love the ads, lovey
xiii Become the world's greatest adman

Be a phoenix

Advertising novitiates are notoriously overeager, optimistic and enthusiastic about the projects in which they get involved. Every whippersnapper is in a tearing hurry to get some successes under his belt, some triumphs on his curriculum vitae. I shared these healthy ambitions, but my early career was a string of disasters.

I was account executive on the launch of Admiral, one of the least successful cigarette brands of the 1960s. (No, you won't find it in your local tobacconist.) I was account executive on the re-launch of Astral soap and cream. (You won't find Astral on your supermarket shelves either.) I was account executive on the launch of Crosby Income Units, at that time the biggest and most expensive unit trust launch ever. (The trust still exists, but the launch lost a fortune.) I was account executive on the launch of the Doncella cigar range. (Haven't seen them around for quite a while.) I was account executive on the launch of Limmits Slimming Chocolate Meals (a daft idea if I ever heard one). I was account executive on the launch of Dentifresh, the only toothpaste for both natural teeth and dentures (even dafter).

I missed copy dates. I put unit trust advertisements into newspapers with the prices wrong. I missed trains, and even occasionally planes, on the way to important meetings. I arrived at meetings late (I mean *late*), and often tired and emotional to boot. The first time I ever addressed a huge sales conference, with an audience of about four hundred, my fly zip was undone.

It is too shaming to continue. The memories make me cringe. Recalling my happy-go-lucky behaviour, the risks I took, the cheerful insouciance with which I stumbled from catastrophe to catastrophe now brings me out in a shaky sweat.

And yet, and yet. The experiences were not wasted. You can learn a great deal more from bungles and bloomers than you can from victorious successes. Inquests concentrate the mind wonderfully. The reasons for successes tend to be specific, the reasons for failures are general. I now wince whenever marketing people say 'We launched Burpo successfully in Wigan, so Wigan's bound to be right for Bilge.' The many factors in a marketing mix that contribute to a triumph cannot be isolated – like magic ingredients – and transposed to other situations. Nor is the plagiaristic repetition of a formula which has proved effective on one occasion likely to prove so effective the second time round.

Whereas things that have gone wrong once will invariably go wrong again. So high-quality smasheroo fiascos are always worthy of detailed analysis. From that point of view my freshman years in advertising were a lengthy series of blessings in disguise. We all have our ups and downs, and after so many downs I guess I was due for a few ups. The thing to fear most about failure is being frightened of admitting it. A good drubbing will make even the most bumptiously bouncy brat pause for mental refreshment.

Not that my life is nowadays bloomer-free – far from it. But I generally remember to check my zip before public speaking.

Beware of ultimata

A few months back a particularly talented young advertising man accepted an obviously lousy job as managing director of an obviously lousy agency. I was puzzled. Why, I asked one of his closest friends, why?

'He was desperate to be a managing director,' came the reply. 'He had set his heart on becoming an MD by the age of thirty-three and became terrified he wasn't going to make it. He just wanted the title. He would have accepted managing directorship of a public loo if it was all that was on offer.'

How dumb, I thought. How could anyone so intelligent behave so foolishly? Then I remembered I had done precisely the same myself. Only worse.

At twenty-nine I came to the conclusion that it was essential for me to be appointed, not even managing director, but deputy managing director of my then agency, Robert Sharp & Partners. I asked for the job. I was refused. I was astonished. I was miffed. I issued an ultimatum. If I were not made deputy managing director within twelve months I would resign. My resignation was accepted. I was doubly astonished. I was quadruply miffed.

But I was not worried. The late 1960s were bonanza days for advertising. I was young and confident. I would easily obtain another job within twelve months. Nor, I post-rationalised, would a move be a bad thing after nearly a decade with the same agency. The job offers would come flooding in. They didn't.

On the contrary, prospective employers manifestly found my situation and my behaviour incomprehensible. At twenty-nine I was a director of a thriving high-profile agency, owned 25% of the shares, received a large salary and bounteous perks, drove a company-owned Aston Martin DB6 – and was proposing to leave, in pique, because further instant promotion had been denied me.

The weeks passed, and the months. It became clear to my Robert Sharp colleagues that other agencies were not clamouring for my services. My pride would not permit me to withdraw my resignation. Nor was I by any means certain that an offer to withdraw would be accepted. I started to imagine – was it imagination? – that my colleagues found my predicament rather amusing. I was receiving my comeuppance, being punished for my hubris.

In the end I took the only job I could get, with MCR Advertising. It was a smaller agency, a less good agency – and I wasn't even to be deputy managing director.

Another lesson learned. I never again issued an ultimatum without knowing precisely what I would do if it were rejected. Lots of advertising people do though. We are all far too impetuous. (And far too obsessed with titles.)

Haughty is naughty

And far too obsessed with status – frequently to our own detriment. We worry about the size of our office, the size of our desk, the size of our chair, the size of our fountain pen; doubtless some of us even have hang-ups about the size of our stapling machine. We hate to share secretaries, we don't like to pour out the tea in meetings, nor to carry artwork bags, nor to switch on projectors, nor to pay taxidrivers, nor to pick up and answer phones which other people should be picking up and answering.

Most of these status-conscious foibles are relatively harmless and matter not a jot or title. But there is one haughty status game which is decidedly naughty: trading up when dealing with clients. Those who play this silly game make it obvious they would sooner deal with senior client management folk than with juniors – even to the point of delaying things when senior folk are unavailable.

In one fell swoop this displeases the seniors, who do not want to be plagued with trivial issues that could be better dealt with by their subordinates, and earns the eternal enmity of the juniors who are bypassed. Woe betide the agency status-seeker when one of the juniors becomes a senior.

Far better to do things the other way around. Trade down. Deal with juniors whenever possible. They are flattered; they get things done; their bosses are pleased to be left alone; the agency enjoys a solid bedrock of support in the client organisation; and when they are promoted, they remember.

Get a little famous

When Peter Muttlebury retired and I took over as managing director of MCR Advertising, I recognised – it hardly required clairvoyance –

that the agency was anonymous, that its name was unmemorable, and that hordes of clients were therefore unlikely to hack a path to our door. Financially the agency was in the mire, making advertising, or even direct mail, an unaffordable luxury. The only answer was to garner free publicity.

In those far-off days the British advertising trade press was not much good. (Today it is absolutely spiffing, it seems wise to say.) Then, the trade magazines lazily published agency press releases, uncritically accepting everything they were told. With the launch of *Campaign*, in 1967, things changed radically. Far from publishing every agency puff, *Campaign* magazine initially seemed to relish biting the hands that fed it. The editor of the time told me that the most important quality in a journalist was scepticism. 'Not the ability to write?' I replied, surprised. 'Writing's unimportant,' he said, 'subs can do that. Scepticism is what counts. When you're a journalist – any kind of journalist, but particularly a trade press journalist – people lie to you all the time. You can never believe a word. Scepticism is the beginning and end of good journalism.'

This somewhat cynical credo permeated *Campaign*'s news reporting for several years, making it much feared (and avidly read) within the advertising village. But while its news was lively – and sceptical – its features were dull and predictable. Writing provocative features, then, appeared to be, and proved to be, a comparatively simple – and exceedingly cheap – way to raise the agency's profile. I started penpushing at once.

In the media, as everyone knows, a little fame spawns a little more fame. I soon found myself being invited to make conference speeches, to write for national newspapers and magazines, to broadcast occasionally, to sit on committees and run seminars and even to write books. Before too long clients had heard of me, and of my agency, and business began to trickle in. There can be no doubt that my articles – I have published about eight hundred in the last twenty-five years – have consistently and considerably enhanced my career.

It was not quite as effortless as it seemed at the beginning, though. I made three inviolable rules, by which I still try to abide, and which may be helpful to anyone thinking of pursuing a similar route to publicity:

i   *Never write in office hours*, otherwise the people around you will complain that you never do any work because you are always too busy writing. I do all my writing at weekends, mostly on Sundays, when everyone else is playing golf.
ii *Never re-publish old articles*, because eventually you will be found out, and editors will cease to trust you. This rule has proved harder as I have grown older.
iii *Never write for publications which massacre your copy.* This is only partly vanity. All journalists (and amateur journalists) learn to accept that their deathless prose will be shredded to some extent, without consultation, by sub-editors. But if your copy gets crudely hacked about there is no point in having it published. As an amateur you are not writing for money, but to publicise your opinions. If these get distorted, forget it.

As we saw earlier, all my publicity skills were desperately needed when I set up my agencies. It is not so easy nowadays – particularly since the recent recession forced trade magazines to slim down – for young agency people to get their writings, or their speeches, published. It can still be done though, if you try, try and try again.

And although my writings have enhanced my career, I suspect I have published rather too voluminously. For a time I became a sort of rent-a-pen. A modicum of restraint might have both improved the quality and implied some exclusivity. That's yet another way I intend to do better next time.

Give back a smidgeon

I mentioned a moment ago that no sooner had I started publishing than I found myself invited to sit on committees, to run seminars and the like. In any industry people take opposing views about such activities. Many consider them utterly unproductive and unprofitable – the words they use are cruder than that – and consider those who thus waste their time to be narcissists who passionately love the sound of their own voice and are puffed up with their own self-importance. Naturally those are not views I share.

Having been president of the Institute of Practitioners in Advertising, on the council of the Advertising Standards Authority, chairman of the Advertising Association, a member of far more committees than I can remember – and honorary president of the Yorkshire Publicity Association – the evidence suggests that I believe trade activities to be a bit worthwhile.

The portentous quasi-ethical excuse for putting so much time into such extracurricular works is that they offer an opportunity for you to put something back into the industry which has provided your livelihood. Yes, it is unprofitable – that is why it is worth doing. I subscribe slightly to that sentiment. But my main motives have been much more selfish.

First, you learn a lot. The first committee on which I sat was called the IPA Development Committee. It was chaired by Denis Lanigan, then chairman of J. Walter Thompson, now a director of Marks & Spencer, among others. He chaired the meetings marvellously. I had never seen anyone run meetings so well. Almost everything I know about chairing meetings I learned then from Denis Lanigan. I am still grateful. And that type of learning has recurred dozens of times, on dozens of committees, in subsequent years.

You also learn a lot about what is going on in the industry. You are kept up-to-date with trends, developments, threats, opportunities. Occasionally you acquire useful gossip. This is particularly important if you are working in a small, or new, agency. My diary of the time records that when I left Ted Bates friends advised me to give up any trade association work, because building a new agency would be so arduous and time-consuming. I consciously took the opposite decision, fearing that otherwise I would become blinkered and rapidly lose touch with major industry issues.

Second, you get to know, and can appraise, many of your competitors. Simultaneously – and many top agency people use this repeatedly – you meet prospective employees, often of high quality, and can become acquainted with them (without the involvement of headhunters). This especially applies to creative awards juries, where much covert job-swapping begins.

Third, whatever the knockers may say, playing a leading role in industry affairs generally enriches your relationships and reputation with clients. Shortly before becoming IPA president I asked one of my most eminent predecessors, Chris Hawes, then chairman of Davidson Pearce Berry & Spottiswoode, whether the IPA presidency was so time-consuming that it had deleteriously affected his agency's ability to win business. 'Not at all. On the contrary, it will help your agency win business,' he answered. 'It will keep you out of the way, and let the others get on with the job.' It did. And the same has proved true during my chairmanship of the Advertising Association.

All in all, serving on trade associations has been both stimulating and educative. But of course I mostly do it to put back a little of what I have taken out. . . .

Don't worry about marrying the job

The Hollywood mogul Sam Goldwyn liked to employ husband-and-wife writer teams because he could rely on them working on their scripts late into the night in bed, when otherwise they might have been otherwise engaged. That way, he said, they worked overtime for free. In contrast, David Ogilvy states emphatically in his *Confessions* that immediately two of his staff get married one of them has to leave. Preferably the wife, he adds rather coyly, to breed. (I daresay he wouldn't dare say that in this post-feminist era.)

Naturally office romances complicate office life, both while they last and when they stop. While the relationship lasts each partner will be unreliable *vis-à-vis* the other. Confidential information will be shared (however much both parties deny it), they will side with each other against others, and it will be difficult to fire either one of them, should this become necessary. Then when they part, all the opposites pertain, which can be more destructive still.

Despite which, I am with Sam Goldwyn. A couple working

together are likely to be doubly loyal; any joint work is likely to be quickly and efficiently carried out; if either of them needs to work all night, or at weekends – an endemic occurence in advertising – the other will acquiesce. And if the wife finally heeds David Ogilvy's advice and leaves to breed she will continue to understand and be interested in her spouse's work.

It is puzzling why the prejudice against dirtying your own doorstep (the nastiness of the phrase says it all!) is so widely prevalent in business, while marrying the girl next door occupies such an esteemed position in novelette mythology. It seems incomprehensible. But then I married the art director.

Choose the right DNA

It is doubtful whether employees in any other line of business spend quite as much time as advertising people discussing the merits and demerits of companies in their industry. To outsiders, overhearing the incessant burble in pubs and at parties, the intensity of admen's conversations sounds veritably obsessive. Around and around the debate will spin, as the participants dispute whether Hype, Hope and Bamboozlem's star is on the rise, while Isaacs and Isaacs' is on the wane, whether Burton, Orr & Gilbernetti is still the hottest shop in town while ACM has passed its peak.

The corollary of all this chatter is that everyone in advertising carries with them, encapsulated in their CV, the DNA of their previous employers. And if you have worked for crummy agencies (equals agencies whose DNA is perceived to be crummy in adland), you are woefully disadvantaged.

Not everyone can pick and choose their employers, but the best people can. So that a second-rate agency on your CV means that either:

    i   you have no judgement, and cannot differentiate high ground agencies from swamp shops or,
    ii you had no choice, because no high ground agency would have you.

It may be possible to overcome the disadvantage, if you manage to get to an interview and have the opportunity to proffer a plausible explanation. ('Hype, Hope and Bamboozlem promised they were going to transmute themselves into a hot shop, and I was going to be part of the Transmutation Project Team.') But you will be pushing water uphill. (As indeed would Hype, Hope and Bamboozlem had they really tried to transmute themselves.)

In every industry the reputation of companies as previous employers matters. In advertising it matters massively. Doubtless I am especially dumb but I did not appreciate this until late in my career. With the wisdom of hindsight, I should have been wiser.

Be blameworthy

It must be because advertising people are so strongly success-orientated that they are so strongly blame-averse. I find blame-aversion tiresome. It is cowardly, it involves lying, it necessitates self-deception. In a fast-moving business everyone makes mistakes incessantly. There is no point in trying to deny this undeniable truth so far as you yourself are concerned.

Moreover, in advertising there are great benefits to be gained from lumbering yourself with the responsibility for the agency's bloomers and bungles. By shouldering blame you absolve others – particularly your clients and your bosses – which will enhance your lovability more than somewhat; by shouldering blame you save swathes of time that would otherwise be wasted in witch hunts; by shouldering blame (most of the time) you are much more likely to be believed on those occasions when you refuse to shoulder the blame because you are truly not guilty.

There is another great advantage to be gained from carrying the can without demur. It makes clear that you are, and believe yourself to be, responsible for results: you are saying, in effect, 'the buck stops here'. If you take responsibility, you will be given responsibility. And only by taking the responsibility for disasters can you legitimately claim the responsibility for triumphs. If you are continuously dodging brickbats, you won't be able to catch the bouquets. Responsibility is indivisible.

Conferences, si!

Although the recession slowed things down a little, the advertising fraternity have always been gluttons for conferences. The merest announcement of a forthcoming get-together and they fill in the perforated form, lob off a small fortune, and get themselves enrolled at the double.

If the shindig is to be sited in some down-at-heel and dreary dump – like Madrid or Marbella or Montevideo – then nasty cynics (and left-behind spouses) may not find the explanation for their enthusiasm too hard to twig. However if, as is all too often the case, the venue is wonderful Wembley, beautiful Birmingham or even balmy Banbury the attractions of the jaunt may need to be elucidated by a Maigret or a Freud.

Being an inveterate conference-goer myself, I have introspected long and hard on the subject. What is it that persuades me that passing interminable hours on uncomfortable chairs, listening to the pious, prosaic parrotings of panjandrums is time well spent and a bundle of fun?

No doubt conference organisers have researched the matter in depth. Having not seen any such scientific studies, the best I can do is hypothesise. There appear to be three basic motivations for conference attendance.

First, you occasionally pick up specific hints or tips that can be put to profitable use. Such hints rarely emanate from the platform performers. If they had any truly original ideas for making their businesses more profitable, the last thing they would do is broadcast them to thousands of others, including their competitors.

Gossiping with other delegates, however, both helps keep you in broad touch with trends, attitudes and current happenings, and provides the occasionally profitable tip. A few years ago we won a complex account which we handled on a fee basis. It rapidly became apparent that we had grievously underestimated the costs and were losing money by the bucketful. Having only recently gained the business, at the pre-quoted stipend, we were loath immediately to go back to the client to up the bread. At a conference I bumped into the heads of the two other agencies who had pitched for the account.

Diligent work in the bar established they had both sought far higher fees than we had. My attitude to the problem changed forthwith.

Second: networking – particularly networking with prospective clients. One of the less attractive audio-visuals at advertising conferences is the sight and sound of agency principals laughing gleefully at the witticisms of their putative prey.

To this survival-of-the-fittest-type behaviour clients respond in one of three ways. Most of them nervously seek the safe shelter of their existing agency chums. A few see it as a legitimate opportunity for freeloading and book as many lunches as their diaries can carry. But from time to time real opportunities for business do occur – which would not have occurred had you not attended the conference.

The third and not to be denigrated, reason for tripping off to pow-wows is the one cynics find most suspect. Conferences are skives, breaks, mini-holidays – not really work, but sufficiently work-orientated to be conscience-salving.

So delegates feel compelled to decry them, to protest that attendance is a dreary drudge. Invariably they protest too much. Like the international jet-setters who endlessly try to convince everyone how much they hate flying Concorde and staying in the Plaza Athenee, conference-goers return from each fray determined to persuade their colleagues of how tedious it has been, of how hard they have worked, of the many long hours they've sweated over hot gins and tonics (and lukewarm Alka-Seltzers).

Palpably much of this bunkum is yet another yawn-inspiring manifestation of the British puritan ethic. (Americans admit quite cheerfully that conventions are for having a ball at, not for being bored at.) I never saw anyone being frog-marched into a conference chamber.

Nettle-grasping

Unless you are especially sadistic you will never get accustomed to, let alone enjoy, firing people. Nor should you. One evening I bumped into the finance director of an agency who boasted that he had just had the best day of his life. He had fired forty-seven people and slashed costs commensurately. He was in high spirits and manifestly expected me to share his joy and congratulate him warmly. When I didn't he seemed puzzled. I have no idea what has happened to him since. I hope he's on the dole.

The volatile nature of the agency business ensures that you are unlikely to climb many rungs of the ladder before you find yourself having to sack somebody. It will be unwelcome, unpleasant, and you will probably procrastinate. Most people do. But if it must be done, do it as rapidly as possible. Macbeth, whose advice one would normally treat with circumspection, at least got this one right: 'If it were done when 'tis done then 'twere well It were done quickly'.

My first assistant – golly I was proud of having been given an assistant – proved even more accident-prone than his boss. Working together, the two of us were a shambles. It rapidly became clear one of us would have to go. He was the newer arrival, the younger, and the more junior. The managing director of the agency said that as I had hired him, it was my job to fire him. I then discovered his mother was extremely ill, which doubtless explained his lack of concentration and his inefficiency. I delayed. He placed a series of unit trust advertisements in the newspapers with all the prices wrong. I took the blame and delayed some more. I had never fired anyone before, had no idea how to go about it, was scared of the responsibility, liked the bloke, and filibustered to avoid taking action.

Predictably, a few weeks later, he put another batch of unit trust advertisements to press with the prices wrong again. 'Accidents will occur in the best-regulated families,' said the client, echoing Mr Micawber, 'but I've had enough.' He refused to pay for the campaign. The agency's managing director said he too had had enough and I would have to act. I explained to the lad that everyone had had enough so he would have to go. I felt nervous and slightly sick. He seemed unperturbed. I thought he might need a drink – I did – so suggested we visit the local. As we sipped our tipples he explained that he was quite relieved to have been fired because he had been concerned about the agency's lack of a pension scheme. His father, before he died, had apparently advised him never to work anywhere without a good pension scheme. He was nineteen. We had a few more drinks and off he wandered, cheerfully, into the night.

Maybe I was fortunate, because after that the prospect of firing people was less daunting. But few subsequent sackings have proved so painless. When I joined Ted Bates the agency was heavily and demoralisingly overstaffed. Almost immediately I asked the board to cut the personnel roster by 20% – about sixty people. *Campaign* made it front-page news, describing me as a 'butcher' and was surprised when I complained. 'Advertising people revel in looking tough,' the editor said. Baloney.

Nothing can make firing people pleasant, but here are three tips which may marginally ameliorate some of the nastiness:

i *Take sufficient time* – explain the reasons for the dismissal fully, put as much blame as possible on to the organisation rather than on to the individual, and be financially generous to a fault.

ii *However much they have been expecting to be fired, it always comes as a surprise* – this is a symptom of human beings' remarkable ability to carry contradictory thoughts in their minds: they may know it is going to happen but cannot bring themselves to imagine it really happening.

iii *After they've gone they will be embittered* – no matter how apparently reasonable their initial reaction they will soon, understandably, build up a welter of resentment and quite probably contact their legal advisers. This is no excuse for not being generous and fair – but you must be cautious not to say anything which might be used in evidence against either you or your company. (Once people realise they are being sacked they anyway only half listen to what you are saying – they are already worrying about their future, how they will explain their dismissal to their spouse and to their children, how they will be able to continue to pay off the mortgage, how they will face life at all.)

It's not only retail that's detail

Ambitious young advertising tycoons rapidly discover that little (if any) of their working time is spent planning profound strategies and analysing the meaning of marketing in the twenty-first century. Such discussions must be relegated to pub time. Their working hours are spent checking: checking media schedules, checking sizes, checking dates, checking artwork, checking proofs, checking meeting times and attendances, checking typing, checking incoming invoices and checking invoices departing. Compared to their previous lives in college – fiercely debating the profundities in Dickens, Dante, Descartes, and Donizetti over a few cans of Tesco own-brand lager in the early hours of morning – checking is spine-crackingly tedious. But that's the job.

It used to be aphorised that 'retail is detail', though I have not heard that said much of late. Perhaps retailers have come to feel it belittles them, now they are mighty powers in the land. Perhaps they would nowadays prefer 'retail is planning profound strategies and analysing the meaning of marketing in the twenty-first century', despite its lack of scansion or rhyme.

I have no such qualms about claiming that 'advertising is detail' (despite its lack of scansion or rhyme). Advertising is detail in two distinct ways, both equally important – and both, in my case at least, took some learning.

In few if any other occupations do baby executives handle such large sums of money. Working on major consumer goods accounts you quickly find yourself involved in the spending of hundreds of thousands, maybe millions of pounds. It is difficult to get such budgets in perspective. You need to keep reminding yourself that it is real, not Monopoly money. You have probably never had more than a few hundred quid in your bank account. Yet you find yourself in meetings nonchalantly debating whether to spend £500,000 or £1,000,000 on this or that campaign.

You have to learn to sail between the Scylla of being too terrified of the huge sums involved and the Charybdis of being too cavalier. The final decision, to spend or not to spend, will not be yours. But the responsibility for pressing the buttons which send the campaign into orbit may well be. At that point cock-ups can be catastrophic.

Earlier I recorded how my assistant and I put to press a flurry of unit trust advertisements with the prices wrong. That bungle cost, at today's prices, some £200,000. Shortly afterwards somebody (not me, for a change) neglected to cancel a peak-time television spot that should have been cancelled. That cost, at today's prices again, over £40,000. A little later in my career – it has only happened once, thank goodness – a client rejected a commercial after it had been filmed. Cost, £160,000. In every case the mishap could easily have been avoided. In every case details had been ignored. Naturally agencies are insured. But to a young executive such calamities are – and should be – agonising. They are not exactly cheering to middle-aged executives come to that.

Advertising is detail in a second way, too. The public (viewers, readers, customers – that lot) may pick up tiny signals in advertisements which can detract from, or *in extremis* nullify, the desired communication. This phenomenon was called 'vampire video' when I was a lad – a metaphor which indicated that some trivial prop in a commercial had so absorbed the viewers' interest that it devoured the sales message. If, for example, an actress in a detergent commercial wore a diamond ring, viewers might be so transfixed by its beauty, or its cost, that they would fail to register anything at all about the detergent.

In the early days of television advertising, 'vampire video' seemed to occur frequently, or so it was believed. Nowadays advertising people are more careful. They have learned the hard way to pay attention to every detail. That is one of the reasons why commercials and print advertisements so often take what appears to outsiders to be an inordinately long time to produce. Everyone worries endlessly about everything. So they should.

Love the ads, lovey

When starting in advertising (and maybe even when finishing), your relationships within the agency are more important than your relationships with clients. To be more accurate, unless your relationships within the agency – particularly with the creative department – are excellent, your relationships with clients are bound to be terrible.

To keep this constantly in mind, for many years I referred to the agency in which I was working as 'the factory'. My colleagues thought this was designed to deprecate, or at least to put back in their boxes, the more bumptious creatives. Not at all. It has always been plain to me that no manager, no salesman, no businessman of any kind can succeed unless their factories are running smoothly. So it is in advertising. And to keep an advertising factory running smoothly it is essential to keep massaging the operatives.

As Chapter 5 showed, the creative operatives care more about their output, their advertisements, than they care about themselves. That is why, to reach the highest ground in advertising, it is vital to be obsessional about advertisements. Outsiders may feel this to be a blinding glimpse of the obvious, to feel it odd that I find it worthwhile making so trite a point. It isn't odd. To succeed in most walks of life it is *not* necessary to be obsessed by the product your company produces. That is why most top executives can and do switch from industry to industry without undue effort. In only a few occupations is it necessary to be obsessed with the product.

Nor is it the case that all top advertising people care much about advertisements. Far from it. Many, perhaps most, are fascinated by advertising, by the process – but have little interest in the advertisements themselves. If this sounds strange, consider whether a margarine manufacturer needs to be obsessed by margarine, or a lavatory cleanser manufacturer obsessed by lavatory cleansers. (Car makers, on the other hand, are at least as obsessive as admen!)

Advertising may not be a vocation, but there is little point in working in it if you do not enjoy advertisements. And you won't succeed unless you let this be known, to all and sundry. Otherwise the folk in the factory will notice. They will not like it. Your own effectiveness will be impaired. And you will not like it.

Become the world's greatest adman

In 1978 David Ogilvy published his autobiography, *Blood, Brains & Beer*. At that time he bestrode the advertising world like a Colossus. He had written his first advertisement at the age of thirty-nine, and in the subsequent twenty-eight years had built an agency billing nearly £1,000,000,000, with a thousand clients in twenty-nine countries. In 1978 Ogilvy & Mather, his agency, was already one of the world's top five, and was still growing strong. He was the supreme all-round advertising man, the only advertising man of real world stature, the greatest.

But *Blood, Brains & Beer* was a dreadful book. And in a far from kind review in *Campaign*, I said so. The review gave credit to Ogilvy's outstanding advertising achievements, but dwelled rather lengthily on his vanity. Analysing his personal qualities, as revealed all too fulsomely in *Blood*, I listed thirteen characteristics which appeared to be essential for anyone seeking, like Ogilvy, to be the world's greatest advertising man:

>   Arrogance
>   Charm
>   Confidence
>   Contacts
>   Creativity
>   Diligence
>   Enthusiasm
>   Literacy
>   Looks
>   Oratory
>   Resilience
>   Self-Publicity
>   Wit

Not all the characteristics which I ascribed to Ogilvy, as can be seen, were insulting; but neither were all of them, as can be seen, flattering.

Despite the unfriendly tenor of my review the book's publishers invited me to meet the author at a publicity party at the Savoy. It was an invitation I could not refuse. At the party's entrance stood the great man, waiting to greet his guests. The publisher introduced me: 'This is Winston Fletcher, he wrote . . .' 'I know damn well what he wrote,' Ogilvy rudely cut her short. Without a pause, without a further word, he spun on his heels, turned his back on me and strode away. I was deeply impressed. Often had I read, in novels, the phrase 'he spun on his heels and strode away' but never before had I seen it in real life. It was superb – and well deserved.

A couple of weeks later I received a letter from Château Touffou, David Ogilvy's French pile. In it he contested several of my review's views. I had got things wrong, he contended, I had failed to understand. I replied, defending my position. For a few weeks hostile missives flew back and forth across the Channel until we both grew bored of it and gave up.

During a mildly bibulous dinner one evening shortly afterwards I mentioned the correspondence to the editor of *Campaign*. He was enthralled. Well a little enthralled, anyway. Could he publish the letters? Of course, I answered, if David Ogilvy agrees. Will he agree? Who knows? I'll phone and ask.

It took me several days to buck up sufficient courage to telephone Château Touffou. The last time we had met Ogilvy had turned his back on me. It seemed unlikely, in the cool light of morning, that he would now receive my call with affability and good cheer. I braced my telephonic ear for a blast of icily dry vitriol.

'No, I cannot give you permission to publish those letters,' he replied affably and with good cheer. 'They were petulant, puerile letters. Private letters. They would look awful in print.'

'All right.'

'But it was good of you to have asked. Not everyone would have done so.'

Years, as the phrase goes, passed and I attended a dinner at which Ogilvy was guest of honour. (It was the dinner at which he admitted his horror of losing clients.) As soon as he spotted me in the crowd he strode – not away – but towards me. Hell, I fidgeted, what have I done now?

'You were right,' were his first words. 'About *Blood, Brains & Beer*, I mean. It was a failure. I still have no idea why it was a failure. It seemed OK to me. But it hardly sold a copy. So you were right.'

That was one of the characteristics needed by successful advertising people that my review list had omitted: blunt self-criticism. And it neatly brings us back to the first section in this chapter.

A final PS: When the *Blood, Brains & Beer* review was published a close friend phoned and said I had omitted the most important quality of all – energy.

'Without energy,' he pointed out, 'all the other qualities are ineffectual.' Certainly advertising demands and devours energy. Certainly Ogilvy had – still has – boundless energy.

So I energetically added energy and self-criticism to my original list of David Ogilvy's qualities. If you have all fifteen in plentiful supply, you could easily become the world's next greatest advertising man – or woman.

12

Playing Politics

It is a truth universally acknowledged that political advertising was invented by Saatchi & Saatchi, in cahoots with Margaret Thatcher, when they plastered the billboards with an infamous poster called 'Labour Isn't Working' in 1979. Unfortunately, like many universally acknowledged truths, it is not true. (The poster was not true either, which was why it became infamous. The people depicted were not unemployed and impoverished but were tricked-out models and Saatchi personnel. Nonetheless the poster was a fine specimen of negative-is-the-best-way-to-be-positive political advertising, of which more in a moment.)

Aeons before Charles and Maurice Saatchi, or Lady Thatcher, were twinkles in their great-grandparents' eyes, the advertising agency Charles Barker, which was founded in 1812 and was floated on the London stock market in 1986, ran press campaigns for parliamentary candidates. In 1832 Sir Edward Knatchbull and Sir William Geary each spent more than £100 on their election advertising. (The reason for such lavish expenditure may be found in a complaint, made in Parliament by Sir Matthew Ridley, that in those days newspapers charged political advertisers twice their normal rates.) So that far from political advertisers copying baked beans and detergents, as the oft-repeated cliché has it, baked beans and detergents have been copying political advertisers, for ages. This should not be surprising. Persuasive communication is the essence of politics, and has been since the dawn of time. The marketing of branded consumer goods is a relative newcomer to the scene.

Nonetheless there have been seminal changes in the ways in which politicians have sold themselves during recent years. Through their use of television and of market research, in particular. Television and market research emerged as power players in politics in the United States immediately after World War II.

Earlier, in the 1936 US presidential election, candidate Landon had, for the first time ever, used radio spots in his campaign against Franklin D. Roosevelt – unsuccessfully, as it turned out. Nothing much then happened until 1948 when the chairman of Colgate, E. H. Little, generously offered Thomas Dewey a complete, multi-media campaign created by Colgate's own agency – my old employers – Ted Bates. At that time Bates was one of the hottest shops in town. (It is a nice irony that Ted Bates was later bought by Saatchi & Saatchi – at that time one of the hottest shops in town!)

Dewey rejected Little's offer – and lost. These two facts may have been causally connected, or they may not. It was a risk Dwight D. Eisenhower's managers were unwilling to take. In the following presidential election in 1952 Eisenhower's spin doctors returned to the Ted Bates agency and got chairman Rosser Reeves – then an advertising whizz-kid who also captained the US chess team in Moscow – to devise their candidate's television commercials. That is when the shenanigans really got going. Like Dewey, Eisenhower did not relish becoming a geriatric electronic huckster. Between takes he sat shaking his head despondently, and said: 'To think that an old soldier should come to this.' Reeves, however, was suitably eulogistic about his own work. 'If only Dewey had known these things,' he boasted later about the techniques that had been used, 'he too would have been president.'

That was puffery, and probably inaccurate puffery to boot. As knowledgeable commentators have since noted, Eisenhower was a cast-iron certainty, which was why the Republicans chose him. He would have won with or without Reeves' help. Equally, Dewey would almost certainly have lost.

Politicians worldwide, however, have never been interested in such subtleties. The lessons they learned were simpler. Without advertising, Dewey bit the dust. With advertising, Ike romped home. *Ergo*, advertising wins elections. The era of high-pressure, all-singing-and-dancing political persuasion had arrived, particularly in the US, but on a lower key throughout the Western democratic world. Harold Macmillan's UK triumph in 1959 followed by Kennedy's in 1960 appeared finally to clinch the argument, if any sceptics still needed convincing.

Harold Macmillan's 1959 campaign, devised by Colman Prentis and Varley, at that time one of the hottest shops in town (it's an established political tradition), employed the great slogan 'Life's Better With the Conservatives. Don't Let Labour Ruin It.' This encapsulates the claim that must be made by any party in power and seeking to retain power: things are good, don't risk a change. The 1959 Tory slogan has repeatedly been copied, always more clumsily.

In 1979 the Labour government proclaimed "Keep Britain Labour And It Will Keep Getting Better', but the voters were unconvinced. In 1987 the Tories, after Mrs Thatcher's Wobbly Thursday, went back to basics with the slogan 'Britain Is Great Again. Don't Let Labour Wreck It', and won a clear parliamentary majority.

Notably, the two successful Tory slogans employed a knocking, negative element ('Don't Let Labour Ruin/Wreck It') which the more gentlemanly, unsuccessful, Labour slogan eschewed. I am not suggesting that this simple difference was the cause of the Tory successes, or of the Labour failure. Election advertising is not that important. But the phraseology in each case reflected the parties' entire campaign stance. Tory campaigns have always attacked mercilessly, taking no prisoners and giving no quarter. (The most recent Tory examples being the 'Labour's Tax Bombshell' and 'Labour's Double Whammy' posters in 1992 – both of which powerfully clobbered Labour's taxation policies, forcing them on to the defensive.) It may sound depressingly negative, but in political advertising the high ground is always captured by negative copy.

The explanation usually proffered for this phenomenon is that voters – particularly in Britain – now have such a poor opinion of politicians that they will only believe negative advertising. Only derogatory, pejorative words, it is argued, realistically reflect the public's present political perceptions. There may be truth in that hypothesis, but it is not the whole truth.

When a political party avoids attack and instead asserts its own virtues they sound like candy floss, like motherhood and apple pie. (Like advertising agency philosophies.) Economic growth, caring social policies, low inflation, low unemployment, better education, better health care, realistic defence policies – they all sound well meaning but uninspiring. Nor do they differentiate one party from another. All political parties espouse all of them. Nowadays the differences between the parties lie not in the ends but in the means. And means are difficult to dramatise.

In manifestos and pamphlets, at political meetings and in speeches, the nuances and niceties of a party's policies can be explained at length. But advertising must communicate in succinct, swift messages. And a punch to the opposition's solar plexus will be a whole lot more swift, and succinct, than a sermon extolling one's own righteousness. Though party politicals are considerably longer than product commercials – interminable, you may often feel – the nature of the medium demands clarity and compression: ideal for disparagement, poor for the complex exposition required by most modern political policies.

This is one of the two principle reasons why centre parties find it so difficult to advertise effectively, as I gloomily discovered while working for the SDP and the Alliance during the 1980s. (The other principle reason, of course, is lack of loot.)

The essential advertising problem for a party in the centre of British politics is that it never knows who to be negative about, who to attack. If it attacks Labour it looks as though it supports the Tories. If it attacks the Tories it looks like a wimpish Labour party. To attack both simultaneously looks both feeble and confusing. (The 1983 SDP/Liberal Alliance election posters tried to do this. They were not an unqualified success.) So negative advertising cannot be done. And for the middle-of-the-road SDP, the communications problem was further aggravated by the carefully balanced, non-extremist, somewhat sanctimonious nature of its messages: competition with compassion, toughness with tenderness, on the one hand and on the other.

In addition to sackfuls of money and an unabashed willingness to indulge in below-the-belt copy, there is a third prerequisite essential to high ground political advertising. A clearly defined and single-minded chain of command. In politics this transparently obvious necessity is rare. (In the SDP/Alliance it was nonexistent.)

First, politics and politicians normally operate by way of committees and meetings. Politicians imbibe the need to carry others along with them, with their mothers' milk. They post-rationalise their predilections for committees, and claim them to be aspects of democracy at work. Well maybe. But they are a lousy way to achieve effective advertising.

Perhaps unsurprisingly, Labour and Liberal Democrat/SDP/Alliance campaigns have been continually bedevilled by committee-itis. But even the hierarchical Tories have not been immune. What was Wobbly Thursday but Mrs Thatcher interfering in the chain of command, and in the strategy that had previously been agreed?

Second, and contrary to present-day conventional wisdom, most politicians do not much like advertising and PR people. Thatcher was, as so often, an exception. Michael Foot's refusal to be dressed up by image-makers, though extreme, was much more typical. And to some degree the politicians' inclinations are admirable. They want to be natural, they want to be themselves, they do not want to be – they fear being – packaged and polished up into gleaming, gimmicky, glitzy glad-handers.

From the moment they launch themselves into politics they learn how to win friends and influence people, how to earn people's confidence, how to cajole and persuade and convince, how to captivate a crowd and how to trounce an opponent. They feel no need to learn such things from callow soap salesmen who have never stood on a soapbox in their lives. So the relationship between politicians and their advertising advisers is far from easy-going. Dwight Eisenhower's distaste has been echoed a thousand times, albeit often silently, in the subsequent decades.('Do I have to do this?' John Major is said to have groaned and grumbled during photo-opportunities in 1992.)

Moreover – and here we come to the second seminal change of recent years – politicians believe they know better than anyone else what voters think about everything because they wallow in market research. It is market research, rather than advertising, which has most influenced the nature of political marketing since 1945. It is noteworthy that immediately the ex-Communist bloc nations threw off the shackles of the Berlin Wall their politicians began (and continue) to undertake opinion polls and political surveys.

Politicians of all hues pore over the floods of data which flow from the pollsters' computers; they read, mark, learn and inwardly digest the voters' views on everything from abortion to zebra crossings. Nobody – no businessman or marketeer, no sociologist or journalist – studies market research more assiduously than the modern politician. (Especially if the research happens to be about himself.) President Clinton has recently been described by the *Wall Street Journal* as being, 'awash with market research data' – as were his predecessors.

Back in the days of Sir Edward Knatchbull and Sir William Geary, the three ways in which politicians could learn the voters' views were via the local press, via their postbags, and via political meetings. All three provide biased, shallow information. Doubtless Sir Edward and Sir William firmly believed they had their ears to the ground, and believed themselves to be in close touch with their constituents – just as MPs do to this day. In truth they only converse with political activists, mostly their own supporters; only a tiny number of voters write to them; and the local press will have its own axes to grind. Market research changes all that.

The burgeoning of opinion polls over recent years has bought home to politicians, with a precision never before available, exactly how well (or how badly) the electorate understands them. Hence politicians have grown increasingly aware of the yawning chasm between their own, as they see it, sensible and defensible policies and the voters' lack of appreciation of their virtues. Consequently the politicians have reluctantly turned, when they can afford it, to paid-for advertising to communicate their messages. And consequently commentators have come to believe that political advertising is powerfully influential. But is it? Does it achieve anything apart from goading the enemy?

Advertising mythology now claims not only that Saatchi & Saatchi invented political advertising, but that their campaign was instrumental in the Tories' 1979 triumph. Balderdash. The Tories were consistently well ahead, miles ahead, in the polls from 1976 onwards, long before Saatchi's made any input. Indeed the Tories' popularity dipped slightly during the course of the campaign, from which you could deduce, if you so wished, that political advertising is counter-productive. Nor did Neil Kinnock's celebrated 'Kinnock' party political broadcast in 1987 achieve the impact with which it is widely credited. Neil Kinnock's own poll ratings improved a couple of points, but the Labour Party itself did not gain one iota. Since 1959 the Tories have won six general elections employing agencies and heavy advertising. Labour, on the other hand, have won four elections without (until now) employing an agency and with minimal advertising. Hardly convincing evidence, either way.

In the year following its launch the SDP captured a third of its market, the electoral vote, with virtually no advertising at all. At that time the advertising-less SDP was probably the fastest-growing political party in British history. The welter of press and television publicity hugely exceeded the possible influence of any advertising the SDP could have afforded. And this blitzkrieg of political news and comment occurs at every general election, nearly drowning the advertising. (The same never applies to consumer goods.)

All this having been said, political advertising is not utterly ineffectual. It may not be as powerful in politics as its protagonists proclaim, but neither is it insignificant. As I mentioned a couple of chapters back, every SDP market survey, from 1982 onwards, consistently established that nowadays the electorate wants to be wooed. Voters today expect a party (particularly an infant party) to be seen to promote itself. The very act of advertising is almost as important as the message. It encourages supporters and convinces waverers that the party really means business. In my view the SDP venture was scuppered in 1987, by the narrowest of margins, at least partly because it failed to make marketing and advertising a priority. (I guess Mandy Rice-Davis would not be surprised by that opinion.) Having been launched with a flurry of marketing activity, it more or less gave up marketing entirely.

One of the fundamental differences between political and other advertising lies in its discontinuity. This makes measurement of its effects, if any, all but impossible. While commercial advertisers can and do test their advertising by desisting from it in regions of the country, for measured periods, such experiments are not available to political parties. Even if a party were to carry out controlled experiments, during one election, by differentiating its campaigns regionally – and that would be a very brave, not to say foolhardy course of action – who can say whether the results would still be applicable in utterly different circumstances five years later? The likelihood is they would not.

So nobody knows, nobody can know, exactly what election campaigns achieve. The only relevant experiment I have discovered was carried out in Illinois in 1972. On that one occasion there was no television advertising, and the results suggest that the newspaper advertisements swayed 3% of the voters from one candidate to the other. But it was a local election, the turnout was low, and Illinois isn't Britain.

The chances are, then, that advertising probably encourages an imperceptible percentage of voters to change sides. It undeniably activates the activists and supports the preconceptions of supporters. They are uplifted and galvanised into ever-greater exertions by seeing their side's slogans on hoardings as they wearily slog round the streets. And they love to see their side biffing the enemy. In a tightly fought election such small effects would be sufficient. Every vote then counts.

13

Joys and Woes

'Why, Mr Fletcher, do you want to work in advertising?' asked one of the panel of pompous old codgers at the far end of the intimidating table.

'People,' the pre-digested reply tripped off my tongue, 'I love people. They're wonderful, aren't they, don't you think, people? That's what advertising is all about, in my opinion, people.'

'Don't be such a hypocritical young pillock,' replied another of the pompous old codgers less than pompously. 'Money's the answer. Why d'you think we work here? Shekels. Swag. Spondulicks. If you're not interested in money you'll never succeed.'

'Well, yes,' I mumbled, 'and there's that too, in my opinion . . .'.

So I had better begin my brief dissertation on the pros and cons of working in advertising by admitting that my little buff monthly envelope is a definite pro.

With that confession out of the way, let's get back to the people. In my late twenties Robert Gavron, until recently chairman of St Ives Group printers and unquestionably one of the country's most successful businessmen, strongly advised me to change my career.

'There are far too many clever people in advertising,' he argued. 'Look for an industry which is less competitive. It makes no sense to pit your wits against the brightest, when there are dozens of easier options. Quit advertising and you'll make your fortune. I'll help you.'

I didn't. (And he didn't.) It was probably wise, and certainly generous, advice. But greatly as I admire and respect Bob Gavron, I could hardly disagree with him more. Working in a business in which the people were tedious would fill me with gloom and grief.

Advertising is, as has been said, a people business. It is what economists call a labour intensive industry (which is not to say that all of the labourers labour all that intensively). Many of the people in advertising are, as Bob Gavron implied, clever, energetic, witty, sophisticated, charming and a joy to be with. Many aren't. Many are infuriating, neurotic, petulant, childish, conceited egotists in constant need of flattering and a punch on the nose. Fortunately the former exceed the latter. And even the latter, exasperating and maddening though they can be, are rarely dull.

Most of the people in advertising are there, naturally, to produce, or to help produce, advertisements (though not all of them seem to know that). For me, as I admitted earlier, being involved in the production of advertisements is one of the perks of the job. But it is only fun if they are good advertisements. (Equals advertisements I like.) Unfortunately, although you may think this is incontrovertible evidence of spinelessness, any agency which produces hordes of advertisements will occasionally be forced to produce advertisements it dislikes. Squabbling with clients who are pushing you to produce advertisements you believe to be wrong is one of the non-perks of the job.

However, when things are going well clients are a source of joy and delight. 'Going well' in this context means that the client is displaying warm and loving enthusiasm for the agency's advertisements — and preferably spending lots of money on running them. Almost nothing makes an agency happier than a nice happy client.

Except perhaps a nice happy new client. The winning of a new client raises an advertising agency's excitement level — which always borders on the frenetic — to fever pitch. The champagne flows, the local pubs do a roaring trade, good cheer is universal. Even those who had nothing whatsoever to do with the victory feel a flush of pride and triumph. It is the same warm glow you feel when your team wins and you know they couldn't have done so had you not been out on the terrace rooting for them.

The converse of all of which, as my geometry teacher used to say, is necessarily also true. Waves of dismay, distress, despondence, desolation and despair surge through an agency (and especially through me) when a client ceases to be happy, and then rapidly ceases to be nice. When clients become ex-clients they become especially nasty. Most ex-clients are odious, malevolent things. Agency people never buy or use the products of clients who have fired them. Such revenge is sweet, if utterly pointless.

Almost paradoxically, however, even losing clients bolsters one of advertising's basic blessings – its diversity. Working in advertising you will one day be dabbling in mayonnaise, the next be immersed in hot chocolate, the next be entangled in investments, then be chewing into confectionery, then be confused by computers, then be tearing into toilet rolls or bickering with a brewer. And when you lose a client there is at least a spot of satisfaction in knowing that you won't have to worry about his problems any more, and you can rapidly move on to something new. Advertising people are innately scatterbrained.

And while advertising is hardly a public-spirited vocation – it isn't exactly nursing, or teaching, or preaching – it does a little good. It creates economic wealth and helps keep the wheels of industry spinning – even if it sometimes makes them spin so rapidly they overheat. We do our bit to improve society's well-being: rather more than wallpaper manufacturers, perhaps, rather less than biochemists.

One of the recurrent themes of this book has been the number of unanswered – often unanswerable – questions prowling around the advertising jungle. How much further will retailers' own brands grow? How many advertisements do you see each day? Are multinational campaigns generally more cost-effective than national campaigns? What is the future of advertising agencies? How should they be remunerated? How can the quality of advertising be evaluated? How can creative people be controlled? What does advertising testing really test? How can target markets be pinpointed more sharply? Can testing ever be a science? Is there a future in launching new agencies? Who should sell creative work to clients? How stubborn should agencies be in defending their work? How does advertising really work? (A whole chapter, that one.) What are the qualities needed to succeed? Does political advertising achieve anything?

These and many more knotty questions have cropped up and been answered, half answered or deliberately left unanswered. To me the uncertainties inherent in such enigmatic issues are endlessly exhilarating.

As I said earlier, I started to write about advertising for the cheapest of motives: to gain publicity. But writing makes you think. The more I have written the more I have thought. The more I have thought the more I have realised how much there still is to think about. Almost every year – almost every day – I decide I know as much as there is to know about advertising, so it's time to give up. This never proves true. Most people, from Claude Hopkins to this day, deplore the ambiguities of advertising. Not me.

Nice and nasty colleagues, winning and losing clients, good and bad advertisements, the answerable and unanswerable questions – all contribute to the lurching unpredictability of advertising, to which I have referred maybe all too frequently. Recently, interviewing an exceedingly bright twenty-seven-year-old, I asked how his career to date compared with whatever he had expected when he left university six years previously.

'The peaks are much higher and the troughs much lower,' he replied. 'I had never expected to be made nearly so happy, nor nearly so unhappy, by incidents and happenings which – in the great scheme of things – are really not that important.'

The next day, as if to prove his point psychically, we won a major client, were short-listed by another major client, and very nearly lost a major client – in a couple of hours. My partner Greg Delaney assures me that as I get more experienced I will grow accustomed to this mercurial volatility. I don't believe him.

If you have read Joseph Heller's *Catch 22* you will remember Dunbar. Dunbar wanted to be bored perpetually so that his life would go more slowly and he would live longer. Well working in advertising ensures you die terrifically quickly. Tedium is in short supply. Crises, chaos and confusion are piled high.

Advertising is a business which, for me anyway, has provided little in moderation, almost everything in excess – a palindrome in which all the advantages create their own mirror-image disadvantages. Except, as the pompous old codger so wisely put it, for the little buff monthly envelopes. I can see no disadvantages in them. Long may they continue.

Index

Abbot Mead Vickers 132, 140
account planners 54
advertising
  awareness levels 16, 126, 127-8
  by-products 186-7, 188
  clutter 15, 16
  consumer benefits 185-6, 222
  consumer reaction 173, 175
  cost-effectiveness 106-7
  how it works 172, 173, 174-5, 185, 186
  intrusive/non-intrusive 176, 179, 180, 182
  long-term benefits 184
  memory-dependent 184-5
  originality and aesthetics 96-7
  public's tolerance of 15-16
  quasi-scientific laws 116-17
  response levels 106, 107-8, 184
  selective perception 175-6, 180
  short-term results 184
  volume 13-14
  waste 106, 107
advertising history 8-9, 11-12, 171-2
aesthetics 96-7
agencies
  advisers or suppliers? 63, 64
  agency philosophy 154-6
  British 39-43, 45-6
  client numbers 66
  creative agencies 45-8
  current problems 35
  current role 55
  generalists and specialists 46-8
  losing clients 167-8, 222
  management issues 144-5
  media specialists 44-5, 58, 101
  multi-service agencies 48-51
  multinational agencies 37-40
  objectives 53-5, 156
  polarisation thesis 36
  types of 37
  winning clients 221
  see also agency finances; launching an agency; working in advertising
agency finances
  charging systems 56, 57
  commission system 42, 43, 44, 57, 58, 59
  'excessive' profits 41
  income sources 56
  performance-related payment arrangements 57, 58
  time-cost fees 57, 58
agency/client relationship
  client conflict 76-7
  complacency 65-6
  confrontations 163
  entertaining 136-7, 165-7
  healthy/unhealthy problems 162-3
  long-term 64-5
  partnership sourcing 76
  presentation and selling of new ideas 158
  sycophancy 163, 164
  tournament system 65
  trust 67-8, 76
AIDA (Attention, Interest, Desire, Action) 185
Ambler, Tim 72-3
Amstrad 73-4
awards 87-8, 95-6, 97, 159, 173
N. W. Ayer 59

Baker, Chris 127

Charles Barker 59, 212
Bartle Bogle Hegarty 132, 146
Ted Bates 42, 135-6, 150, 156, 163, 205, 213
Baxter, Marilyn 153
Bayley, Stephen 80
Bernbach, Bill 29
Billet Consultancy 7
Bloom, John 64-5
Bogen, Joseph 82
Bozell Worldwide 11
brands
   brand advertising and market expansion 188
   brand-image advertising 108, 184, 187-8
   consumer loyalty 6-7
   heavy users 103-4
   market segmentation 101-2, 103
   market share 3, 7
   new brands 122
   product quality 3-5, 7
   purchase levels 104-6
   re-launches 122
   role of advertising 2, 4
   valuation 5-6
briefs
   clients' briefs 74
   content 53-4, 93, 94
   drafting 54, 92
Broadbent, Simon 6, 127, 173
Brodie, Bill 75
Buck, Stephen 2
Bullmore, Jeremy 167, 172
business-to-business advertising 100, 179-80

Campaign 95, 196, 205, 210
car advertising 8
Chinn, Stephen 128-9, 130, 173
classified advertisements 176-8, 181
client service people 161
clients
   agency switching 65
   briefing the agency 74
   consistency 74-5
   cost-cutting 52, 68-9
   enthusiasm 75
   ex-clients 167-8, 222
   flexibility 72-4
   getting their own way 69-70
   the 'good client' 68-9, 70
   honesty 71
   motivating the agency team 70, 75
   objectives? 68
   or customers? 66-7
   rejection of advertisements 62, 72, 158, 159-60
   toughness 71
cold calls 141
Collins, Christopher 75
Colman Prentis and Varley 214
competitive pitches 139
conferences 202-3
coupon response 16
CPC Foods 157
creative agencies 45-8, 58
creative boutiques 36, 51
creative people
   briefing 53-4
   controlling 86, 91-4
   dealing with clients 161-2
   financial motivation 90-1
   freelance creatives 47
   intelligence and creativity 87
   motivating 88-91, 97
   and multinational campaigns 38-40
   perfectionism 87, 94
   personality traits 86-7
   providing clear briefs for 92-3
   stereotypes 80, 84-5
   time schedules and budgets 93, 94
creativity
   aesthetics 96-7
   bisociation theory 82, 83
   the brain and the creative function 82-3
   clash with business management 84
   irrationality of 84
   lateral thinking 83
   nature of 80-1
   originality 96
   synectics theory 83
Crewe, Ivor 129-30

database marketing *see* direct mail
Davis, Evan 186
De Bono, Edward 83
Delaney, Barry 134, 136, 137, 138, 142
Delaney, Greg 74, 134, 136, 137, 138, 167, 223
Delaney, Paul 78, 79-80, 133, 147

Index

Delaney Fletcher Dolancy 133–4, 135, 136–40, 141–3, 146–50
delegation 145
Dentsu 152
DFSD Bozell 133, 150, 156
direct mail 9, 10, 107, 140–1
direct-response advertising 120, 131, 184, 185
Dowds, Bob 136, 137
Doyle Dane Bernbach 158
drug efficacy tests 123

Eastern Europe 24, 47
Ehrenberg, Andrew 104
Eisenhower, Dwight D. 213
Ellis, Havelock 85
English, Michael 164
entertaining 136–7, 165–7

Feldwick, Paul 127–8
financial advertisements 179
financial advertising 8, 16, 120–1
Financial Times 23
Foreman, Sir Dennis 84
future of advertising
 agenda 17
 predicted obsolescence 1

Gavron, Robert 220
Gazziniga, Michael 83
geodemographic cluster analysis 113
Glynne-Jones, Peter 163
Goldwyn, Sam 115, 199
Gordon, William 83
Goya Perfumes 75
Gross brothers 42
Gossage, Howard 90

Hakmiller, Carl 85
handbill distribution 12
Hawes, Chris 199
Heineken campaign 188
Henley Centre 2, 4
Hennessy, Gilles 71–2
hierarchies 144
Hill, William 62
Hillards 136, 137
Hinton, Graham 52
hobby publications 179
Holloway, Keith 76
Hopkins, Claude 116, 120, 185

Hummert, Frank 164

Institute of Practitioners in Advertising (IPA) 43, 52
interactive marketing 11, 99–100
International Distillers and Vintners 72–3
IPA Advertising Effectiveness Awards 95–6, 173
Iran Air 147–9

J. Walter Thompson 43, 59
Jacoby, Robert 42, 89, 136, 156
Japan 33, 47, 76, 77
job advertisements 178
Johnson, Samuel 90

Kay, John 186
Kimberley Clark 161
Kinnock, Neil 218
Kit Kat campaign 21
Koestler, Arthur 81–2

lager market 103–4
Lander Associates 6
Lanigan, Denis 198
launching an agency
 choice of name 134–5
 client contacts 138–9, 142
 growth 146
 management issues 144–5
 multinational partners 146, 150
 offices 142–3
 optimum size 145–6
 partner selection 132–3
 publicity 139–41
 recruitment 143–4
Le Piat campaign 73
leadership 145
Levitt, Theodore 19, 22
Lois, George 191
London Press Exchange 43
lonely hearts classifieds 177–8
Lord, Cyril 64–5

mail order 99, 100
mail shots 13, 107
market segmentation 101–2, 103, 108, 109, 112
marketing communications
 main sectors 9–11

specialisation 50-1
through-the-line approach 50
Maslow, Abraham 93-4
Mather & Crowther 43
McDonald, Colin 172-3
MCR Advertising 168, 194-6
Mead, Peter 52
media
  increasing segmentation 110-11
  marketplace 114
  media costs 101, 107
  media developments 98
  media specialists 44-5, 58, 101
  media surveys 111
meetings 144
mergers 151
multi-service agencies 48-51
multinational advertising
  campaign categories 25-6
  Consistent Campaigns 27, 29, 33-4, 39
  defining 23, 24-5
  Diverse Campaigns 28-9, 33
  gauging success of 29-30
  globus confusingus 18, 19, 20, 22, 34
  income percentages 25, 39
  language and word-play 22, 28-9
  national differences 18-19, 20-3
  national-to-multinational strategy 31, 32
  risks 30-1
  Universal Campaigns 26, 29, 32, 33
  volume of 22-3, 24-5
multinational agencies
  billings 37-8
  and creative people 38-40
  split operations 39
  worldwide networks 37
Muttlebury, Peter 169, 170

Naismith, John 19
networking 203
Newspaper Proprietors Association (NPA) 44-5
Nokes, Barbara 92-3

office politics 145
Ogilvy, David 28, 75, 95, 96, 126, 146, 155, 158, 164, 199, 209, 210-11
Ogilvy & Mather 146, 209
Olivetti 168-70

opinion polls 129-30, 217

patent medicine advertisements 180
Pedigree Chum campaign 27
Perry, Sir Michael 4
personalised newspapers 98
petfood 101-2
political advertising
  agency/politician relationship 216-17
  Conservative campaigns 212, 214, 217-18
  discontinuity 218-19
  effectiveness 219
  Eisenhower campaign (1952) 213
  Labour campaigns 214, 216, 218
  negative advertising 214, 215
  opinion polls 129-30, 217
  SDP/Alliance campaigns 177, 215, 218
post-testing
  Reel-of-Ten tests 126
  twenty-four-hour recall tests 125-6
Powell, Chris 35, 52
Premier Beverages 75, 157
presentations
  by creative people 161
  new business 139
  re-pitches 168-70
prize-winning campaigns 94-6, 97
psychological cluster analysis 122-3
publicity 139-41, 196-7

QVC Network 99

Raymond, Charles 118
re-pitches 168-70
Reeves, Rosser 213
Register MEAL 14, 106
Reliable Advertising Services 10
research
  area tests 131
  awareness tracking studies 126-8
  classifying the population 111-12
  colour research 21
  coupon response 131
  defining the sample 120-2
  dubious data 120, 124-5
  fallibility 118-19, 130
  influence of the researcher 122-4
  intention-to-buy questionnaires 110
  manipulative respondents 128-30

INDEX

mechanical aids 119
opinion polls 129-30, 217
pitfalls 118, 119
post-testing 125-6
predicting purchase behaviour 121
qualitative research 122-3
quantitative research 123
Reel-of-Ten tests 126
scientific status? 117-18
twenty-four-hour recall tests 125-6
The Research Business 15
retail advertisements 178-9
retailers' own brands
    benefit of manufacturers' brands 6
    market share 2, 3, 7
    quality 3-4
Robert Sharp & Partners 143, 194
Robertson, Andrew 53, 63

Saatchi, Charles 165
Saatchi, Maurice 141
Saatchi & Saatchi 41-2, 140, 141, 143, 212, 217
sales promotions 9
Segel, Joseph 99-100
selective perception 176-6, 180
selling an agency 151
Shelton, Sir William 133, 149, 167
Smirnoff campaign 188
Smith, William 12, 16
sponsorship 9, 10
Star, Jonathan 186
status 195
Storr, Anthony 87
Strand cigarettes 126
style manuals 23
Sugar, Alan 73-4

targeting
    defining the target market 103, 120-1
    keeping close to the customer 109
    market analysis 112-13
    minimising waste 110, 113
    precision targeting 113, 115
    weeding out non-purchasers 110
technology, impact of 59, 98
telemarketing 9, 11
telephone selling 141
television
    channel switching 15
    clutter 15
    commerical breaks 14, 15
    interactive marketing 11, 99-100
    media rates 107
    narrow casting 100
    time-length for commercials 181
Thatcher, Margaret 112, 216
Townsend, Robert 158
trade association work 197-9
trade press 196
Trollope, Anthony 9

ultimata 193-5
Unilever 69
United States 15-16, 32-3, 115
USP (Unique Sales Proposition) philosophy 156

VALS (Value And Life Styles) system 111-12
'vampire video' 207
Vogel, Philip 82

Weisman, Richard L. 13
Willott Kingston Smith 56, 57
wimpishness 71, 72
women in advertising 152-3
working in advertising
    agency relationships 208-9
    attention to detail 206-7
    choosing the right employer 200-1
    firing people 204-6
    game plan 191-211
    how to be the world's greatest adman 209-11
    husband-and-wife teams 199-200
    joys and woes 221-2
    profiting from conferences 202-3
    recruitment 143-4
    taking responsibility 201-2
    women 152-3
writing for publications 196-7
Wynne-Williams, Jack 42

Yellowhammer PLC 152